Polish Immigrants
and Industrial Chicago

Polish Immigrants and Industrial Chicago

Workers on the South Side,
1880–1922

Dominic A. Pacyga

University of Chicago Press
Chicago and London

The University of Chicago Press, Chicago 60637
The University of Chicago Press, Ltd., London
Copyright © 1991 by Dominic A. Pacyga
New Preface © 2003 by Dominic A. Pacyga
All rights reserved.
University of Chicago Press edition 2003
Printed in the United States of America
12 11 10 09 08 07 06 05 04 03   1 2 3 4 5

ISBN: 0-226-64424-3 (paperback)

Library of Congress Cataloging-in-Publication Data

Pacyga, Dominic A.
    Polish immigrants and industrial Chicago :
  workers on the South side, 1880–1922 / Dominic A.
  Pacyga.
        p.   cm.
    Originally published: Columbus : Ohio State
    University Press, 1991, in series: Urban life
    and urban landscape series. With new introd.
    Includes bibliographical references and index.
    ISBN 0-226-64424-3 (pbk. : alk. paper)
      1. Polish Americans—Illinois—Chicago—History.
    2. Working class—Illinois—Chicago—History.
    3. Chicago (Ill.)—History—1875– I. Title.

  F548.9.P7P33   2003
  977.3'110049185—dc21

                                    2003050720

For my parents and grandparents

Contents

Illustrations

Preface to the Paperback Edition

E ven now, at the beginning of the twenty-first century, Polish is the language of choice for thousands of Chicagoans as they make their way along Milwaukee or Archer Avenues on the Northwest Side or the Southwest Side of the city. Polish businesses, churches, parochial schools, Saturday language and culture schools, and fraternal organizations still come together to create community and to solidify Chicago's Polonia—an important ethnic community in "the city that works." New immigrants mingle with the children, grandchildren, and great-grandchildren of those immigrants who arrived in earlier waves. They mix not only on the streets of traditional Polish neighborhoods but now often in Chicago's suburbs and beyond to exurbia. These most recent arrivals to Chicago bring new energy and a sense of continuity to Polish Chicago. Although language skills may fade in the second and third generations, traditions have been maintained—even if in an Americanized form. The Christmas Eve meal with the breaking of the *opłatek* (Christmas wafer), the blessing of baskets to celebrate Easter, the polka at weddings (where there's always an "open" bar)—these all remain part of being Polish American in Chicago. And these customs have been adopted by other ethnic groups in Chicago. It is not uncommon for "American" Catholic parishes to bless baskets and hand out packages of wafers at Easter and Christmas. Everyone in Chicago knows what *pierogi* and *kielbasa* are, even if they could not find Poland on a map or tell you anything about Poland's history or the background of Chicago's Polonia. From the last half of the nineteenth century until today, Polish Americans have made their influence felt in Chicago.

This influence has much to do with the ongoing economic relationships among Chicago, Poland, and the vast economic system that emerged out of Western Europe. First published in
1991, this book argues that both Chicago and Poland were
brought together by the creation of capitalism—they found
themselves tied together through changes in the grain trade, various technological revolutions, and changing immigration patterns. That bond, once established, has continued to exist, as
seen in the rarely interrupted exchange of populations since the
last half of the nineteenth century. Mary P. Erdmans has traced
the latest manifestation of that migration chain in her sociological study *Opposite Poles: Immigrants and Ethnics in Polish Chicago,
1976–1990*, just the most recent exploration of Chicago's Polonia.[1] In her book, Erdmans traces the interaction among several
generations of Polish Chicagoans. The members that comprise
the older ethnic leadership group in her book are the children
of the Polish workers discussed in this book as well as those immigrants who arrived in Chicago after World War II.

There is a great divergence between the Polish immigrants
that Erdmans studies and those that were the focus of *Polish Immigrants and Industrial Chicago*. This difference is more basic
than even the time periods studied. Erdmans's immigrants arrived in Chicago just before, during, and after the struggle of
the Solidarity labor movement in Poland. They are collectively
referred to as the "Solidarity immigration." These new Chicagoans tended to be more urban and more educated than the
earlier waves of rural peasants who emigrated from Poland. In
turn, these recent arrivals were more upwardly mobile. However,
many Solidarity immigrants first found employment in low paying service occupations as janitors and cleaning ladies or in the
underground economy that is an important part of the Polish
American community. Only later did they move into professional
positions and to the fringes of the city or to the suburbs. This new
story illustrates a changed pattern of immigration in Chicago—
as the city becomes more and more the home of the rich and
the poor, upwardly mobile newcomers often move out beyond
Chicago's borders. Here they join second and third generation
Polish Americans who witnessed a good deal of upward mobility

in the years after World War II. Much of this mobility was based upon the second and third generations' struggle for both community and an effective labor movement earlier in the century. Successful unions provided benefits that allowed for college educations and that offered professional positions for the third generation.[2] While many boast that Chicago contains one of the largest Polish populations in the world, the reality is that over seventy percent of all of those claiming Polish heritage today live in the suburbs. The old Polish immigrant working-class neighborhoods discussed in this book—South Chicago and the Back of the Yards—are today primarily Latino and African American in population.[3]

The immigration discussed by Erdmans is of course only the latest wave in the ongoing population transfer that has existed between Poland and Chicago since the mid-nineteenth century. Their numbers remain small compared to the great economic peasant migration of the nineteenth century. In Chicago's Polish American organizations these new immigrants have begun to challenge the older leadership of both the American-born children of the economic migration and the World War II immigrants who arrived as refugees after the horrors of the Nazi occupation and the Soviet-imposed regime. As Erdmans illustrates, these groups have clashed over various issues concerning Polonia and its relationship to the latest immigrants. Post–World War II immigrants often point to the fact that the Polish Americans from the latest wave of immigration were raised in a communist society and stereotype them as somehow dependent—first, on the communist state and then, on Polish American charity—and as inferior in their Polishness to the older generation. A similar conflict also marred the relationship between the World War II immigrant generation and those who had arrived in the United States as part of the peasant economic immigration before World War I. The post-1945 immigrants felt superior because they spoke better Polish and were for the most part better educated. Their interpretation of who was a Pole put them at odds with the traditional Polish American community. Despite these conflicts, however, Polonia has shown a great deal of unity and stability through the various waves of immigration and different rates of assimilation. As Donald Pienkos has shown, Polish American institutions have long come to the aid of both new immigrants and those who still live in Poland.[4]

All Polish immigrants should also be viewed in terms of the larger worldwide Polish diaspora that has created Polish communities in many different places including France, Germany, Brazil, Cuba, Australia, Kazakhstan, India, and Turkey. Emigration has played a major role in the history of Poland over the last two centuries. It continues today—Poles were recorded as the largest legal immigrant group and the second largest illegal immigrant group in Chicago in the mid-1990s.[5]

Polish Immigrants and Industrial Chicago deals with the economic migration of Polish peasants to Chicago's Union Stock Yard and Steel District in the era 1880–1922 and their transformation into American workers. It discusses the struggle to build stable working-class communities and the labor movement out of peasant immigrant populations. The book was an attempt to shed light on larger processes in urban, ethnic, and working-class history by using Polish South Siders as an example. One of the questions it looked at was how these peasants became industrial workers and how they dealt with their new urban milieu.

Since *Polish Immigrants and Industrial Chicago* was published, there has been a good deal written about whiteness theory and the assimilation of ethnic groups into the dominant white culture. The works of Noel Ignatiev on the Irish and Karen Brodkin on Jews as well as the theoretical discussions by David Roediger, Mathew Frye Jacobson, and others have pointed to race, especially in the case of African Americans, and its impact on assimilation of immigrants in the United States. Most recently, Thomas A. Guglielmo has studied the Italians and race in Chicago. My own work on Polish workers—this book and an article on Chicago's 1919 riot—has contributed to this discussion. Polish workers in Chicago came to see themselves and to be perceived as "white" only after passing through the cauldron of a race riot and the labor movement.[6]

Poles in Chicago lived among many different ethnic groups—of which African Americans were only one. As I argue in this book, Polish immigrants had to create their own communities (a process I call the intramural response) before reaching out effectively to other groups. This eventual interaction with other European ethnic groups varied over time and place. Ron Bayor set the stage for my discussion with his classic *Neighbors in Conflict*—a look at several of New York's ethnic groups. And truly, Poles intermingled with many groups on the city's streets and in its industrial plants. Dorota Praszałowicz, in *Stosunki Polsko-Niemieckie Na Obczyźnie,* takes an excellent look at the Milwaukee Polonia and has pointed to a good deal of cooperation between Poles and Germans. Her argument is persuasive and provides ethnic historians with more research regarding the interaction among white ethnic groups. Praszałowicz's earlier work explored the same kind of cooperation that existed in German and Polish parochial schools. These works all substantiate the description of the American city as a mosaic of ethnic groups and cultures. Some of these groups, such as the Poles, Germans, Jews, and other Central and Eastern Europeans, had long histories of both conflict and cooperation in Europe; others groups knew little of each other before contact in Chicago and other American cities. The building of community (the intramural response) made possible the eventual extramural responses such as active participation in the labor movement.[7]

Others have written about both the Poles in Chicago during the time period covered and about the neighborhoods discussed in this book. Edward Kantowicz's pioneering study *Polish American Politics in Chicago,* as well as his later work, set the standard high for looking at this community. Kantowicz described an inward-looking ethnic community that never reached beyond its borders to grasp either political or ecclesiastical power. For Kantowicz, the Poles were too parochial and unable to build bridges to other ethnic groups and to organize effectively to build a multiethnic political base in the city or in the Catholic Church—as the Irish and even the Czechs were able to do in the Democratic Party.[8]

Victor Greene's book *For God and Country* appeared at the same time as Kantowicz's but described a regionally fragmented community in Chicago that only later identified itself as Polish in Chicago. The streets of Chicago created ethnic consciousness in a peasantry that had tended to identify with their village and region rather than with the larger concept of Poland. Religious disagreements and the split between nationalists and Catholics played an important role in Greene's book as it did in Joseph Parot's *Polish Catholics in Chicago*. Parot described in greater detail the conflict among Polish immigrants over the definition of *Polskość* (Polishness) and the role of Catholicism in that definition. All of these works focused on the North Side where the oldest and largest Polish community lived. A more recent book by Joseph Bigott, *From Cottage to Bungalow,* investigates the housing patterns and politics of Chicago's industrial south suburbs. In addition to Bigott's excellent investigation of working-class housing, his discussion of Polish American politics is a valuable contribution to the literature. None of these works, however, touches on the labor movement or focuses intensely on the steel and meat packing industries of Chicago's South Side.[9]

James Barrett's book *Work and Community in the Jungle* explores the labor movement in the Chicago Stock Yards during the same era covered in *Polish Immigrants and Industrial Chicago*. Barrett's work looks at workers in general but doesn't focus on any particular group. His interpretation did not take into full account the importance of religion and traditional community building in the Back of the Yards. The excellent study by Thomas Jablonsky, *Pride in the Jungle,* in turn, delved into the geographical and historical roots of that same community—making an excellent connection between the physical environment of houses, churches, and stores and the creation of the various ethnic communities. Having both public and semi-public space helps to establish community; it also enables ethnic communities to first, have a place of their own and second, use these places to create a public forum in which to discuss issues. These concepts are crucial to understanding the immigrant and working-class history of Chicago and industrial America. Like *The Back of the Yards* by Robert Slayton, Jablonsky lays out the origins of the Back of the Yards Neighborhood Council; founded by Saul Alinsky, Joseph Meegan, and Bishop Sheil in the late 1930s, the council was a reaction to much of what is discussed in *Polish Immigrants and Industrial Chicago.* Both of these studies paint an important picture of the opportunities afforded in the 1930s to create an extramural response to conditions in the industrial city. My own work finds

these themes in the Steel District's South Chicago and the establishment of the Russell Square Community Committee as part of
the legendary Chicago Area Project to combat juvenile delinquency, but I explain once again that only a rooted mature Polish
community could reach out past the parochialism described earlier by Kantowicz.[10]

Since the appearance of *Polish Immigrants and Industrial Chicago*, various other scholars have researched the experience of
Polish workers in America. Maria Anna Knothe has illuminated
the role of Polish women in Chicago. Adam Walaszek continues
to be a leading Polish scholar of Polish immigration to the
United States—his study of Polish Cleveland is an important
look at a major industrial American city. His earlier overview of
the Polish American working class supports many of the themes
in this book, and he explores them further in his study of Cleveland. The immigrant letters collected by the Kula family, which I
translated and quoted in this book, have been more skillfully
translated by Josephine Wtulich and published in English. They
remain a crucial source for the understanding of Polish immigration. John Bukowczyk's overview of Polish immigration, *And
My Children Did Not Know Me*, is the best concise overview of Polish immigration to the United States. His edited collection *Polish
Americans and Their History* is a fine contribution covering many
aspects of Polonia's history and culture.[11]

The history of Polish immigrants in the United States and in
Chicago is long and intricate. From the pioneering sociological
work of W. I. Thomas and Florian Znaniecki to Mary Erdman's
look at the most recent immigrants, this history has proven to be
central to an understanding of the American ethnic experience.
Polish Immigrants and Industrial Chicago looks at an important part
of that story.[12]

Notes

1. Mary Patrice Erdmans, *Opposite Poles: Immigrants and Ethnics in
Polish Chicago, 1976–1990* (University Park: Pennsylvania University
Press, 1998).

2. Dominic A. Pacyga, "Polish America in Transition: Social Change and the Chicago Polonia, 1945–1980," *Polish American Studies* (Spring 1987): 38–55.

3. For a look at the Mexican community in Back of the Yards see the special advertising supplement by the 47th Street Chamber of Commerce, "4th Annual Mexican Independence Day Celebration," *Chicago Sun-Times*, 2 September 1999.

4. Donald M. Pienkos, *For Your Freedom Through Ours: Polish American Efforts on Poland's Behalf, 1863–1991* (Boulder, Colo.: East European Monographs, 1991).

5. For a thorough discussion of the Polish Diaspora see Adam Walaszek, ed., *Polska Diaspora* (The Polish Diaspora) (Kraków: Wydawnictwo Literackie, 2001).

6. Noel Ignatiev, *How The Irish Became White* (Cambridge: Harvard University Press, 1995); Karen Brodkin, *How Jews Became White Folks and What That Says About Race in America* (New Brunswick, N. J.: Rutgers University Press, 1998); David R. Roediger, *The Wages of Whiteness: Race and the Making of the American Working Class* (London and New York: Verso, 1991); Mathew Frye Jacobson, *Whiteness of a Different Color: European Immigrants and the Alchemy of Race* (Cambridge: Harvard University Press, 1998); Thomas A. Guglielmo, *White on Arrival: Italians, Race, Color and Power in Chicago, 1890–1945* (Oxford and New York: Oxford University Press, 2003); Dominic A. Pacyga, "Chicago's 1919 Race Riot: Ethnicity, Class, and Urban Violence," in *The Making of Urban America,* 2nd edition, ed. Raymond Mohl (Wilmington: Scholarly Resources, 1997), 187–207.

7. Ronald Bayor, *Neighbors in Conflict: The Irish, Germans, Jews, and Italians of New York City, 1929–1941* (Baltimore: Johns Hopkins University Press, 1978); Dorota Praszałowicz, *Stosunki Polsko-Niemieckie Na Obczyźnie: Polscy I Niemiecy Imigranci w Milwaukee, Wisconsin (USA), 1860– 1920* (Polish-German Relations Abroad: Poles and German Immigrants in Milwaukee, Wisconsin) (Kraków: Prace Instytutu Polonijnego Uniwersytetu Jagiellońskiego, 1999); Dorota Praszałowicz, *Amerykańska Etniczne Szkoła Parafialna* (Ethnic American Parochial Schools) (Kraków: Wydawnictwo Polskiej Akademia Nauk, 1986); Dominic A. Pacyga, "To Live Amongst Others: Poles and Their Neighbors in Industrial Chicago, 1865–1930," *Journal of American Ethnic History* (Fall 1996): 55–74.

8. Edward R. Kantowicz, *Polish-American Politics in Chicago, 1888– 1940.* (Chicago: University of Chicago Press, 1975); Edward R. Kantowicz, "Polish Chicago: Survival Through Solidarity" in *Ethnic Chicago: Revised and Expanded,* ed. Melvin G. Holli and Peter d'A Jones

(Grand Rapids, Mich.: William B. Eerdmans Publishing Company, 1984), 214–38.

9. Victor Greene, *For God and Country: The Rise of Polish and Lithuanian Consciousness in America, 1860–1910* (Madison, Wis.: State Historical Society of Wisconsin, 1975); Joseph John Parot, *Polish Catholics in Chicago, 1850–1920* (DeKalb: Northern Illinois University Press, 1981); Joseph C. Bigott, *From Cottage to Bungalow: Houses and the Working Class in Metropolitan Chicago, 1869–1929* (Chicago: University of Chicago Press, 2001).

10. James Barrett, *Work and Community in the Jungle: Chicago's Packinghouse Workers, 1894–1922* (Urbana: University of Illinois Press, 1987); Thomas J. Jablonsky, *Pride in the Jungle: Community and Everyday Life in Back of the Yards Chicago* (Baltimore: Johns Hopkins University Press, 1993); Robert Slayton, *Back of the Yards: The Making of a Local Democracy* (Chicago: University of Chicago Press, 1986); Dominic A. Pacyga. "The Russell Square Community Committee: An Ethnic Response to Urban Problems," *Journal of Urban History* (February 1989): 159–84.

11. Maria Anna Knothe, "Recent Arrivals: Polish Immigrant Women's Response to the City," in *Peasant Maids/City Women: From the European Countryside to Urban America,* ed. Christiane Harzig (Ithaca and London: Cornell University Press, 1997), 299–338; Adam Walaszek, *Światy Imigrantów: Tworzenie Polonijnego Cleveland, 1880–1930* (The World of the Immigrant: The Making of Polish Cleveland) (Kraków: Nomos, 1994); Adam Walaszek, *Polscy Robotnicy Praca I Związki Zawodowe w Stanach Zjednoczonych Ameryki, 1880–1922* (Polish Workers: Work and Unions in the United States, 1880–1922) (Kraków: Wydawnictwo Polskiej Akademia Nauk, 1988); Witold Kula, Nina Assorodobraj-Kula, Marcin Kula, *Writing Home: Immigrants in Brazil and the United States, 1890–1891,* ed. and trans. Josephine Wtulich (Boulder, Colo.: East European Monographs, 1986); John J. Bukowczyk, *And My Children Did Not Know Me: A History of Polish-Americans* (Bloomington: Indiana University Press, 1987); John J. Bukowczyk, ed., *Polish Americans and Their History: Community, Culture, and Politics* (Pittsburgh: University of Pittsburgh Press, 1996).

12. Eli Zaretsky has edited and abridged a version of the Thomas and Znaniecki study. William I. Thomas and Florian Znaniecki, *The Polish Peasant in Europe and America,* ed. Eli Zaretsky (Urbana: University of Illinois Press, 1984).

Preface

Polish Chicago has often been studied from the perspective of its large North Side settlements and through the experiences of its religious and professional leadership. The South Side Chicago Polish experience is most often mentioned in passing or in studies of labor history dealing with mass production industries. Little was known, though much was assumed, about Polish packinghouse and steel-mill workers. This book is an attempt to explore the impact of the industrial city on Polish peasant immigrants during the height of the so-called new immigration. This period not only witnessed the greatest immigration of Poles to the United States but also included a very active time in both immigrant community building and labor union activity. It also coincided with Chicago's emergence as a major American urban industrial center. For these reasons the Polish experience on Chicago's South Side seemed to present a unique opportunity to explore the emergence of the industrial city and the immigrants it attracted.

This book began as a dissertation at the University of Illinois at Chicago in the mid-1970s. The patience, guidance, and above all friendship of Leo Schelbert helped me to carry it through some very difficult times. Schelbert forced me to see beyond theory to the very humanity of the immigrant experience. If this study is successful at all, Leo Schelbert deserves much of the credit.

Perry Duis first suggested that I look at South Chicago as well as the Back of the Yards. Further, Duis gave me a firm grounding in Chicago's history and guided me to many unexplored sources. Glen E. Holt proved to be a good colleague and friend. Much of this work resulted from long conversations with Holt as we worked together on a study of Chicago's South Side neighborhoods. Edward C. Thaden introduced me to Polish and East European history. His kindness and wit drew me into graduate school and helped me to remain. Thaden taught me to put Polish immigrants into a larger European historical framework. John C. Kulczycki has proved to be a fine friend. He came to the University of Illinois at Chicago in time to sit on my dissertation committee. Since then Kulczycki has offered encouragement and advice and lent impossible-to-get books. Richard M. Fried gave me the background to understand Polonia in the context of twentieth-century America. Robert Remini came to my aid during one of those unavoidable crises in graduate school. His colloquium helped me to explore nineteenth-century America.

Many people have read the manuscript during various stages of its development. Edward Kantowicz has been a kind and patient reader. Sometimes I think he read it more often than I did. Robert Asher, Melvin Holli, Thaddeus Radzilowski, and Louise C. Wade all have commented on this book. This final version is better for their suggestions. Dorota Praszałowicz and Marcin Kula have helped me through long and interesting discussions, and through their own work, to formulate ideas concerning Polish history and the immigrant experience. Władyslaw Miodunka made it possible for me to see modern-day peasant Poland by inviting a contingent of scholars through the Polish American Historical Association to visit the Jagiellonian University in 1986. James Pula and M. B. Biskupski offered friendship and collegiality. Five friends from graduate school—Arnold Hirsch, Peter Mclennon, Mark Freidberger, Philip Kozlowski, and Adam Rogulski—shared in long discussions concerning both Poland and Chicago. Ellen Skerrett gave freely of time, advice, encouragement, friendship, and even primary sources. Andrew Greeley provided encouragement and goodwill.

I know of no one who has recently written about Chicago's history who does not owe a great debt to Archie Moteley of the Chicago Historical Society. Archie is a valuable resource as well as good friend. As editor of *Chicago History* Fannia Weingartner published my first article. She guided my early attempts at writing. Larry Viskochil, also of the Chicago Historical Society, came through in a pinch with photographs. I want to thank the archivists and staffs of the Chicago Historical Society, the Regenstein Library of the University of Chicago, the University of Illinois at Chicago, the Archdiocesan Archives of Chicago, and the Polish Museum of America, especially Jacek Nowakowski. Les Orear of the Illinois Labor History Society also provided valuable assistance.

The late Aloysius Mazewski, president of both the Polish American Congress and the Polish National Alliance, encouraged and helped me to finish the dissertation phase of this manuscript by obtaining funding from the Polish American Congress Charitable Foundation for various studies of the Polish community in which I was involved. He is sorely missed by myself and Polonia. Other funding came from grants from the Kosciuszko Foundation and the Polish American Scholarship Fund. I also received a teaching assistantship and a fellowship from the University of Illinois at Chicago. President Mirron Alexandroff of Columbia College in Chicago brought me to the staff of the Southeast Chicago Historical Project in 1982 to further study South Chicago. Both the National Endowment for the Humanities and the Illinois Humanities Council helped fund the venture. Later Alexandroff welcomed me to the highly creative atmosphere at Columbia College. Lya Dym Rosenblum, Bert Gall, Les Van Marter, and my colleagues in the Liberal Education Department have heartened and helped me by making my stay at Columbia College most pleasant and rewarding. I want to thank Columbia College for a subvention to pay for illustrations and other costs. Without Zane Miller, Henry Shapiro, Alex Holzman, Lynne M. Bonenberger, and Alexander Metro, this book would not have been published. I owe them much. Diane Williams and Shelley Brown typed several early drafts of this manuscript. Mario R. López drew the map that helped to put the two Polish communities in perspective.

Friendship and family have played important roles in the history of Polish America. The same must be said of this project. My two grandmothers, Mary Walkosz and Bernice Pacyga, provided me with memories of Polonia's early years. They also imbued me with a love for Polish culture and the Polish language. I cannot thank them enough. My parents, Joseph and Pauline Pacyga, helped in many ways. When certain Polish phrases seemed indecipherable, a quick phone call home cleared the way. My parents taught me to respect the past, but also the truth. My aunt, Rita Walkosz Hurley, contributed much to this work. She has been a source of comfort as well as information. Theodore J. Swigon provided photographs from his family's collection, help with ideas, and above all the kind of friendship indispensable to such an endeavor.

Another group of friends taught me much about the Union Stock Yards. From the summer of 1969 until the fall of 1971 I worked in various capacities for the Union Stock Yard & Transit Company. Walter "Ferpo" Konkol, Ben Dees, Steve Scanlon, "Happy" Durrant, Charlie Brasil, Tom Hartnett, Mr. Cook, and my fellow workers at docks A, J, and K helped me to understand much about life in the yards.

Finally I especially want to thank my wife, Kathleen Alaimo. She has provided insight, ideas, encouragement, and editorial assistance. Kathy helped in so many ways that this book would have been impossible without her. Our daughter, Johanna, also has placed her mark on this book. She made sacrifices that must be made by a child of two historians. Somehow, writing books has always been part of our collective lives. Kathy and Johanna have made all that worthwhile. Many individuals have helped to make this a better book. I, of course, am solely responsible for its faults.

Introduction

In 1877 the Zulawski family settled into the area just southwest of Chicago's Union Stock Yards. Seven years later the Donitskis built a cottage on Throop Street near 48th Street. The Hanaskis, Humuskis, and Manuskis also built homes in the area. A discernible Polish community began to stretch along the streets that had been dominated by Irish and German laborers since the founding of the Union Stock Yards in 1865. At this same time, enough Poles lived in South Chicago for the establishment of their own Roman Catholic parish, Immaculate Conception, near the massive lakefront steel mills.[1] In the last decades of the nineteenth century, Polish peasants became industrial workers in the United States. This study explores the process of how these packinghouse and steel-mill workers adjusted to the industrial milieu and joined the American urban working class.

In 1918 William I. Thomas and Florian Znaniecki published the first volume of their monumental five-volume work, *The Polish Peasant in Europe and America.*[2] This path-breaking study of Polish immigrants helped to establish the Chicago school of sociology. It also presented a model for the study of immigration and the impact of modern industrial capitalism on traditional societies. Thomas and Znaniecki's study of Polish peasants on both sides of the Atlantic Ocean presented a group of rural folk made over by the modernization of the economy. In doing this the two sociologists set important precedents for the study of industrialism and the peasantry.

Thomas and Znaniecki attributed changes in the structure of Polish peasant society in the nineteenth century to the break-

1

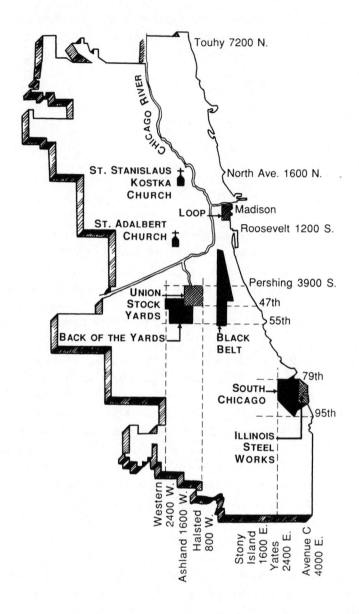

Chicago, 1917. This map shows the location of the Back of the Yards and South Chicago on the city's South Side, and their relationship to the original Polish settlement at St. Stanislaus Kostka Church, the second major Polish settlement at St. Adalbert Church, the Loop, and the Black Belt. *(Drawn by Mario R. Lopez)*

down of the historic isolation of rural village life and the gradual development of the market economy. The authors presented a traditional society in transformation. Old values and norms came into question as Polish peasants became more integrated into the European capitalist system. Emigration evolved as a further step in this process whether or not the emigrant planned to return to his or her home.

In delineating the Polish peasants' experience of modernization in Poland and in the United States, primarily in Chicago, Thomas and Znaniecki searched for an answer to what was commonly referred to as the "immigrant" problem. Many observers and commentators saw immigrant communities in the United States, particularly those with Eastern and Southern European roots, as unassimilable and as major contributors to urban social problems. Immigrants had a great impact in cities such as Chicago, where immigrant stock residents made up nearly 80 percent of the population by 1910.[3] Thomas and Znaniecki described Polish peasant society as passing through a three-stage process of organization, disorganization, and reorganization. From an outsider's point of view, the apparent disorganization of the immigrant communities was part of a process leading to a new system.[4] The two sociologists suggested that the emerging Polish American community might look forward to the formation of a cooperative society as the next stage in its evolution. Thomas and Znaniecki made the further point that personal and familial disorganization did not necessarily mean societal disorganization. They implied that some aspects of Polish peasant society had survived the trauma of modernization in Poland and emigration to the United States. Polish peasant society contained the seeds of its reorganization into a new and viable form in the United States and in Europe. No solution could be imposed on the immigrant problem; an answer would have to arise out of the community itself.[5]

The Polish Peasant in Europe and America had a great impact on the early development of sociology and on the historiography of American immigration. The discussion of disorganization and dysfunction of individuals, families, and societies in the face of capitalism, industrialization, and emigration helped to shape generations of scholarship on both immigrants and later African American migrants to the city. It influenced historians through the work of Oscar Handlin and the consensus school of American history, whose members sought experiences in the past that generated values transcending group distinctions in American society.[6]

The Polish American community often reacted negatively to the work of the Chicago school of sociology. The documentation of the disorganization of Polish immigrant families seemed to play into nativist hands. Polish American leaders would have preferred a more filiopietistic view of their community. Mistrust of sociologists ran deep in Polonia. Sociological studies by Ernest W. Burgess, William Thrasher, and Clifford Shaw enraged Polish Americans. Despite Thrasher's and Shaw's argument that ethnicity and juvenile delinquency were not related, Polish Americans saw the investigation of working-class Polish communities in America in general and in Chicago in particular as a form of nativist slander.[7]

Thomas and Znaniecki presented an original and influential picture of peasant Poland. As Eli Zaretsky has pointed out, however, missing in their interpretation was the manor house and its gentry inhabitants. Also missing was the reality of European class conflict. This seems odd since Polish peasant activists and socialists had already made their mark in Polish communities in Europe and America. Polish history, folktales, and literature were filled with examples of conflict between the peasantry and the gentry. Poles played an important role in the Russian Revolution of 1905. Furthermore, Polish immigrants took part in many industrial conflicts in the United States. Some of these events occurred rather close to the University of Chicago offices of William I. Thomas. Yet peasant radicals, labor unions, and socialists hardly appear in the five-volume study.[8] Although Thomas and Znaniecki contributed much to the study of immigration, their approach prevented them from seeing class conflict as a key factor in the shaping of both Polish and Polish American society. Neither traditional Marxists nor consensus historians adequately portrayed the development of immigrant communities. Eli Zaretsky cites both the successes and failures of Thomas and Znaniecki in

his call for a new synthesis to explain immigration and its relationship to modern American industrialism.[9] My study attempts
to view the Polish peasant in light of migration, conflict, urbanization, and the continuing importance of the communal tradition. Communalism did not disappear with either the decision to
emigrate or the landing at Ellis Island. Preindustrial, premigra-
tion attitudes and values continued to have an effect even in the
shadow of Chicago's packinghouses and steel mills.

Polish Chicagoans brought much cultural, social, and ethical
baggage with them from Europe. Traditional peasant culture
had a major impact on urban working-class neighborhoods, institutions, and labor movements. Industrialization, immigration,
the workplace, and the home dynamically interacted to form a
new society. Institutions such as the Roman Catholic church, various labor unions, fraternal groups, as well as saloons, gangs, and
other less structured organizations—some of which seemed to be
part of the disorganization of immigrant communities—created
an intense social web. Out of this emerged an ethnic working-
class community able to reach out to other communities in a common cause.

Social, cultural, technological, and economic forces transformed the world in the nineteenth century. The capitalist system exploded across Europe and the rest of the globe. Polish
peasants saw their lives altered by vast changes in the economic
order. While the Polish economy shifted in response to new realities, Polish peasants found themselves released from many feudal
obligations. Opportunities beckoned and the Polish peasant
responded.[10]

Migration was a positive response to the new economic parameters available to Polish peasants in the last third of the nineteenth century. Immigration, as one response to industrial capitalism, brought Poles to the neighborhoods that surrounded the
giant packinghouses and steel mills of Chicago. They went there
not because they were "uprooted" or even "transplanted," but because they made what seemed to them to be sound decisions to
better themselves within the framework of the available economic
opportunities.[11]

Once they immigrated, the South Side Poles faced an urban

industrial order that was not of their own making. The Poles responded in two basic ways. First, in what I call the communal response, they established small inward-looking communities that fostered stability and strength. This was a necessary precondition for the development of their second response: extracommunalism. The growth of class consciousness among Polish workers and their integration into the American working class represent an extracommunalism that rests firmly on the foundations of an already established cohesiveness. In their extracommunal response Polish Americans reached out to other working-class ethnic groups and even middle-class reformers, such as settlement-house workers, in an effort to survive and better the conditions under which they worked and lived. Both reactions, deriving from long-lasting traditions in Polish peasant society, marked the entrance of these formerly rural folk into the industrial working classes of both Europe and America. These responses also fitted into well-established patterns of American urban working-class society and its forms of protest.

Both the communal and extracommunal responses are crucial to understanding the Polish American experience in Chicago. The creation of a sense of community based on traditional folkways gave the Polish settlement a solidarity that it needed in order to take an active part in urban working-class society. Both Catholicism and nationalism played an important role in this process. At times though, an extreme form of communalism crippled Polish American participation in the wider urban society. Nevertheless, this study finds Poles reaching out, after a period of adjustment and acculturation, beyond their self-contained communities to ally themselves with others. In doing this they hoped to influence the urban industrial society in which they and other immigrants now played integral roles.[12]

The immigrant emerges as one who proved capable of dealing with the new industrial order and who attempted to take advantage of it by migration to another one of the Polish lands, to a different part of Europe, or in this case to the United States. Polish peasants felt liberated by the vast changes of the nineteenth century and responded in a rational way. This response included emigration and participation in peasant and working-class movements in Poland and abroad.[13] Of course, the element of liberation involved in peasant migrations should not be exaggerated. Although immigration can be viewed as a freely chosen response to changing economic circumstances, many factors, including poverty, limited the maneuverability of peasant immigrants.

The extracommunal response speaks to the question of working-class solidarity. A recent study of Chicago's packinghouses argues that the union helped to integrate various ethnic groups into American society. Furthermore the multiethnic kill floors fostered interethnic cooperation based on a common work experience.[14] This argument, although persuasive, does not take full account of the European experience of the Poles and other immigrant groups. The culture of Polish immigrants must be understood in order to trace accurately their response to American industrial society. This study tracks the emergence of what some would call premodern patterns of collective behavior and protest among immigrants. I argue, however, that although some of these forms of organization were rooted in preindustrial traditions, they provided a firm base for the labor movement in Chicago and certainly for the concept of community and a sense of neighborhood in an urban setting. I maintain that Polish Americans created an experience of working-class and neighborhood solidarity out of older rural communal peasant traditions that sought unity in the face of an uncompromising foe such as the management of Chicago's major packinghouses and steel mills.[15] Strike actions, riots, even street gang activity often addressed this need for unity rather than fomenting communal disintegration or dysfunction.

For the historian it quickly becomes evident that the labor movement that emerged after the Haymarket tragedy was strongly based on a sense of neighborhood. Even before 1886, the Knights of Labor supported local working-class institutions in which it could root its organization.[16] The success of organized labor during the First World War was in large part due to a strong sense of place and group as well as class. Organizers founded the unions of both steel and packinghouse workers on vital communities

united along lines of common interest. Polish Americans established a feeling of community and then reached out to form a
sense of neighborhood and class.

The term *neighborhood* is slippery and hard to define. This is
especially true for Chicago's history; studies of the city's neighborhoods are numerous.[17] The Polish experience on the South
Side provides good examples of the development of urban immigrant communities and neighborhoods. Large mass-production
industrial concerns dominated the Back of the Yards, adjacent to
the giant packinghouses, and South Chicago, home to steel mills.
To many outsiders the possibility of creating a sense of community and neighborhood under these intensely urban and industrial conditions seemed impossible. Sociologists and other contemporary observers such as Upton Sinclair, who looked back to
an earlier rural sense of both neighborhood and community,
could see little hope for these urban no man's lands.[18]

This study defines *community* as a group of individuals who
share a common language, beliefs, traditions, experiences, and
goals. *Neighborhood,* on the other hand, is a geographical term
that includes various communities. It is necessary to distinguish
the definitions of *neighborhood* and *community.* In many cases terms
have been used interchangeably, but this is inadequate as no ethnic group, except in the case of racial segregation, totally monop-
olized American urban neighborhoods.[19] In the case of both the
Back of the Yards and South Chicago, the presence of many Roman Catholic, Protestant, Orthodox Christian, and Jewish places
of worship attests to this reality.

It is essential to realize that although different ethnic groups
shared the same geographic space they did not necessarily interact with one another socially or emotionally. The relations among
the various groups often proved to be unsubstantial. Each group
lived without interference.[20] Here lie both the strength and the
weakness of the immigrant/ethnic communities. The tendency
toward a feeling of gemeinschaft remained important despite the
reality of a gesellschaft world. Still it is wrong to focus simply on
communalism as the only response of rural immigrants to the industrial city. The actions of Chicago's Polish American workers
during the period covered in this book stood rooted in their Pol-

ish peasant past, but they were also shaped by the American industrial setting. Therefore terms such as *tradition* and *modernity*
are not flexible enough to serve historians well.[21] Polish immigrants were not "new" men and women, but neither were they
simple reflections of the feudal past. Chicago's Polish areas were
not simply reconstituted Eastern European villages; they were industrial urban neighborhoods made up of working-class communities shaped by both the European and American experiences.
Continuity and change remained constant elements for European immigrants in the United States.

The urban working class cannot be treated in a vacuum. Although peasants tended to have an underdeveloped class consciousness, they did have a sense of the meaning of social conflict.
Social conflict left an indelible mark on the memories of Polish
peasants turned workers. Some of the events immediately following the First World War resembled not only industrial conflicts
but preindustrial jacqueries. The participants were acutely aware
of this. Premodern attitudes often helped determine modern
working-class reactions to industrial conditions and role definitions. Precapitalist traditions concerning community, work, and
social relations provided a base for the Polish response to industrial Chicago. The Chicago experience in turn transformed these
actions. In this way Poles helped to shape both the American city
and the response of American workers to the problems inherent
in a capitalist/industrial society.

One aim of this study is to challenge any attempt to reduce the
American urban working-class experience to a uniform one. Ethnicity emerges as a vital variable in understanding the development of the urban working-class experience in the United States,
just as other historians have demonstrated the centrality of gen-
der and race.[22]

This book deals with the structure, ways of life, disposition,
and collective actions of Polish workers in Chicago.[23] Outsiders
identified the two South Side Chicago neighborhoods of my
study with the industries that dominated them. Chicago's packinghouse employees and steelworkers lived in neighborhoods
that surrounded the huge industrial plants. Everywhere these
immigrants went, the smells, sounds, and images of meatpacking

and steelmaking followed them. The small shopkeepers, saloon proprietors, priests, and ethnic professionals who depended on these workers also called the Back of the Yards and South Chicago home. They shared many of their fears, hopes, and concerns. Indeed they often came from the same class background.[24] The events of the workplace shaped the events of the neighborhood. Even those not working in the plants found their experiences molded by the affairs of the industrial workplace. Therefore despite the truth of the claim that the Industrial Revolution had divorced the workplace from the home, the relationship remained an intimate one. I argue that this link proved crucial first to the creation of neighborhood identity and later to workers' unity. It was also a crucial factor in the formation of what I shall call communal strikes in these neighborhoods during the early part of the twentieth century.

Industrial capitalism transformed Western society. It created Chicago and shaped its history. Polish peasants turned workers found themselves in the midst of this upheaval. Like all upheavals it presented both problems and opportunities. By emigrating, Polish peasants hoped to better their economic position. Many hoped to accumulate wealth in America and then return to Europe; they hoped to purchase more land and join the higher ranks of Polish rural society. In the United States they attempted to better their position in the urban workforce through both collective and individual action. In each case the tumult of the Industrial Revolution provided peasants with an opportunity to better their conditions, a goal not always realized. These changes, however, also threatened their cultural and ethical life styles. Their response to these threats included the creation of tradition-based communities as a form of psychological and economic protection.

Various observers have argued that working-class ideals favored mutuality over individualism.[25] The fact that the peasant communal past called for unity even at the expense of the individual is important for understanding how Chicago's Polish workers fit into the pattern of both neighborhood and labor union development in the period 1880 to 1922. The Eastern European peasant experience was a communal one. Roman Catholicism

provided a communal theology and culture for Polish immigrants. The peasants described by the Polish author Ladislas Reymont in his Nobel Prize winning novel, *Peasants*, were a communal people.[26] In this type of society the individual understood his
fate to be that of champion of the common good. Communalism
seems to have survived the impact of industrial capitalism and
migration in the two Chicago neighborhoods surveyed here.

The connection between the environments of the home and
the workplace is critical. Before theorizing about class experiences, we must explore the entire world of Polish workers on
Chicago's South Side.[27] Ethnic groups could both affect and be
affected by their surroundings. They might be both unsuccessful
in resisting change and successful in coping with the new world
in which they found themselves.[28] Despite the fears of family and
communal disintegration expressed by Thomas and Znaniecki,
the Polish family offered a sound foundation for coping with the
tremendous changes brought about by industrialism. Through
chain migration and family and group identity, Polish immigrants forged strong links that carried over into the workplace.
Polish women proved central to this working-class community.
Both women and children actively participated in the process of
community building and in its defense. Polish workers in the
Back of the Yards and South Chicago failed to recreate their native villages. This attempt, however, made it possible for group
members to confront and humanize the new society in which
they now labored. It also allowed them to become active participants in American urban industrial society. By extending the
scope of this study to include not only the workplace but also the
home and the community of immigrant laborers in Chicago, we
can reflect on the complex nature of urban working-class life.
The world of Polish immigrants in Chicago's industrial neighborhoods was dirty, crowded, and poor. Yet in this world, men,
women, and children struggled against these onerous conditions,
empowered by older rural traditions and modern urban forms,
in an effort to emerge as something more than victims of urban
industrial society.

In the end the basic question is how did Polish packinghouse
and steel-mill workers affect Chicago and its working class be-

tween 1880 and 1922. They obviously took part in the major labor movements of the period and helped to create a sense of neighborhood in the city's industrial districts. Observers saw them as among the most active and radical participants in the labor movement. Their neighborhoods were described as intensely communal. John Kikulski, a Polish labor organizer and fraternal group leader, not only organized workers but ran for political office under the short-lived banner of the Labor party in 1919. Kikulski paid the ultimate price for his deeds. He was murdered near his home in 1920. Polish women confronted the Chicago police in a display of solidarity during the packinghouse strike of 1921–22. I argue that this was as much a result of traditional Polish peasant culture as it was of class consciousness. The past shaped the present as Polish newspapers depicted management as the equivalent of the old gentry in Poland. Collective action, whether industrial, political, or social, had its roots in the communalism of peasant society and laid the foundations for community in America.

Chapter 1 deals with Poland, Chicago, and the world capitalist system with which both were involved. It defines the economic and social parameters that formed the world of Polish peasant/immigrant workers in the late nineteenth century and in the early part of the twentieth. The next two chapters portray their work and living experiences in Chicago's stockyard and steel districts. Chapter 4 discusses the communal response of Polish workers to the city's South Side. It explores old world rural attitudes and follows their migration to the new urban industrial neighborhoods of the Back of the Yards and South Chicago. Chapter 5 examines the attempt by these communities to reach out to other working-class and even middle-class people in order to have an impact on their environment. This extracommunal response leads to some sense of class consciousness. Neither the packinghouse nor steel-mill neighborhoods were ethnically segregated. Certainly various ethnic groups, including native-born whites, worked in the two great industries that dominated these two districts. A good deal of interethnic, and even to a limited degree interracial, contact and cooperation took place both in the neighborhood and on the job.[29] Politics is also dealt with in this chapter.

Success for Polish Americans in politics proved to be an especially difficult goal. In part this was because of the failure of the extra-communal response, a response that proved inadequate for the type of ethnocentric politics practiced in Chicago. It proved easier for Poles to unite with others on the shop floor than at the ballot box. Chapter 6 deals with the period 1918–22, when the Polish working-class community experienced several intense crises that threatened its existence. It reacted by defending itself through both strike action and communal rioting. The conclusion attempts to draw some lessons from the Polish experience on Chicago's South Side and to explain immigrant community building and its impact on the American city.

CHAPTER ONE

Poland, Chicago, and the New Economic System

The nineteenth century witnessed several revolutions. Innovations in technology and finance shook the world and remade Eastern Europe. These same transformations created Chicago on the shores of Lake Michigan. Poland and Chicago found their destinies intertwined by economic and technological changes. They became intimate partners in an international market system that brought social and economic upheaval to one and tremendous growth to the other. They became so involved with each other that Chicago, in many ways, became a Polish city, but a Polish city like no other.

The publication of Adam Smith's *An Inquiry Into the Nature and Causes of the Wealth of Nations* in 1776 and the growing tide of free market capitalism ushered in the new era. The revolution in economics centered on Great Britain and northwestern Europe. London became the financial capital of the new order as that order spread its influence worldwide.[1] Capitalism expanded its realm to include all of Western Europe and the Eastern seacoast of the United States as the two-pronged revolution in economics and industrialism continued. By the mid-1850s these areas were part of the investment and manufacturing nexus of what will be referred to as the Atlantic center. An intricate relationship also developed between the Atlantic center and certain outlying areas or borderlands.[2]

The areas of British settlement in North America and the Pacific might be called the Anglo-borderlands. The nations of Southern and Eastern Europe fit into the European borderlands category. Africa, Asia, and Latin America are most properly referred to as the colonial borderlands.

Each of these outlying districts had a unique relationship with the Atlantic center. In general, however, the capitalist core organized raw materials, investment, the trade in products, and even the movement of peoples through the world market. For example, one of the borderlands might provide immigrants to be distributed either to the Atlantic center or to one of the other borderlands as needed. Investments from the center often controlled the rate of migration, natural resources, agricultural products, and profits.[3] This system did not always work smoothly, but the relationship between the different borderlands and the center stayed fairly stable throughout the century from the end of the Napoleonic Wars to the outbreak of World War I, the period often referred to as Pax Britannica.

The progress of the nineteenth-century revolution can be traced in iron, stone, and mortar. Perhaps the growth of the modern transportation system provided the most obvious example of economic and technological change. Once again, the transformation originated in the Atlantic center. The development of railroads in Great Britain, Western Europe, and the United States completely altered marketing practices. Advances in transatlantic travel paralleled those on land. In particular, the development of the steel-hulled steamship revolutionized both migration and shipping. People, natural resources, and industrial products now flowed much more easily through a capitalist market system that had been developing over several centuries.

One result of this was the migration of millions of individuals. This occurred first in the Atlantic center, then in the borderlands as capitalism and industrialism needed more and more men, women, and children to satisfy their voracious appetites for cheap labor and expanding markets. Western European capitalism conquered the world in the period from the sixteenth to the nineteenth century. The Atlantic empires appeared simultaneously with the rise of capitalism and saw their greatest expansion in both economic and political terms in the nineteenth century. At this precise juncture Poland and Chicago became connected in terms of the world system.

Once this vast transportation and market system linked Poland and Chicago, human migration could proceed easily. American historians speak about a transportation revolution that opened up the American West, but it should also be remembered that the railroad made movement across Eastern Europe easier. This was not the only reason for migration from the "other" Europe, but it was a factor. Along with emancipation, railroads allowed peasants to be more mobile.

In the last half of the nineteenth century, changes in economic and social conditions in Poland motivated large numbers of people to emigrate. An estimated 3 million Poles left between 1850 and 1914. The American migration, which was the largest, was only part of the greater movement of Poles to areas in Europe, Asia, and the Western Hemisphere.[4]

Polish immigration to the United States reached its peak in 1912, when roughly 175,000 people entered the country from all parts of Poland. Perhaps the most reliable estimate states that between 1,148,649 and 1,780,151 Poles entered America between 1899 and 1932.[5] In 1920 it was calculated that there were approximately 3 million inhabitants of Polish heritage in the United States. By 1930 the U.S. Census counted 4,227,734 Poles.[6]

Poles in particular were well aware of the problem of crossing national frontiers, a result of the intricacies of the political situation in Eastern Europe. Since the end of the eighteenth century the old Polish Commonwealth had been absorbed by three states: Prussia, Russia, and Austria. These powers divided the Polish lands among themselves in three partitions. The first partition took place in 1772 without resistance. This was followed by programs to reform both Polish government and society. Their tardiness and perhaps even their success were soon apparent. The partitioning powers acted quickly to prevent the emergence of a strong Poland. A second partition took place in 1793, and the Polish state finally vanished from the European map in 1795. Poland reappeared in truncated form during the Napoleonic period but disappeared again after 1815. In that year the Congress of Vienna attempted to restore the old European order, that is, the political system before the rise of Napoleon. The new Europe included a newly partitioned Poland and the reestablishment of the eighteenth-century balance of power in Eastern Europe. The settlement established the Congress Kingdom of Poland, which comprised about one-sixth of the territory of the commonwealth before partitioning. The Congress of Vienna bound this new political entity permanently to the Russian Empire with the czar reigning as king in Warsaw. Austria occupied Galicia, in the south of Poland, and Prussia assumed control of Poznania and other parts of the western and northern sections of the old Polish state. This arrangement lasted until the end of World War I, when Poland regained its independence.

Though the Polish state had perished, the nation did not fade as a cultural entity. Nor did Poles cease to try to recover their lost political freedom. This movement had an important effect on the peasantry and in turn on emigration from Poland.

Congress Poland, although united with Russia, maintained its own army, retained a separate administration, and enacted a liberal constitution. The Poles were to rule themselves under the guidance of the czar's brother, the Grand Duke Constantine. In practice, the constitution soon became a dead letter, and the Russian disregard for many of its provisions led to an armed revolt against the Romanovs in November 1830.[7]

This outbreak, fought by and for the Polish gentry with little support from the peasantry, ended in defeat in eleven months. The resulting Organic Statute of February 14, 1832, superseded the Polish constitution of 1815. Now the Congress Kingdom became a more thoroughly integrated part of the Russian Empire.[8] Rebellions also took place in 1846 and 1848 in the Austrian and Prussian partitions, but they too failed and resulted in suppression of the national movement.

In 1863 another uprising took place. This one differed from the 1830–31 Russian-Polish War in that groups not directly connected with the landed aristocracy initiated the uprising. The intellectual proletariat in the growing urban centers of Russian Poland played an important role in the movement, and medical students in Warsaw stood among the first to answer the revolutionary call.

The revolt began on January 10, 1863. One of the first acts of the insurrectionists gave the movement a social revolutionary flavor; they granted the peasants title to their own land. This attempt to win the peasantry over to the insurrection proved to be, for the most part, a failure. Some peasants did take part in the fighting, but the majority did not trust the educated Poles or the gentry and remained neutral, if not hostile, to the patriotic groups.[9]

The significant step of land reform did not, however, go unnoticed by the czarist government. The Russians used it to permanently divide the Polish gentry and peasantry. The granting of peasant lands, or *uwłaszczenie*, by the Polish rebels on January 22, 1863, provided a call to arms not only for the peasants of Congress Poland but also for those in the former Polish territories to the east, the so-called Russian western *guberniias* of Lithuania, Byelorussia, and the Ukraine.[10] These peasants, most of whom were not ethnically Polish, had suffered drastic evictions during the Russian reforms of 1861. The St. Petersburg government, fearing the possibility of peasant support for the Polish insurrection in these areas, decided that the conditions of their emancipation needed to be considerably improved.

The czar published a new decree on March 1, 1863, affecting the three western districts. With this statute, the Russian government acted to return to the peasants that land taken from them in 1861 by the Polish gentry who still predominated in the area. The main purpose of the new dictate was to undermine the influence of the large landowners who were the major exponents of Polonism in the countryside. Within two months the Russians extended the Lithuanian decree to the Ukraine in order to gain peasant support there against the Poles.

In the Congress Kingdom, Czar Alexander I was more reluctant to act without the support of the Polish nobility. As the rebellion spread, however, the czar issued four decrees concerning the Polish peasantry. The orders of February 19, 1864, were important steps toward the modernization of Poland.

The first of these decrees outlined the general principles of emancipation. It declared that all peasants would become full owners of their land and that all holdings taken illegally from the peasantry would be returned. Also, all unfarmed land that belonged by right to the peasantry would be divided among the landless peasants. Finally, the title of the land was a gift by the czar to his Polish subjects. The decree included a land tax to be used to compensate the gentry for their losses. The other three decrees outlined the procedure to effectuate the proposed land distribution.[11]

These laws sealed the fate of the insurrection. The peasantry flocked to the Russians for protection. The important fact, however, was not that the revolt had failed but that peasant land reform had been achieved.

The realities of land reform in Russian Poland are somewhat difficult to judge. Official czarist records seem to inflate the impact of the granting of land to the peasantry. Nevertheless, it is estimated that 140,000 landless Polish peasants received holdings because of the reform. These averaged about three morgs, or roughly four acres. The Russian authorities had originally promised them land from the national domains and then broke this promise. There was actually little land to distribute. Authorities favored peasants who had been loyal to the czarist regime during the insurrection or were veterans of the Russian Army. In 1864 large ownerships comprised 10.4 million morgs, or about 56.5 percent of the Congress Kingdom's arable land. Small landholders held 7.9 million morgs in 514,113 holdings, or about 43.5 percent.[12]

The years following emancipation in Russian Poland saw changes take place throughout the countryside. Russian Poland began to develop somewhat within the framework of capitalist competition though peasants were still considered to be a separate estate with special obligations and privileges. One provision limited the right of any peasant to divide his holdings below six morgs among successors. Also all land granted by the Russian ukase could only be inherited or bought by other peasants. These laws, however, proved to be hard to enforce.

An immediate outcome of the liberation of the peasants was a temporary marked improvement in their standard of living. Housing, clothing, and food seem to have improved, especially for the well-to-do peasants. A sharp rise in the peasant population also followed emancipation. This resulted, however, in the partitioning of peasant properties as one generation succeeded another. Some peasants were able to purchase more land, but many could not hold on to their property. Until the 1880s there were few instances of parcellization of large estates in Congress Poland. In the twenty-five years after the reform, peasant land increased by only about 400,000 hectares (one morg equals 0.5 hectares, or roughly 1.4 acres), or by 8.1 percent. In 1904, some forty years after emancipation, the number of small farms in Russian Poland equaled 1,094,519. This included 957,521 held by peasants, 83,995 owned by middle-class farmers, and 53,003 controlled by petty noblemen. Farms of 2 hectares made up 24.9 percent of these holdings, those of from 2–5 hectares equaled 39.5 percent, farms of 5–20 hectares made up another 33.3 percent, and large farms of over 20 hectares made up only 2.3 percent. Small farms of up to 5 hectares made up 64.4 percent of all farms and at the same time occupied only 16 percent of the total acreage. Landless peasants grew in number from 220,000 in 1870 to 849,000 twenty-one years later. An agrarian proletariat appeared in the Polish countryside. For those lucky enough to hold on to their land the average size of their holdings decreased.[13]

The consequences of shifts in landownership and size of holdings have been the object of much debate. According to Lenin's theory of class division, some peasants began to act as small capitalists by augmenting and improving their operations, employing wage labor, and joining the ranks of the lower middle class. The poorer majority of the peasant class gravitated toward proletarianization. Other observers, including Stefan Kieniewicz, argue that holdings began to assume a uniform average size. In either case Russian Polish peasants exhibited a good deal of land hunger in the years between emancipation and the First World War.

The 1870s were years of rising grain prices and of increased production for better paying crops such as wheat, barley, and sugar beets. This encouraged farmers to try to increase production and their holdings. The world crisis in grain prices did not affect the Congress Kingdom until the mid-1880s. During the next decade a severe agricultural depression ensued. Grain prices dropped 50–60 percent. For the first time in four centuries Central Poland stopped exporting wheat to Western Europe. This resulted in the violent displacement by wheat from overseas, which shook the Polish economy. Instead of supplying wheat to the West, Poland became a supplier of textile goods to the Russian Empire and of emigrants to various parts of the world economic system. The spread of industrialization accompanied this change, as did a switch to wage labor for large groups of Polish peasants. A major change in Russian Poland's relationship with the world capitalist system occurred.[14]

The problems facing Polish peasants in Russian Poland also confronted their cousins who lived under different historical conditions in the German and Austrian partitions. The partitions indeed present a problem for a clear understanding of the status of Polish peasants in the nineteenth century. The fact that Poland did not exist as a political entity for much of the modern era meant that Polish peasants faced various types of economic and legal conditions in the three separate partitions. The peasants of German, or Prussian, Poland enjoyed emancipation in 1807. In Austria the Polish peasant gained emancipation in 1846. Both these events took place under vastly different conditions than did the Russian Polish emancipation of 1864. The abolition of compulsory labor and other feudal obligations often took longer to occur. Many of these issues were settled differently according to local custom. One reality, however, remained generally the same. The relationship between the peasantry and the large estates continued to be one of inequality in all three Polish areas of Eastern Europe. The large estate did not disappear after emancipation. In fact its position in the economy improved as it became more of a capitalist institution.

The German partition indeed saw large estates grow at the expense of land once held for use by the peasantry. Furthermore Germany under the leadership of Bismarck looked to replace the Polish peasantry with German colonists and to strip the Poles of their native culture. Bismarck's program of *Kulturkampf*, while also aimed at German Catholics, included an aggressive policy of Germanizing the Polish sections of the Reich. Polish farmhands often had difficulty obtaining full-time employment in Prussian Poland. In the county of Swiecie in western Prussia the income of a working village family was estimated at 280 to 300 marks annually in the late 1870s, whereas minimum expenses were calculated at 400 marks per year.[15]

In Galicia, that part of the old Polish Commonwealth under Austrian control, the Polish countryside suffered from overpopulation caused by the maldistribution of land. This was most obvious in 1902, when Galician emigration began to grow. In that year 79 percent of the farms in Galicia contained five hectares (12.5 acres). They covered a mere 29 percent of the land. Large holdings of between twenty and one hundred hectares covered 7 percent of the land. Estates of over one hundred hectares covered 40 percent of Galicia. Illiteracy was rampant in the Austrian partition. In 1900, 67.7 percent of the Galician population was illiterate. In 1888 Stanisław Szczepanowski wrote that a Galician works to maintain half and eats to nourish one-fourth a man. Under these conditions emigration provided a reasonable answer to the "Galician misery." Money from emigrants overseas sent home to Galicia eventually played an important role in that partition's economy. Reemigration and seasonal migrations by Galicians also added to the wealth of this portion of southern Poland.[16]

Prussian Poland supplied the first source of Polish emigrants to the United States and other parts of Europe, as well as Latin America. After 1871 and the creation of the German Empire this migration quickened. The 1880s were the time of greatest overseas migration from Prussian Poland. The movement spread to Russian Poland in the 1890s and to Galicia at the turn of the century.[17] Generally the emigration from the Polish lands was rural to urban whether to a European industrial center or one in the United States or Canada. Still some of it remained rural, as was the emigration to Brazil. Also the Polish provinces saw a good deal of seasonal migration. Indeed Poles who eventually settled in the United States often migrated in stages.[18]

The movement from Prussian Poland reached its greatest heights in the 1870s. At the end of the decade Poznania suffered a population loss of 41,000. By the 1890s this migration to the United States began to lessen and the emigration of Poles from Russia increased. Prussian Polish migration to the Ruhr, however, continued. Between 1890 and 1892 approximately 70,000 left the Congress Kingdom. After 1900 the Galician emigration gained momentum and that part of Poland supplied the greatest numbers going to the United States. In the period 1899 to 1910 some one-half million Poles left Galicia for the United States. The greatest single year of outmigration from the area was 1910, when over 60,000 persons departed.[19]

The Polish peasant in the nineteenth century lived through a period of immense change that altered Poland's relationship with the rest of the capitalist world. It no longer served as a catalyst for Western European urbanization by acting as the Atlantic center's breadbasket. The American Midwest now played that role. Poland became the frontier between the industrialized world to the west and the great rural expanse of Russia to the east.

This affected Polish peasants in several ways, the most important of which was emancipation. This in turn led to competition and land hunger, which led to emigration as a positive answer to new problems. Polish peasants acted both individually and as a social group to decide their own destiny. The old order crumbled and "liberated" the peasant, but to what end? Migration became one answer as Poland's economy readjusted to yet another shift in the capitalist system. Chicago too began to adjust.

The same forces that transformed Eastern Europe created Chicago. As an early settlement it was a trading post for the American seacoast, and ultimately for the European fur market. Later, with the expansion of the Atlantic center to include the northeastern United States, Chicago acted as a go-between for the new economic giant to its east and the natural-resource-rich Midwest and West. The opening of the Erie Canal in 1825 provided the original takeoff point for the city's economic growth. The canal made Chicago the western terminus for future east-west trade routes that took advantage of the natural waterway link provided by the Great Lakes. The Chicago–Erie Canal–New York City connection came as close to being a Northwest Passage as North America would ever have. Chicago's future looked bright as the first shipment of wheat headed for eastern markets in 1830. The city had become the agent of the Atlantic center in America's Midwest.[20]

Chicago's role as broker can be seen most clearly in the original

ethnic makeup of the settlement, its sources of financial investment, and the relationship between the emerging city and both
its hinterland and the Atlantic center.

The men and women who settled Chicago after the War of
1812 and the Fort Dearborn massacre of the same year hailed
primarily from New England. This fact established the ethnic
tensions between Chicago and the rest of Illinois that eventually
resulted in present-day regional politics. The names of those
families important in the early city's economic life, such as Wentworth, Newberry, Field, Armour, and Swift, all had roots in New
England or the Middle Atlantic states. The Chicago area first became a colony of the East shortly after the American War of Independence. The British had destroyed the old French ascen-
dancy. They in turn were replaced by their cousins from New
England. These Chicago families had intimate ties with the emerging economic centers of the East Coast.

A sure sign of this situation is the source of investment for the
enterprises of the early, young, and even mature city. Chicago
was a child of the East nurtured on loans from Boston, New
York, and Philadelphia. Eastern money, set free after the War of
Independence, searched out new investments. The West, with its
entrepôt Chicago, proved to be among the most profitable. Family and business connections solidified the link.[21]

What was Chicago's role in the new world economic system
created by the 1830s? The answer is in the emerging city's relationship with its hinterland. The Erie Canal, connecting New
York and Chicago, allowed midwestern farmers to supply the
East and ultimately Europe. The Great Lakes trade, however,
was affected by the seasons in a way that the Mississippi River
trade centered on St. Louis would never be. Saint Louis and even
little Galena looked more important than Chicago, with its population of about 5,000 in 1837. Chicago attempted to overcome St.
Louis' natural advantage by digging its own depression-plagued
canal between 1836 and 1848. The route of the Illinois-Michigan
Canal further points to Chicago's future role. Heading to the
southwest to link the sluggish Chicago River with the Illinois
River and ultimately the Mississippi River, it was designed to
better Chicago's position as broker between Yankee markets and

midwestern farms. As the canal neared completion, however, Chicago businessmen came upon a new technology that quickly made the canal obsolete—the railroad. Once again the east-west link proved crucial.

When the secondhand Pioneer steam engine made its way west from Chicago in 1848, it ushered in a new phase in the history of the city. Within six years Chicago found itself the hub of the nation's railway industry. Like a giant spider web, the railroad network connected east and west at Chicago. Saint Louis and other competitors fell to the wayside as Chicago became the full-fledged outpost of a rapidly expanding American capitalism.

This process involved three major steps in the nineteenth century. The first saw Chicago simply as a trading post delivering agricultural products to the East and finished industrial goods to the West. In the second phase the city actually produced goods for distribution to its hinterland. The prime example of this is the opening of the McCormick Reaper Works. Finally, Chicago began to exploit the West and Midwest for production of goods to be distributed throughout the capitalist world system. Although these developments often worked simultaneously, the final stage fully emerged only after the Civil War and the Chicago Fire of 1871. Once again, eastern investment proved of paramount importance. This final stage saw the city's population explode as Chicago became a primary example of an American industrial city. The city attracted hundreds of thousands of American and foreign-born workers in the process.[22]

Two examples of this final stage of capitalist development are the meatpacking and steel industries. They developed as great industries in the years between the Civil and First World wars and to a large part symbolized Chicago to the nation and the world. These industries also attracted large immigrant populations and from 1880 to 1920 were crucial in the development of a large part of Polish Chicago. For these reasons, a close look at steel and meatpacking will help to explain Chicago's and Poland's connection with each other and the Atlantic center.

By 1900, Chicago had clearly demonstrated its dominance in meatpacking and its challenge to Pittsburgh in steel-making. The industrial complex which had grown up since the end of the Civil War was so impressive that many came to the city not to witness its beautiful lakefront or magnificent park system, or even its notorious vice district, but to see the packinghouses and steel mills of Chicago's South Side.

The growth of the South Side industrial nexus began long before the turn of the century. Both the meatpacking and steel industries originally had been located closer to Chicago's business district. With the opening of the Union Stock Yards on Christmas Day 1865 and with the establishment of the North Chicago Rolling Mill Company's South Works in South Chicago in 1880, the emergence of the huge manufacturing districts of the South Side began.[23]

Chicago was the dominant meatpacking center in the United States even before the establishment of the Union Stock Yards, surpassing Cincinnati in the slaughter of hogs as early as 1861. During the Civil War, many plants left the war zones and moved to Chicago, thus greatly expanding its meatpacking industry. Prior to 1865 Chicago's livestock buyers and sellers transacted business at several yards around the city. These proved to be too small and inefficient for the rapidly expanding industry; therefore, plans to organize a large and conveniently located market took shape during the war. The packing plants had originally been established along the north branch of the Chicago River; the Civil War era packinghouses were located on the south branch about two and one-half miles from the site of the new yards.[24] After the creation of the Union Stock Yards, the packing industry gravitated toward the same location. The period from 1865 to 1890 was one of steady growth. Major packers such as Armour, Swift, Morris, Libby, and Cudahy established their plants and general offices near the Chicago stockyards.[25]

The site chosen for the new stockyard stood in a marshy region to the southwest of the city and, at the time, just outside its limits. The land was originally considered next to worthless, and the 320-acre site was purchased from John Wentworth for $100,000. The Union Stock Yard and Transit Company (U.S.Y. and T. Co.) was chartered on February 13, 1865. Work on the new livestock market began on June 7. Plans included construction of pens to hold

21,000 cattle, 75,000 hogs, 22,000 sheep, and 200 horses. Surrounded by railroad tracks, the new location included a hotel, a restaurant, and later a post office and bank. To expand the idea of a self-contained unit, company officials even developed plans to build housing for the expected increase in workers.[26]

Chicago celebrated the Christmas Day opening with much fanfare. A special train from the city brought visitors to the yards for the occasion, with special guests enjoying dinner at the Hough House, the market's new hotel. On the next day commission men put 761 hogs on sale in the pens. On December 27 the first cattle and sheep joined 3,700 hogs on exposition. By Saturday, December 30, 1865, the old yards closed forever and Chicago had its central livestock market.[27]

The Union Stock Yards and the industry grew rapidly. In 1866, the Chicago yards' first full year of operation, they handled 1,564,293 head of livestock. The number grew to 14,622,315 in 1900 and reached an all-time record for a livestock market in 1924 with 18,643,539 head. By 1900 the original 320 acres had increased to 475 acres with a pen capacity of 75,000 cattle, 50,000 sheep, 300,000 hogs, and 5,000 horses. At this time the stockyards and packinghouses employed approximately 32,000 people.[28]

The 1922 edition of *The Packer's Encyclopedia* listed several major considerations for the successful establishment of a packinghouse. Livestock markets had to be within easy reach; the distribution of the finished product was to be achieved economically; railroads had to be near and well developed; the labor supply was to be plentiful; the cost of power reasonable; water in ample supply; and finally, drainage and sewerage facilities had to be well developed. The Chicago location met all these conditions, especially the three most critical ones: railroad facilities, labor supply, and access to livestock markets.[29]

Well-developed railroad facilities served the Union Stock Yards. More than twenty-two railroads entered the yards and more than one hundred and fifty miles of track spanned stockyard property. The Union Stock Yard and Transit Company operated the Chicago Junction Railroad, which served all the railroad lines that touched Chicago. The company provided excellent facilities for the unloading of livestock from railroad cars. Hundreds of chutes allowed a fast transfer of animals to holding pens. Large overhead ramps connected the railroad docks with the main pen area and simultaneously with the packinghouses. The facilities guaranteed that many trains could be serviced at the same time and a speedy transfer guaranteed.[30] As to the labor supply, the second postulate, the *National Provisioner* stated accurately in 1894: "A great advantage of Chicago over country towns is the availability at the Union Stock Yards of all the labor that you want, for which you pay by the hour, and only use the labor as long as necessary."[31] The district surrounding the yards attracted diverse ethnic groups who eagerly searched out the available jobs. This in turn attracted others to the area.

Third, livestock was easily available at the Chicago location. The Union Stock Yards provided the primary market for the nation's livestock industry. The numbers and types in Chicago attracted buyers not only from the Chicago packinghouses but from off-market packers as well, especially those who catered to the kosher meat trade on the East Coast.

The volume of livestock trade was tremendous at the Chicago yards. From 1890 to 1933 yearly receipts did not once drop below 13 million head of livestock. In 1890 workers unloaded a record 311,557 railroad cars at the stockyard docks. Daily livestock runs also reached outstanding proportions. The record run for one day's receipts of hogs was 122,749 (December 15, 1924); of cattle, 49,128 head (November 16, 1908); and of sheep, 71,792 head (October 16, 1911).[32] In all, in its 106-year history the Union Stock Yards received over 1 billion head of livestock for sale in its pens.

There was, however, a fourth factor in the development of Chicago's meatpacking industry not mentioned in *The Packer's Encyclopedia*: technological change. The invention and successful demonstration of the refrigerated railroad car ensured Chicago's supremacy in the industry. While the G. H. Hammond Company shipped the first beef in a refrigerated car in 1868 from Detroit to Boston, Chicago's Swift and Company perfected the cars to revolutionize the industry. Gustavus F. Swift, the founder of the company, began experimenting with the cars in the 1870s. Both Swift and Armour and Company soon dominated the manufacture and distribution of the railroad cars. The railroads, fearing a loss on the shipments of livestock along their lines, refused to build them. At first, they also would not haul them. The Grand Trunk Railroad finally agreed to move the cars along its line, eventually forcing others to handle the cars. This transportation network provided a solid foundation for the meatpacking industry, and the Chicago packers used it to extend their control over the national market.[33] Many of these same factors were also central to the successful establishment of Chicago's other great industry, steel.

South Chicago had originally been a camping ground on the shores of Lake Michigan for the Potawatomie Nation and later developed as a fishing village for white settlers. There had been little industry located in the area before 1880, when the steel industry transformed the small settlement then called Ainsworth.

Earlier industrial developments included the establishment of the Northwestern Fertilizing Company in 1867. Two lumberyards and some small grain elevators also provided employment for a growing number of Irish and Swedish workers in the area. In 1869 the Calumet and Chicago Canal Company began operation primarily as a land development company. The federal government, in turn, deepened the Calumet River and improved the harbor, thus making the area more attractive to industry. By the mid-1870s, some small steelworks appeared in South Chicago along with the buildings of the car shops of the Baltimore and Ohio Railroad, but the major industrial event occurred in 1880 with the opening of a plant by the North Chicago Rolling Mill Company.[34]

The firm, which operated plants on both Chicago's North Side and in Milwaukee, began to look for a new plant location in 1879 and chose the mouth of the Calumet River. The company built four blast furnaces in 1880. A Bessemer steel mill and a rail mill started operating in 1882. In 1889 the North Chicago Rolling Mill Company and the Union Steel Company merged, purchased the Joliet Steel Company, and formed the Illinois Steel Company. The South Chicago plant, often referred to as the South Works, had expanded by 1898 from an original site of 74.5 acres to one of approximately 260 acres.

In 1898 the South Works was one of the most modern mills in the industry. Thirty-six miles of standard track served the gigantic mill, along with six and one-half miles of 3′0 gauge track. The south slip handled water shipments running in from the Calumet River. The north slip connected the plant to Lake Michigan. The ore yards reached by the south slip had a capacity of 300,000 tons, the north slip yards a capacity of 700,000 tons. Ore received in 1897 totaled 1,629,865 tons. Because of winter ice on the lake, the season for ore shipments ran only from April 15 to December 15.

The blast furnace provided perhaps the most symbolic feature of this or any steel mill. Described often in dramatic terms, it represented the heart of the steel-making process at the turn of the century. The South Works had the capacity to produce 80,000 tons per month, or 960,000 tons of steel annually. The secret of the mill's success was put simply but accurately in 1898: "The situation of the plant gives unexceptional opportunities for receiving and shipping materials, which are unsurpassed by its competitors." By the turn of the century, 3,500 men worked in the South Works.[35]

Other firms followed the lead of Illinois Steel and located in the Calumet District. These plants gave the entire region the appearance of a steel town: they dominated its skyline and the whole scenery of South Chicago.[36] The industry expanded across the state line into Indiana, where after 1900 the huge United States Steel Corporation created a new town called Gary. A merger that combined the resources of Carnegie Steel, National Steel, Federal Steel, and an assortment of finishing companies formed U.S. Steel. The new corporation included Illinois Steel and brought the giant trust to South Chicago. Eighty percent of domestic steel production was now united in one corporation.[37]

By 1900 both the steel and meatpacking industries were solidly established in Chicago. The steel industry expanded from the mouth of the Calumet River to cover the entire lakefront south of 79th Street. The meatpacking industry centered on the Union Stock Yards near 47th Street and Ashland Avenue. Both produced goods that moved throughout the economic system, which was being transformed by technological change and the free market.

By the time immigrants reached Chicago they had a long and tiresome journey behind them. Although the means of transportation had improved considerably by the last quarter of the nineteenth century, the journey could still be a difficult one.

The immediate problem for Polish emigrants from areas outside the German Empire was to cross the imperial frontiers so as to reach the great ports of Northern and Western Europe. Until the first decade of the twentieth century, Liverpool led the other European cities in the immigrant traffic, but by the time Polish emigration reached its peak, the German ports of Hamburg and Bremen had the most embarkations for the United States. The Prussian government was instrumental in directing the emigrant flow to ports in Germany and Belgium, where conditions for emigrants were felt to be the best.

After 1892, the German government involved itself more in the immigrant traffic by setting up control stations at its eastern borders. Germany instituted these checkpoints for fear that immigrants would carry cholera from the interior to the ports. In 1897 the Reichstag passed another law concerned with the trade: it dealt with the agents, ships, rights of emigrants in the ports, and their medical inspection.

The increased complexity of American health regulations made it more important to deal effectively with illness and other physical or mental deficiencies at the ports, or even earlier at the frontiers. In 1907 authorities rejected almost 12,000 people at the German border and nearly 40,000 at the various ports, leaving 13,000 for American inspectors to turn back at Ellis Island in New York. Obviously, doctors at European ports and border stations did a very effective job despite the crowds and the intricacies of American laws.[38]

One of the border control stations was located at Myslowitz at the junction of the German, Russian, and Austrian empires in Poland. Both Austrian and Russian Poles passed through that station to reach the German ports. At the control stations emigrants walked through a narrow corridor where they met three men: an agent of the steamship lines, a Russian policeman, and a German officer. The emigrant gave his or her tickets to the agent and then entered a large hall. The Germans kept Austrian and Russian Poles separate. The room had tiled floors, high ceilings, and colored-glass windows and was heated and ventilated. At night electric lights kept it lit. Around the hall were wooden benches on which emigrants might sleep if they could find a place. Others lay down on the floor or on their baggage. Vermin covered the walls and a strong likelihood existed that baggage or clothing would be infected. Nothing was charged for these "accommodations" during the stay at Myslowitz.

Once the emigrants entered the border station they could not leave except to board the train taking them farther west. A canteen, whose stock consisted mostly of beer, wine, and alcohol, provided the only food. It was high priced and of uneven quality.

German law required immigrants to pass a medical examination at Myslowitz. It consisted primarily of a quick look in the eyes of the traveler. Guards sometimes disinfected the clothing and baggage of the emigrants. Authorities segregated Jews on the trains leaving the checkpoints.[39]

Other Poles who crossed the frontier often did not visit the border stations. At different times, when one of the imperial governments opposed emigration, it was necessary to slip across the border. Others simply chose, for one reason or another, to avoid border inspections. This could be dangerous as well as difficult. One letter written in 1891 comments:

When leaving home be careful, especially at the border. I am not sure what it is like there. I have been told that everyone must escape across it. If you must do so and the soldiers chase you, do not run, but stand still or they may shoot. It is best to get good papers.[40]

In some cases guides took emigrants across the frontier. It was often a perilous business for both the guides and their customers. One emigrant reported:

From Zielonij we went to Zielun, we stopped at Mother's, had dinner and met two guides. I went with them to the border near Budy Kraszewskie. I asked how much it would cost to get across. They said five rubles. I talked them into doing it for three. We came to the border in the afternoon and I watched for Russians for six hours, until I was relieved at six p.m. We crossed the frontier at eight in the evening.[41]

Once emigrants crossed the border their adventure had just begun. The emigrant was faced with the trip across Germany to one of the ports in order to take passage to America. Emigrant trains were uncomfortable and often were filled to capacity. There also might be some confusion, especially if trains had to be changed along the way. One immigrant explained to his wife in the 1890s:

My dear wife, I cannot tell you which of the five train stations to go to in Berlin. Ask a Prussian conductor and tell him you wish to go to Antwerp. He will explain which station to go to and where to buy a ticket.[42]

After making it to the port, emigrants had to cope with a new environment. On arrival they were ushered into a room for another medical examination. Again, a doctor looked into their eyes while an officer noted their description and place of birth. Another asked questions concerning age, employment, addresses of friends or relatives in America and Europe, and amounts of money on hand. The emigrants also gave proof of a valid ticket. While waiting to be processed, they were taken into a large room and served rye bread, fruit, marmalade, and tea.[43]

If the immigrant was unfortunate enough to have a long wait at the port, it could be a very expensive venture. Those going to the United States were forewarned: "You should have at least forty rubles with you," wrote Jozef Markiewicz, "because in Bremen you must pay for your own expenses while waiting for the ship."[44] The ports, especially Bremen, were great stately places and they often made a lasting impression. One emigrant commented:

Bremen is a very rich city. There are no wooden houses or cheap boarding houses. Every home looks like a beautiful palace and the entire city stands on a canal. How big the city is we cannot say because it is so immense. If you were to come here you would be amazed at its richness. The railroad station is lit with electric lights and colored lamps. From Bremen to the sea is a two-hour train ride.[45]

Bremen gave many immigrants their first real taste of nineteenth-century urban life, and many liked it. "For room and board we spend one mark and two troyki per day. The mode of life is good here."[46] Another wrote of the meals in Bremen:

This is the kind of breakfast we have: three buns and all the coffee you can drink up to ten cups; for lunch potatoes, cooked carrots, potatoes in sauerkraut, very fat pork and a little bread; for supper, bread with butter and all the coffee that you want.[47]

The port also held many dangers. Travelers were warned about people in Bremen and at the other ports who would try to cheat them out of their money and baggage.[48] Another danger centered on big city life. One young Pole from Małopolska, for example, came to Hamburg with money given him by his parents for his trip to America. Instead of buying a ticket, he spent his money in a house of prostitution. Penniless in the great city, he found work and eventually made his way back to his village.[49] But the great majority of Poles boarded their ships without incident and made their long ocean voyages.

Some described the crossing as pleasant, though sometimes rough. One man warned his wife about the dangers for children on board:

I warn you, my dear wife, be careful with the children. Do not let them run on board the ship. While it is sailing quietly it is alright for them to go on deck . . . however, when the ship is rocking it is best for them to lie in bed. When the sea is rough, quite a few people are thrown about and break their heads. On the ship I was on, one lady ran down the steps and fell. She broke her legs and died three days later.[50]

Stanisław Kazmierkiewicz wrote that emigrants should stay near the center of the ship, "where it will be healthier than at either end." He also advised travelers to take the lower berths because the smells of the quarters lingered near the ceilings of the rooms.[51]

The letters warned the peasants not used to the sea about seasickness. They often fell prey to nausea and vomiting. "Take with you on the ship—sugar, tea and Hoffman Stomach Drops—so that you can help yourself when you cannot eat."[52]

By the 1890s the trip to America from northwestern European ports seldom exceeded twelve days. Few died on the crossing. Discomfort proved to be the main problem. The crowding could be excessive, especially in steerage, though even third-class passage had become quite tolerable.[53]

Once the immigrants made the crossing, they had to pass through yet another receiving station. In New York City this was Castle Garden on the tip of Manhattan, or after 1892 Ellis Island just off the coast. "When you land you will be recorded in a large building called Castle Garden. Give this address to a man there. He speaks Polish and he will send you to me," one immigrant wrote.[54] Another wrote to a friend: "When you will come to America they will give you a ticket for your clothes. Do not lose the ticket. When you get to the off-loading area, I will go for your clothes."[55]

As there were people trying to cheat emigrants in the European ports, there were also the so-called runners in New York City. Immigrant letters warned new travelers: "When you get to Castle Garden, there will be agents who will try to take the new arrivals with them for a place to sleep. Do not go with them. If you do, you will pay plenty."[56] Another wrote in 1891: "If someone wants to take you some place, do not go. They invite you to dinner, and then it costs you plenty. It is best to buy a ticket at Castle Garden and come straight to me."[57]

Immigration authorities required immigrants to pass another physical and mental examination at the point of disembarkation. At New York, barges brought immigrants from the ships to Ellis Island, where attendants guided them into the inspection lanes. Four medical officers performed the preliminary examination. They stood at the front of the lines while two others waited at the far end where the lines merged into two exits. Every immigrant passed two medical officers.

The first officer looked for any obvious physical or mental problem. In 1917 an investigator described his duties as follows:

It is the function of this officer to look at all defects, mental and physical, in the passing immigrant. As the immigrant approaches, the officer gives him a quick glance. Experience enables him in that one glance to take in six details, namely the scalp, face, neck, hands, gait, and general condition, both mental and physical. Should any of these details not come into view, the alien is halted and the officer satisfies himself that no suspicious sign or symptom exists regarding that particular detail.[58]

Whereas the average immigrant remained at Ellis Island only about two or three hours, many were detained by officers. Medical examiners marked these immigrants with chalk and sent them to another section for closer inspection. Special caution was taken to determine mental illness. "Should the immigrant appear stupid and inattentive to such an extent that mental defect is suspected, an X is made on his coat at the interior aspect of his right shoulder." If the inspectors found definite evidence of mental disease, a circled X would be marked. Other brands were made on an immigrant's coat for different physical deformities or diseases. Certain symptoms, such as a person's temperature, were written out in full. The suspects then went to a room apart from the rest of the arrivals. Here, with the help of an interpreter, the immigrants underwent a more complete examination. Some were held for long periods, some hospitalized, and some released after a more thorough inspection. Others were not admitted.[59]

Those immigrants not detained by the first medical officer faced a second inspector known as the "eye man." This officer also made a quick mental and physical examination and then proceeded to check the immigrant's eyes. If the alien successfully passed this inspection he was then sent to a third official from the Immigrant Service, who questioned him in order to discover whether he was an anarchist, bigamist, pauper, criminal, or otherwise unfit.[60]

Officials did not allow some immigrants to enter for other than physical or mental problems. Three Polish girls entering the United States via Quebec were stopped, and one of them gave her brother-in-law's address in Chicago as their destination. Upon investigation by the Chicago immigration inspector it was decided not to let the girls enter, as conditions were unsatisfactory. In another case, authorities detained a woman first for a closer medical inspection and then for lying to an inspector regarding her destination and marriage in Chicago. Authorities eventually permitted her to enter the country in custody of the Polish National Alliance in New York.[61]

Once the immigrants passed through Ellis Island or one of the other ports of entry they had to make their way to the interior. The trip to Chicago was a long one. According to the advisory committee of the U.S. Bureau of Immigration, newly arrived aliens going to Chicago often rode trains with no decent accommodations and arrived in "deplorable condition." Some immigrants lost their baggage on the trip. Others got lost themselves. Two Polish girls from Galicia, headed for Chicago, never arrived. The Immigrants' Protective League traced them as far as Rochester, New York. Apparently they met a man from Rochester on the train and he offered to help them. The league explained that they had simply disappeared. One seventeen-year-old girl got off the train in South Chicago, thinking she had reached her destination, but she had mistaken that station for the main station downtown. Fortunately, someone came to her aid.[62]

The arrival in Chicago could be a bewildering experience for a new immigrant. As the train approached the city, rapid industrialization was evident everywhere. The train station itself could be a source of confusion. Other kinds of rail traffic often sidetracked the immigrant trains. It was hard to meet those that arrived behind schedule. Furthermore, the great crowds at Chicago made it difficult to find waiting friends and relatives.[63]

Some of the immigrants discovered on arrival that they did not have the full or proper address. One Polish girl knew her destination only to be South Chicago. The police eventually picked her up and brought her to the Immigrants' Protective League, where she was united with her aunt the next day.[64]

Often the immigrant was well-prepared for the trip by travels in Poland or in other European countries for work. Others knew the stories of previous immigrants. One observer pointed out that villagers told the tales of the first peasants to leave for America over and over again, producing both the language and effect of legend. No communication gap existed between those who traveled to the United States or to other foreign places and the people in the home village. In fact, a communications network connected the various areas wherever people of the village settled.[65]

Letters provided the most obvious form of communication, but another soon developed. Immigrants returned to their native village with news of America. The "continual immigrant" was a well-recognized phenomenon. In one village in Małopolska, a villager made the trip eight times, as a local functionary explained: "Mike went to America and before you know it, here he is again. Before a year passes he receives a letter from some friends in America that there is work and away he goes. Mike doesn't stay in one place long."[66]

Villagers referred to others as *obieżyświaty*, or globetrotters. One such wanderer visited America twice and once worked his way to Africa on a tramp steamer. His wife finally put a stop to his adventures.[67] Some, after saving money in America, returned to Poland. One woman and her child went back with the understanding that her husband would follow. When after several years, he did not return to Poland, she traveled to Chicago to find him.[68]

For many the trip to Chicago was not their first stop in America. One South Chicago family originally settled in Pittsburgh. Disappointed in the Steel City, they decided to move to Chicago after talking to some Chicago Poles. When they arrived they found their new home to be much like the one they had left behind in Pennsylvania.[69]

The trip from the train station to the various Polish neighborhoods took place on the city's vast and confusing public transportation system. As streetcars carrying new immigrants approached the Stock Yard District, the Poles had their first taste of life in their new home. The effects of rapid industrialization showed everywhere in the neighborhood, but perhaps the most startling evidence of the meatpacking industry was the strange, pungent odor that filled the air. Different smells came at different times of the day, but they were all simply referred to as the "stockyard smell."[70] Even before they descended from the streetcar, the newcomers were initiated into the world of industrial Chicago by the sights and sounds of the packing industry. The same proved true of the Steel District or the North Side Polonia. Smokestacks from nearby factories, tanneries, and mills dominated the skyline. Everywhere industry reigned dominant.

The immigrant's new environment presented several problems regarding survival. The newcomer had to find food, shelter, and employment. And, of course, the basic human desire for companionship and a sense of community also proved urgent in the new setting.

In order to deal with these problems, different groups created an informal system connecting the various settlements in Europe and America. Often the immigrant who came to the United States arrived on a prepaid ticket. Polish immigrants sent money back to their villages in order to have their family, friends, or fiancés join them.[71] After the first migration had been made from a village, a system of information and mutual aid quickly emerged. Although the village could not be exactly duplicated in the new environment, the would-be immigrant knew that he could find compatriots, or *rodacy*, in the new settlement who would help him to establish himself in Chicago.[72]

The first year in the city was probably the most crucial in determining the success of the individual in coping with the new urban-industrial milieu. The immigrant's ability to deal with the new situation depended on his resources as well as on the help he received from others. The role of friends and relatives was crucial and is stressed in the literature concerning immigrant acculturation. Some suffered cultural shock, a keen experience of disparity between the cultures they left behind and the new environment offered in America.[73]

The creation of what might be called a "workers' commune" often proved to be the first step taken in the creation of an immigrant settlement. Several men rented a building and employed the wife of one of the married men to purchase and prepare food and to do the wash and the housekeeping. Men would move in and out of this arrangement, sometimes leaving to visit Poland, other times leaving once they had married or brought their families from Europe. This way of life was especially important in the early days of the colony, when men far outnumbered women in the immigrant communities.[74]

Both men and women also often rented rooms in the households of previously settled families. This provided one of the chief sources of overcrowding in neighborhoods, which from outward appearances did not seem congested.[75] When the family migrated as a unit, friends could be depended on to help find suitable quarters. After the initial migration from a village to Chicago, immigrants established the so-called neighbor-family or chain-migration system to aid others.[76]

This aid included more than simply finding shelter for the new arrivals. Those who arrived earlier also aided their rodacy to find employment. In the various Polish settlements in Chicago immigrants found their way to the mills, factories, packinghouses, and lumberyards with help from their friends. Often this connection could be crucial in gaining employment. Neither job-hunting nor hiring was highly scientific or selective. More often than not, it was by knowing someone that a job could be secured.[77]

After securing the basics of life, the immigrant entered more fully into the life of the community. For most, this meant joining the local Polish Catholic parish. Once again primary group relations played a key role in the choice of a place of worship. Besides the fact that different ethnic groups often dominated the various Catholic parishes in Chicago's neighborhoods, the immigrant usually chose his or her parish from among several Polish churches because family or friends attended there.[78]

The bond between the new settlement and the old village was especially important for the unmarried immigrants. Instead of searching outside the group for a mate, they looked within. Often they returned to Europe to marry or chose another immigrant from the same village or district to wed. Regionalism continued to play a role even in America.[79]

The fact that there was diversity within the ethnic group as well as ethnic diversity within the neighborhood is crucial for understanding the development of the Polish community. The different regional groups often kept to themselves and argued with those from other parts of Poland. They also often maintained independent social and fraternal groups.[80] Chicago's neighborhoods contained many of these subethnic groups. This variety had a significant effect on the Polish response to the problems facing them in Chicago.

Most of the Poles who came to Chicago settled in five distinct parts of the city. The first to be established was located on the Near North Side, centering on the intersection of Milwaukee and Ashland avenues with Division Street. The second large settlement developed in Pilsen on the West Side near 18th Street and

Ashland Avenue. Polish immigrants established two separate Polish neighborhoods in the Stock Yard District, one in Bridgeport and the other in Back of the Yards near 47th Street and Ashland Avenue. Finally a Polish neighborhood appeared in South Chicago near the massive Illinois Steel Works.[81]

CHAPTER TWO

Working and Living
in Packingtown:
Back of the Yards, 1890–1914

Both the Back of the Yards and South Chicago presented a host of problems to the newly arrived Polish immigrants. The meatpacking and steel industries that dominated the two districts created these difficulties by their very nature. The rapid expansion of industry in Chicago in the nineteenth century did not allow for much planning, neither as to the construction of plants nor as to the neighborhoods that grew alongside them. The search for profit provided the main force behind these developments, and few considered the welfare of the workers in the early days of the city's industrial development. The resulting hasty and haphazard growth led to conditions, both inside and outside the plants and mills, that startled investigators and proved trying for the people who had to experience them daily.

The evolution of meatpacking into a mass production industry centered at Chicago was completed by the 1880s. Economic rivalry between the major packers, although lessened by eventual financial combination, had an adverse effect on the working conditions found in the plants. Because of the low margin of profit inherent in the industry, the easiest place to cut costs and thereby improve financial gains lay in the labor process. By the turn of the century this situation brought a general decline in the wages paid to employees by the packers. It also altered the conditions under which the workers in the plants lived and inevitably changed the ethnic and racial makeup of the workforce. Competition also influenced the status of different types of workers. Increasingly, skilled laborers found their jobs replaced by a minute division of operations that allowed the hiring of cheaper, unskilled workers and thus undermined the position of the skilled in the industry. These changes took place at the very time when Polish workers entered the plants surrounding the Union Stock Yards in the 1880s.

Although some Poles undoubtedly had worked in the industry before, it was in 1886 that they entered Chicago's packing plants in large numbers. In October employees of the major packinghouses had struck in an attempt to preserve the eight-hour day, which they had won earlier during the demonstrations that had culminated in the Haymarket Riot of May 4. The workforce in the yards was at that time predominantly Irish and German, with a considerable number of native-born white workers of uncertain ethnic origins. The failure of this strike, which stemmed primarily from ineffective leadership on the part of the Knights of Labor, meant an end to unionism in the stockyards until the turn of the century. It also allowed the return to conditions that prevailed in the industry before the May Day demonstrations, but with the added insult of the "yellow dog contract," which the packers forced on the returning workers in order to prevent unionization in the future.[1]

There were various ways of garnering a job in the stockyards. Workers, including the new Polish arrivals, were introduced to the industry usually at the crack of dawn outside one of the packing plants. Crowds of hundreds and sometimes thousands of laborers, mostly unskilled, gathered near the various employment offices. They appeared every morning at around six o'clock and waited for about an hour. The employment agent walked among the crowd and picked those who seemed the strongest and best able to do the unskilled work at the plant. The agent did not allow any bargaining over wages or hours; he simply tapped the men he had chosen on the back and said: "Come along!" Generally, the agent picked only a few. The rest of the group would be back the next day. Those hired in this manner often did not know how long they would remain employed. Many returned looking for work after a very short time. Because of the labor surplus, the packers could keep wages low and prevent unionization.

The employment agents were under the direction of the superintendent of each plant. One of his assistants, or someone

Union Stock Yards, 1900. This photograph taken from a hot-air balloon shows the maze of cattle, sheep, and hog pens that made up the Chicago stockyards. Just to the west across Racine Avenue stood Chicago's major packinghouses. *(Courtesy of the Chicago Historical Society)*

designated by him, procured the employment of all help. This man received a request from each of the foremen specifying how many and what type of workers, skilled or unskilled, each department needed. Often the foremen did not know the exact number until the gang had been formed at seven o'clock in the morning. The employment office closed at 8:00 A.M. if at all possible, and the crowds dispersed. According to John E. O'Hern, the manager of the Armour plant, the companies preferred former employees. He also claimed that Armour and Company hired workers on the basis of their knowledge of the industry. This probably proved true when it came to the hiring of skilled men, but the increased use of unskilled labor made this less necessary.

There were other methods for gaining employment in the yards and packinghouses. The denial of the packers notwithstanding, the practice of paying off the foremen and employment agents proved quite common. In 1908 Mike Matkowski swore that he paid ten dollars to a truckman at the G. H. Hammond Company so that he and Anton Humek could get jobs. Management did dismiss the guilty parties when investigators brought such matters before them. Still, this probably was a well-established practice in the yards, at least before World War I. Many workers were hired through the intercession of friends or neighbors who had already secured jobs. This was the way women usually found their employment; occasionally, recommendations from the welfare departments of the packers also helped them get jobs. At times, a priest or some other community leader prevailed on one of the packers to hire someone known to be a hardship case. In any event, the hiring practices of the packers before World War I were hardly scientific and depended more often than not on personal relationships.[2]

Each day's packing operations began the evening before or early in the morning when livestock trains from all over the Midwest and the West converged on Chicago. Union Stock Yard and Transit Company employees unloaded thousands of hogs, sheep, cattle, calves, and horses daily at the chutes and railroad docks located in the yards. Company workers or those of the various livestock commission firms then drove the animals to the sale areas. Here handlers fed, watered, and rested the livestock for the market, which began usually between 8:30 and 9:30 A.M.

Long before the selling began, buyers from both the on-market and off-market packers received their instructions as to type and quantity of livestock to be purchased for that day's kill or for shipment, usually to the East. When the market finally opened, the buyers moved about on horseback from pen to pen, examined the livestock, and made their bids. Once a commission agent accepted a bid, drovers brought the animals to the scales provided by the Union Stock Yard Company. Here scalemasters weighed them and established the exact price for the lot. Then the agents of the packers picked up the livestock and drove the animals over the ramps to the packinghouses or to the train docks for shipment.[3]

It was a difficult chore to drive tens of thousands of animals over the ramps or viaducts to the packinghouses. Observers often accused the drovers of unwarranted cruelty. The *Chicago Tribune* pointed out that it was not enough that the animals were killed but that they were beaten by the employees, and thus their suffering was needlessly increased. The herders faced a difficult job.

The floors in the pens were often slippery from animal drop-
pings, and not infrequently men were injured by falling in the
pens or in the cobblestone alleys that cut through the stockyards.
The wooden ramps also were slippery, and the animals could easily turn on the drovers in the narrow confines through which they
had to drive them. This proved especially dangerous when cattle
panicked and were most difficult to control. Animals that died in
transit or while being taken to the packinghouses lay piled on the
side of the docks and alleys to be removed later, adding to the general unpleasantness of the job of driving animals to slaughter.[4]

Whereas the *Tribune* chided the livestock handlers for treating
the animals with undue cruelty, the packers saw it more as an economic problem. Drovers who beat the animals could cause serious financial loss. Foremen recruited handlers from the mass of
men looking for work every morning and did not require much
skill of them. Nevertheless, a knowledge of the yards and of the
various passageways and ramps was necessary, especially for those
in charge of the gang of drovers. Although the job required little
experience, the packers eventually realized that these men had to
be taught the proper ways of handling the stock because the
abuse of the animals affected the meat produced after slaughter.
Mistreatment could cause damage to the high-priced meat of the
loin and rump of the animal. While the packers knew that severity was sometimes necessary in dealing with cattle gone wild, they
constantly warned their employees against the harsh treatment
of animals. Hogs were especially susceptible to damage when
struck by the drovers. If driven carelessly, hogs would pile up
on one another, thus causing what was known as a "face-bruised
ham." Men driving hogs with whips often became callous and
caused severe markings on the animals. Therefore, the employers developed a canvas slapper that left no mark on the stock and
urged the animals along by a loud slapping noise. Sheep presented less of a problem and rarely had to be beaten. They simply
followed the "Judas goat" to the slaughter.[5]

Once the animals had been selected, purchased, and driven to
the various packing plants, the packers found it necessary to give
them some rest to ensure the quality of the meat. Ideally they
should have been allowed to rest for the night. The packers, how-

Hog kill in a Chicago packinghouse, ca. 1890. Notice the dimly lit room and the blood-soaked wooden floors. *(Courtesy of the Chicago Historical Society)*

ever, more often than not, killed their livestock the day of purchase after giving them some brief rest in the cooling pens adjacent to, and sometimes on the roof of, the packinghouses.[6]

The slaughterhouses stood several stories high. While their walls were generally constructed of brick, their interiors were made mostly of wood. Most floors, although sometimes made of brick or cement, were also wooden. The slaughtering and packing process made them wet and slimy. The buildings were poorly lit, and most rooms needed artificial light at all times. Some of the workrooms in the interior of the buildings enjoyed neither daylight nor fresh air. Rank smells filled these rooms. In these buildings, often haphazardly built and with additions simply tacked on as need seemed to dictate, man and animal confronted each other.[7]

The slaughtering process resembled an assembly line; it had to achieve the most effective processing of the livestock. Workers drove the animals from the resting pens to the kill floors, where others, known as stunners, quickly dispatched them. The carcass then proceeded down the line until the gang completed the operation. Others then transferred the carcass from the kill floor to the cooler.

The cattle kill is perhaps the best example of this. Handlers drove the rested cattle into a narrow pen, which tightly held two animals and allowed for little movement. Men walking on a platform alongside the stunning pens swung steel sledgehammers, with which they hit the animals between the eyes and knocked them unconscious. Earlier in the nineteenth century another form of downing the animal, called spearing, prevailed. The spear, a clumsy and inefficient tool, consisted of a bar of iron about six feet in length, sharpened to a dull point at the lower end. The worker positioned himself above the animal and sent the spear with as much accuracy as possible into the area where the head and cervical column meet, thus severing the spinal cord. But the stunning was not permanent and often several blows were needed. In 1880 the *Chicago Tribune* reported that fully seventy-five out of every one hundred cattle downed in this manner had to be finished off with a sledgehammer. Spearing also did not allow the free bleeding of the animal and caused the blood to settle in the neck, which later had to be trimmed. By the turn of the century the sledgehammer replaced the spear in all the major houses. Once the stunning had been completed, workers raised the sides of the pen so that the cattle fell out onto the floor, where shacklers chained the hind legs. A steam-driven hoist raised the carcass and sent it down the line for the completion of the killing process.[8]

The force of its own weight carried the carcass on a pulley down a slope to the sticker. This worker cut the animal's veins by stabbing it through the chest into the hollow of the neck and cutting through the arteries. This demanded skill and had to be done quickly and accurately. The throat had to be well opened and the blood from both the arteries and veins had to flow freely; otherwise the beef would become discolored. The main danger was that the animal might regain consciousness before it would be stuck, break loose from its bonds, or perhaps awaken even before the chains were secured to its hind legs and run loose on slippery floors covered with steaming blood and filled with men with sharp knives. If this occurred, a man with a rifle attempted to quickly kill the animal and remove the danger from the kill floor. This, however, rarely occurred, especially after the complete replacement of the spear by the sledgehammer in the downing process.[9]

The carcass moved farther down the line on a pulley to the header, who decapitated it. This skilled worker had to make sure that he removed the hide from the head and did not damage the tongue in the process. The slaughterhouses kept the heads in numerical order so that they could be identified with the beefs upon government inspection.

The carcasses passed some 193 men in a gang formed to kill 84 head per hour. The size of the gang varied from plant to plant. Management divided the work up in a minute division of skills that allowed the hiring of unskilled immigrant labor at low rates. In 1905 there were over thirty classifications of men in the killing department. Included were twenty rates of pay that ranged from 50 cents to 16-1/2 cents per hour.

Once the slaughter of animals had begun, the flow seemed endless. After 1886 the packers perfected a way of speeding up the killing process in all the departments. Within a short time the rate of animal processing increased tremendously. In 1884 five cattle splitters in a gang would process 800 head of cattle in ten hours, or 16 cattle per man per hour at an hourly wage of 45 cents. By 1894 four splitters were getting out 1,200 cattle in ten hours, or 30 head per man per hour. This was an increase of nearly 100 percent in ten years, yet the wage rate fell to 40 cents per hour, except for the "pacemakers," who made 50 cents per hour. These men could and did work at fast speeds, thus quickening the entire line. Unskilled workers made up the great majority of workers in the packinghouses. But the packers chose exceptionally skilled or strong men to fill the better-paying positions in the plant. These men, known as steady-time men, did not depend on the number of hours worked per day to make their paycheck worth the effort. The packers paid steady-time men a regular wage each week, unlike the great majority, whose weekly income depended on the frequency of livestock receipts at the yards. They averaged between $24 and $27 per week while the other 90 percent of the workers were paid at a lower rate, by the hour, and on the basis of work done.

The steady-time men felt loyal to the company and formed a sort of aristocracy among the butcher workmen. This diminished the unity of the workers and hampered the growth of labor unions to the benefit of the packers, whose primary concern was increased production at a lower price and, especially, higher profits. The pacemakers opposed unionization because it threatened their privileged position in the workforce.

Wage rates varied during the two decades before World War I, but the differences in wages between the skilled and unskilled did not. The skilled held the most desirable and well-paid jobs in the cattle department. Floormen wielded the knife and by necessity had to be among the most experienced in the yards. It was their job to skin out the breast and remove the hide from the inside of the hind legs and sides. The skinner could do more damage to the animal than any other worker in the plant. A cut in the hide could depreciate it by more than the wage paid per hour to the floormen. A spotted or rough carcass would be the last to be sold and meant the loss of a great amount of money on a perishable product. The splitter wielded the ax or cleaver and had to cut through the center of the backbone. If the cut was not made neatly the wholesaler would not be able to sell the piece quickly, again risking a drop in value.

Whenever possible, management simplified the process. In 1904 in a cattle department of a large Chicago packer, 230 workers killed 105 cattle per hour. Of these, only 11 earned 50 cents per hour, while 3 received 55 cents. The less skilled positions abounded. Eighty-six workers received 20 cents or more. One hundred and forty-four garnered less than that amount. The packers and some of the men benefited from this division of labor. It increased the number of unskilled workers and to some extent the wages of the very skilled. Whereas an all-around butcher might hope to make 35 cents per hour in 1904, the floormen and splitters earned 50 cents. The company could count on those few men and disregard the hundreds of others. But more important, the average wage of the gang, while it would have been 35 cents if all the workers had been butchers, stood at only 21 cents because of the division of labor.[10]

Polish immigrants filled these less skilled positions. They took jobs as washers and wipers, men who cleaned the dressed carcasses of water and blood. Poles could also be found among the truckers who moved material and supplies around the various departments and brought paunches and intestines to the chutes that led from the kill floor to the offal departments. And they were, of course, among the general laborers who assisted the penners, knockers, and hoisters and cleaned the blood from the floors and took the dressed carcasses from the kill floors to the coolers.

Because of the seasonal fluctuations that prevailed in the industry, the unskilled positions were only temporary. When the available livestock did not warrant the maintenance of a full gang in the killing department, foremen laid off unskilled laborers. The more skilled then took over their functions. They received less pay but preferred it to being out of work.

The hog and sheep kills followed the same general pattern as that practiced in the cattle department. Of course their variations arose from the basic differences between the species, but as in the cattle kill, the other departments also witnessed a minute division of labor. From the time that the hogs and sheep arrived in the resting pens until they ended up in the cooler, they too had passed by an army of men.[11]

Once the killing process was completed, the meat and other parts of the animal went to the various departments that made up the packing plant. Despite the varieties of meat products, only about 58 percent of the animal purchased on the hoof ever reached the table. At an earlier time a good deal of waste resulted, but by the turn of the century a by-products industry had evolved, and the packers found a use for practically every part of the animal. Products ranged from fresh meat to tennis and violin strings, and from cosmetics to fertilizers and dog food. The butterine department produced a butter substitute from the fat that had been worked into tallow, of which the Swift plant in Chicago alone produced thirty tons a day. Even horns and hooves,

Hog wheel in a Chicago packinghouse, ca. 1905. Most Poles entered the packing industry as unskilled workers. These "shacklers" had the job of grabbing a hind leg of a hog and shackling it to the hog wheel, which then raised the still-living animal into the air and sent it on its way to the kill floor. *(Courtesy of the Chicago Historical Society)*

which earlier had been discarded, found a ready market. Since newer immigrants filled most of the unskilled positions, all these departments provided jobs for the growing Polish community.[12]

By 1900 a substantial number of women had entered the industry. In 1875 the canning division became the first department to hire female employees. At first management did not allow women to use knives, considered man's tools, and they did not offer women jobs requiring them. In the canning division women painted and labeled cans and jars. They also canned beef and tended the machines that cut the various types of meat. By 1890 only 990 women worked in meatpacking, or about 2.2 percent of the total employees nationwide. Their numbers, however, grew rapidly so that by 1904 over 2,000 labored in the Chicago plants. From 1910 to 1920 the number of women in the industry nearly tripled nationally; the 12,197 female employees in 1920 represented more than 10 percent of all the workforce. Wartime conditions had necessitated their large-scale entry into the industry, but simply accelerated a long-time trend.

Many women entered divisions other than the canning department. During the strikes in 1894 and 1904 management introduced women to many jobs in which men alone had previously been employed. Foreign-born Polish, Slovak, and Lithuanian women now "took up the knife" in the Chicago packinghouses. By the end of the 1920s, women could be found in just about every department, including the kill, where they helped to dress the carcasses, but they still did not take part in the actual slaughter of the animals.[13]

Of the jobs held by women, pork trimming was considered to be the most skilled. It took about a year of experience to become a skilled pork trimmer, whose pay was almost always based on piecework. Women had to lug heavy, meat-filled buckets, which could weigh more than ninety pounds, to a nearby conveyor belt, but this was the first department in which women were allowed to use knives, so women desired this skilled job. Most, however, had to accept less skilled functions such as feeding cans into the machines. These working women checked the cans as they entered the machines to be filled with meat products, and spilled any water found in them on the floor. As a result, workers constantly stood in pools of water. In 1910 women earned $6 per week for this work. Whether skilled or unskilled, women workers in the yards tended to be paid substantially less than their male co-workers.

Officials of one packing house explained that they paid women employed in the gut-pulling department a lower rate because males could be moved to heavier work when needed. Women did not receive equal pay even when they replaced men on a job. They might even earn less than expected because their work proved so irregular. Although an occasional week's earnings could be high, the yearly amount was low. Women, except for the most skilled, had little chance for advancement. Like their fathers, husbands, and brothers, the packers defined them as cheap, or in their case even cheaper, labor to be used when needed and discarded when not.[14]

Children also periodically labored in the meatpacking industry. In 1894, 320 youngsters, including 18 girls, worked in Chicago packinghouses. The following year the number of those under sixteen years of age fell to 242. Armour, Morris, and Swift and Company employed most of them. In 1896 the number of children employed increased by only 5. Armour & Company and the Nelson Morris Company once again led the packers in the employment of children. Swift remained the third largest employer but had reduced its total from 44 in 1895 to 24 in 1896. Libby, McNeill & Libby also reduced the number from 27 in 1895 to only 8 in 1896. Then the number rose again; by 1900 a total of 507 children under the age of sixteen labored in the Chicago packinghouses.

The children worked as common laborers and at the lowest rates of pay. Hardship was often the excuse used for their employment, but studies proved this not to be true in all cases. However, some children did work in their fathers' places. In 1895 inspectors found a child working at a dangerous machine. He gave the explanation that he held the job for his father, who had been injured while tending the device and would lose the position if his son did not take his place.[15]

In 1893, Illinois joined the ranks of the more progressive states by the passage of a child labor law. It made illegal the employment of a child below the age of fourteen and prohibited the employment of children in manufacturing. Children over the age of fourteen, but under sixteen, could not work at any machinery or at any job considered "hazardous," which meant any job that insurance companies would refuse to insure.

In 1897 a new law extended the provisions of the 1893 law to commercial enterprises. The law also limited the working hours of those under the age of sixteen to no more than sixty hours per week and no more than ten hours per day. The act also required the issuance of affidavits by doctors who certified the health of the individual child and his or her ability to perform the work required. By the turn of the century, compulsory school laws strengthened the child labor laws and a new statute prohibited children under sixteen from working more than eight hours per day.[16]

The regulations, however, proved difficult to enforce despite the establishment of the office of factory inspector. On the one hand, the office was simply understaffed, and on the other, both the age and health restrictions could easily be overcome by determined parents. The age of a child could easily be forged on the sworn affidavits with a fee to a notary public. This made it impossible for factory inspectors to enforce the law. At the request of the parents, doctors often issued false statements as to the physical condition of the children.[17] The law which required the issuance of a school certificate vouching that the child under sixteen could read and write English was also easily evaded. As a matter of routine, parish schools, both Catholic and Lutheran, granted such letters once a child had been confirmed.[18]

On family-owned farms, wherever they were, children grew naturally into the world of work. They looked after cattle, sheep, or goats, helped make hay, reaped grains, or prepared firewood. But in the industrial context child labor often became a dire necessity for survival, although factory inspectors tended falsely to view it as a European tradition. Work in the urban industrial world of Chicago differed greatly from the agricultural life of Poland, and many immigrants looked back with nostalgia to those days.[19]

Often the school presented a problem. Teenagers became bored with the subjects offered and saw no purpose in going on. In a 1911 study of why children left school before the eighth grade, 110 reasons out of 330 reflected negatively on the school.

According to the report, "Many said that they could have contrived to keep their children in school had suitable instruction been offered." The study concluded, on the basis of interviews with parents, students, and teachers, that the schools did not adequately address the needs of the children in the neighborhood.[20]

Family income, however, provided a much more pressing problem in the Stock Yard District than the inadequacy of the school system. Although many reformers denied that economic need was the real factor in the problem of child labor, it was decisive in the Back of the Yards.[21]

A good half the reasons given for leaving school before the end of the eighth grade pointed to economic need. The money problems of the family, when combined with the inadequacy of the school system, often proved to be fatal for the academic career of the child, as one investigator testified: "If family resources are fitful, the child's wage is considered to be necessary, and under these circumstances, concrete proof of the school's economic value must be presented before the parents are willing to have their children continue."

It was noted that a generous desire to help their parents was the reason that boys left school. Rent payments and the need to keep the younger children in school presented more pressing worries than a future career opportunity that remaining in school might bring to an older child. Since girls were to become mothers, school was a waste of time. Work, on the other hand, could help them to pay back the family and prepare them financially for married life.[22]

A longer stay in school did indeed not seem to affect the earning power of children under sixteen. Nor was there any connection between age and earning power. After sixteen, the young adult was legally able to perform a greater range of tasks, which was reflected in the wage. However, girls who had completed eighth grade seemed to have been better able to find jobs that paid more than $6 a week than those who left school earlier. In the stockyards, on the other hand, the amount of schooling did not provide an economic advantage; body size and dexterity in a particular type of work had more to do with the wage received than any other factor.

The children of the Stock Yard District did not necessarily find employment in packinghouses upon leaving school. Light industries and offices in Chicago provided much employment. In a study of 131 boys, 50 percent found their first job either as errand boys or with a messenger service. Factories accounted for only 26 of the jobs reacquired after leaving school. Of the sample, only 12 had any chance of reaching a skilled position. Many of the boys worked in the general offices of the packers, where the average starting weekly wage was between $4.00 and $4.50. This seemed to be about the average pay for this type of job in the city during the period. The story of one Polish boy was typical of the experiences of the male child workers. He first secured employment as a messenger in a printing firm for $5.00 per week and left after a week. The boy then worked as a messenger in the yards for four weeks at $4.00. After this, he went to Donnelley's Press as a messenger for the same pay for three weeks. The fact that the child moved from job to job was not unusual. As the boys wandered from one position to another, they often simply moved into factory work, where they remained. The experience of girls seemed much the same, with wages and type of employment the only difference. Generally, the starting wage for female children stood between $3.00 and $4.00 per week. Of 86 girls studied, 52 found their first employment in a factory, usually wrapping or packing candy or soap or making boxes. The girls moved from job to job like the boys, though they seemed less rebellious. Three female friends, who changed jobs eleven times in fifteen consecutive months, were atypical, but restlessness on the job was a common feature, if not expressed as often among the boys.[23]

Whatever the various reasons for child labor, the efforts of the reformers did have a direct effect on it, not only in the packinghouses but in all the industries of the city. The number of children under the age of sixteen working in urban areas in Illinois fell from 8,543 in 1900 to 4,264 in 1904, a drop of 50.1 percent. The decline in meatpacking was even greater. During 1904 about 80 children worked in packinghouses, a decline of 86.6 percent from 1900.[24] Several factors caused this change: inspectors had been most diligent in their prosecution of the managers of the slaughterhouses; the compulsory school attendance law had been strengthened; and the Meat Cutter's Union, which would not admit members younger than sixteen, lobbied for stronger child labor laws. By 1914, child labor had just about disappeared from the stockyards, except for some young boys who worked as messengers in the packers' offices. Of course, those who had given false ages could not be traced.[25]

The decline of child labor in the packinghouses does not mean that children did not enter early into the proletarian status of the community. High school and other educational opportunities, such as night school, had little influence on their lives. One Polish woman did not even know of such a program, which took place in a public school a short walk from her home. The children of Polish workers in the district faced a life of work similar to that of their fathers and mothers.[26]

Industrial accidents stalked packinghouse workers whatever their age, sex, or nationality. Although the injuries encountered in the stockyards were not so violent or severe as in the steel mills, mines, and railroads, they were frequent enough to affect the livelihood of the families in Back of the Yards. When compared to statistics relating to other industries, accidents in the meatpacking industry seem almost negligible, but the figures recorded by the Bureau of Labor Statistics of the State of Illinois do not give a complete picture of the problem.

The laws regarding the registration of injuries changed frequently. At the outset, the bureau recorded only those accidents that caused a loss of thirty workdays or more. Later, mishaps that caused a loss of fifteen or more days were filed with the state, and eventually, an incident that caused a worker to miss at least seven days had to be reported to the Illinois Labor Department. After this compensation act was repealed, the legislators reinstated the old thirty- and fifteen-day definitions of severity. There is also some question as to how reliably management reported accidents. Accurate data concerning nonfatal accidents remained difficult to obtain. For the most part, however, the state accurately reported fatal accidents.[27]

In 1907 the first report concerned with industrial accidents listed beefpacking as a separate industry. For the final six months of the year it recorded 5 deadly accidents in the packinghouses.

When compared to the 100 who had died in the mines during the same period and the 129 killed while working for steam railroads, the figures for beefpacking fatalities seem small, representing only 1.7 percent of the 298 industrial fatalities in the state. During the same period, 17 workers suffered injuries serious enough to lose thirty workdays in the industry, as compared to 287 coal miners and 412 steam railway workers. Nonfatal accidents in beefpacking made up only 1.6 percent of the 1,094 statewide total.[28]

From June 1907 to the end of 1912, 33 men died in industrial accidents in Chicago meatpacking plants. Thirteen of these died in the Swift & Company plant alone, from June 1907 to December 31, 1910.[29]

Many fatal accidents occurred in the industry because of elevators. For example, on March 2, and again on August 16, 1909, Polish laborers died due to elevator-related accidents at the Schwarschild & Sulzberger Company plant. In March of the same year, an elevator killed a Lithuanian in the Swift plant. Machinery caused other deaths, as in the case of John Panszezyk, a married Pole with four children who was caught in the belting of some machinery at Morris & Company on January 12, 1909. Others died from falls or the collapse of walls or platforms. Some nonfatal accidents were caused by falls or by falling objects, others by mishaps with machines. Because of the low and inadequate wages, such accidents—most likely underreported—created near disaster for many families.[30]

The conditions under which the employees labored led to a variety of diseases typical for the industry. Skin infections provided a constant threat. Dermatoconiesis and tubular wart, called in the vernacular of the yards "pickled hands" and "cut worm," haunted workers. Pickled hands afflicted most frequently those who worked in the pickle rooms or who handled pickled meat. Some cases appeared also in the sausage department. Irritated and reddened skin provided the first symptom of the disease. After a few days the skin thickened and cracked. At times the flesh opened to the bone, creating terrible sores on both the palm and the back of the hand. The disease healed slowly and often took as long as two months to cure, even if the worker agreed to leave his job to prevent the risk of reinfection. Cut worm, on the other hand, yielded more readily to treatment because it could be surgically removed. The latter infection prevailed among those who handled cattle and hog intestines; it first appeared as a small tubular wart, which grew rapidly, finally breaking open and creating an ulcer. Other types of skin disease, although less common, also appeared among the workers, all probably attributable to the materials handled in the packing process. Workers did not use gloves for protection before the First World War.

Among the types of sickness that most seriously injured the workers were those that affected the lungs. Leaving the yards was the only cure, a decision impossible for many who could find no other work. Dust irritation occurred among those who worked in the wool and hair houses. A few days after exposure to the dust of the rooms, the men would come down with a dry, hacking cough. The problem probably could have been avoided by wearing protectors. Some workers wore handkerchiefs over their mouths in an attempt to deal with the dust in the hair and fertilizer plants, where the same basic conditions existed, but they often removed them after taking the kidding of their fellow workers. Those who ground bones in the fertilizer departments or worked in the horn rooms suffered from a similar problem. The fine particles of dust found there had very sharp edges and often worked themselves into the flesh and the linings of the air passages, causing a troublesome infection.

Pneumonia affected those who worked in the massive carcass coolers. Workers moved the meat as quickly as possible after dressing to the large refrigerated rooms. Men and women who worked in this section of the plant constantly moved in and out of storage areas between a room filled with hot, steamy air and the cooler. Heavy clothing could do little to temper the effects of the sudden change in temperature. Pneumonia resulted and often ended in death.

Rheumatism also haunted the packinghouse workers, many of whom worked in damp rooms. Workers experienced especially bad conditions on the "killing beds," where blood and water soaked the wooden floors. Even when the packers installed concrete footings or raised platforms, the water and steam necessary for the operation of the departments endangered the employees. Those who worked in the hide department and the scalders in the hog kill worked under similarly bad conditions. The livestock handlers also contracted the disease. Rain and snow often soaked them to the skin, and they had to wade through the mud and manure that covered the pens and ramps of the stockyards.

Other diseases that plagued the workers ranged from ulcers to nervous disorders and tuberculosis and were at least aggravated, if not caused, by unsanitary conditions. Living conditions caused by economic needs also affected and worsened these diseases.[31]

Housing presented a constant problem to the residents in Back of the Yards. In the 1890s the neighborhood resembled a frontier settlement with dirt streets, wooden buildings and sidewalks, and outdoor plumbing. Mary McDowell, who worked in the neighborhood in 1894 as head resident of the University of Chicago Settlement House, referred to the citizens of the community as "pioneers," settlers on the new urban frontier. In 1900 a report on Chicago tenement conditions did not include the Stock Yard District because the author considered it, like South Chicago, to be so bad as to be atypical. In 1905 Upton Sinclair described the same basic conditions in *The Jungle*. Another investigation in 1911 repeated with even more detail the indictment of housing and living conditions in the district. Even a lawyer representing the packers announced as late as 1918: "The only remedy is absolute destruction of the district. You should tear down the district, burn all the houses."[32]

Some of the first cottages had been built near 43rd and Loomis on land eventually sold to the packers for their expanding plants. These settlers relocated near the corner of 46th and Laflin streets. The wooden homes were easily moved to the new location.[33] As housing expanded in the area west of the yards, builders used the same basic wooden balloon-frame construction. The neighborhood was fully settled by 1890 and most of the buildings had been constructed before 1914. A 1939 study of housing in the New City Community Area, which included the Back of the Yards, concluded that 15 percent of the housing then standing had been built before 1885, 54 percent before 1895, 77 percent before

1905, and 93 percent before 1915. Residential structures in this community were generally older than those in the city as a whole.[34]

Housing in the area developed in one of two basic ways: the creation of large residential subdivisions or the erection of individual tenements and cottages by families who for one reason or another wished to live in Back of the Yards. In either case, houses were built of wood in the form of the so-called balloon-frame buildings first erected in the city in the 1830s. This type of construction was a variation of the traditional wooden structure using lighter boards instead of heavy timbers, and nails rather than interlocking mortise work. Closely fitted boards covered the outside of the house. The dwellings were easily assembled, portable, and above all cheap to construct.[35]

One of the influential real estate developers of the city played an active role in the early days of the community. Samuel Eberly Gross entered the real estate business in the late 1860s and soon amassed a fortune. By the turn of the century he dedicated at least sixteen suburbs, and between 1884 and 1894 he sold more than 30,000 lots and built more than 7,000 houses. In addition to being a land developer and builder, he also acted as a financier. Gross, who had come to the Stock Yard District in the 1880s, organized subdivisions in McKinley Park, Bridgeport, and Back of the Yards. The houses Gross offered in these neighborhoods were typical working-class dwellings, cheaply priced.

S. E. Gross's largest and most important subdivision in the Stock Yard District stood in Back of the Yards between 45th and 47th streets and Ashland Avenue and Loomis Street. In 1883 he started building homes for families of moderate means, and soon his New City development in Back of the Yards began to take concrete shape. In 1887 he improved the forty-acre subdivision and ran a brisk business from his regional office on the corner of 47th Street and Ashland Avenue. Over 400 lots priced from $625 were for sale in this development. Most significant for the stockyard workers were the small initial cash outlays and low monthly payments. Gross asked only one-tenth of the full price of the lot, or of a house with a lot, as down payment. The subsequent monthly payments ranged for $8 to $12. Gross would even lend money to the buyer of a lot to erect a home, if one had not already been built, and he did not require a cash down payment if the buyer agreed to build at once. Workers flocked to the Gross development, which lay within a five-minute walk of the packing-houses. By 1891, 350 people had purchased homes from Gross in New City.

For his working class clientele, Gross built wooden one-story cottages, with an attic and a basement raised above grade, on twenty-five foot lots. The floor plan included two bedrooms, a front hall, a parlor, a kitchen—the largest room in the house—and a pantry. The entire structure measured seventeen feet, nine inches in width and twenty-one feet, ten inches in length. Gross divided the basement into two rooms with an outside entrance. This "working man's reward" cost from $1,050 to $1,500 with a $100 down payment and a monthly installment of $9 to $11. Gross pointed out that the monthly mortgage payments equaled no more than rent for an apartment of comparable size. Unlike many of his competitors, Gross seldom foreclosed on a mortgage and many considered him a friend of the working class. He was so popular among workers that leaders of the United Work-ingmen's Societies tried to persuade him to run for mayor of Chi-cago in 1889.[36]

Besides large-scale developers like Gross, individuals came to the neighborhood and built cottages or tenements for the grow-ing population of the district. In 1884, for instance, William Fitzgerald built a two-story frame building at 4225 South Ash-land Avenue. At the same time, a Mr. Doherty put up a frame cottage on 47th Street near Centre (Racine) Avenue, and Mr. Witch replaced his small cottage with a larger two-story frame tenement on Justine Street near 48th Street. In the spring of 1884 the *Sun* commented that the immediate area around the in-tersection of 51st Street and Ashland Avenue was growing so rapidly that some groceries and other types of business already operated there. Even a new hotel, the Ashland House, opened on 47th and Ashland near the Gross subdivision. When Packers Ave-nue opened south of 48th Street, four cottages appeared along the new roadway.[37]

A detailed survey made in 1939 provided a retrospective ex-amination of the building trends that existed between 1884 and

Table 1. Housing Characteristics in Back of the Yards

Type of structure	Total reports	Year built 1905–1914	Year built 1895–1904	Year built 1885–1894
Total reports	7,808	1,607	2,342	3,859
Single family	1,941	293	511	1,137
Multi-family	3,413	819	1,027	1,567
Under 10 units	3,400	814	1,024	1,562
10–19 units	12	5	3	4
20 units or more	1	0	0	1
Business with dwelling	774	147	224	403
Other nonconverted	575	113	209	253
Converted	1,105	235	371	499

Source: Chicago Plan Commission, *Chicago Land Use Survey*, Housing in Chicago Communities—Community Area Number 61, Preliminary Release (Chicago, 1940).

World War I. These data for the New City census area, of which the Back of the Yards is a part, describe housing still standing at the time of the report. Table 1 is derived from the survey.[38]

The number of cottages actually built was larger because many of the later tenements replaced single-family dwellings, but the trend is obvious. After 1885 multifamily dwellings replaced the smaller buildings at an astonishing rate. The figures before 1885 show a greater balance between the two types of structures, with 539 single-family units and 569 multifamily units constructed before that year. After that, the Back of the Yards became a district of tenements rather than of small homes. But most tenements contained fewer than ten units. Nearly 10 percent of the buildings contained a small business, such as grocery stores, shops, and taverns. They could be found on every street, not just on major arteries such as 47th and 51st streets and Ashland Avenue. A study published in 1911 by Sophonisba P. Breckinridge and Edith Abbott of the Chicago School of Civics and Philanthropy confirmed the general pattern; it examined ten "typical" blocks and those that made up Whiskey Row on Ashland Avenue in Back of the Yards.

This report revealed that the average building in that neighborhood was a two-story wooden frame house which covered less than 60 percent of the lot. Of 617 structures surveyed, 144 were one-story, 387 were two-story, and 85 three-story buildings, and only one had more than three floors. Only 46 of them were made of brick. Of 608 homes checked, nearly 58 percent contained one or two apartments, 90.4 percent contained four or fewer apartments, and only one structure had fifteen units. Of 582 neighborhood lots examined, 248 had a building covering half or less of the land; 43 stood vacant. Buildings covered 90 percent of only 25 lots. This neighborhood of small tenements possessed a relatively large amount of open space in Back of the Yards that somewhat concealed the actual congestion of the neighborhood.

The district did, however, suffer from overcrowding. The ten typical blocks were uniform in size, each having an area of 3.3 acres. The most densely populated block had 306 people per acre; the average was 208. Compared to the Polish district on the Northwest Side with 340 persons per acre and the Jewish West Side, the blocks in Back of the Yards seemed less overpopulated, but the actual living space available in the cottages and tenements proved inadequate.

The survey by Breckinridge and Abbott gave the size of 1,616 apartments and homes. Nine hundred five of them had four rooms, 127 two, and 17 only one room. Two hundred thirty dwellings contained five rooms and 159 had more. Twelve hundred ninety-three had four or more rooms. Although the flats contained many rooms, they remained on the whole quite small. Fourteen hundred fifty-nine rooms had less than 70 square feet, the legal minimum under the 1903 tenement law. One man slept in a cubicle with an area less than 18 square feet, while in another house four people slept in a room of only 28 square feet. Five apartments contained less than 120 square feet, considered to be the minimum size of the large room required under the law for apartments constructed after 1903. Nine hundred thirty-five of the rooms did not even meet the required height of eight and one-half feet.

City regulations that dealt with the amount of cubic air space allotted per person supposedly governed living conditions. The minimum amount allowed per adult was 400 cubic feet and for each child 200 cubic feet. Out of 3,730 rooms surveyed, 1,181, or 53 percent, provided less space than the law required for the number of occupants. The investigation unveiled some startling violations. In one apartment, four people slept in a chamber that provided only 333 cubic feet; legally, it could not have been occupied by more than one child under the age of twelve. In another house, five people slept in a cubicle of only 472 cubic feet, and in yet another, seven persons slept in an area that legally should have been occupied by one child and one adult or by three children. Such cases seemed quite common in the Stock Yard District.

Lodgers caused much of the overcrowding. They made up over 27 percent of the neighborhood population according to the 1911 survey. Twenty-two hundred sixty-one men and 322 women lived with 794 families, or 50.8 percent of those contacted. This average of three persons per family caused serious overcrowding in the small apartments. It also led to higher rents for the entire neighborhood because the landlords, knowing the number of boarders, raised the rent. Breckinridge and Abbott did not mention that the lodgers were often family members or former neighbors from Europe. It was not simply an economic system forced on the workers by low wages but part of a communal response to the rigor of emigration and the new industrial order.

The boarders affected the privacy of the families. Toilet facilities were mostly inadequate, and one toilet located in the hall, basement, or yard had to be used by several families—in one case, no fewer than seven. Out of 156 toilets surveyed, only 35 percent served one family only, 52 percent two families, and three or more families used 13 percent. This meant that 22 percent had to be used by five persons and 52 percent by six to ten individuals. In extreme cases a single lavatory had to serve thirty-six to forty people. These overtaxed facilities were often found to be dirty and in disrepair. Those located inside apartments usually stood in a closet that opened on the kitchen, and investigators generally found these to be clean and in good condition. The kitchen provided the center of home activity and the warmest room during the winter months.[39]

The family spent much of its time outdoors or in public meeting places. Children played in the streets and alleys while women

Outhouse on South Marshfield Street in Back of the Yards, early 1920s. This filthy yard outhouse provided the only toilet facilities for the building directly in front of it. Notice the closeness of the outhouse to the neighboring tenement with its open, unscreened window. *(Alice May Miller, "Rents and Housing in the Stockyards District of Chicago." Master's thesis, University of Chicago, 1923)*

conversed on the stoops and in the backyards. The men too engaged in these social activities, but for them the saloon provided a most important institution.[40]

Vile odors enveloped the wooden cottages, tenements, and saloons of the Back of the Yards. Evil-smelling nuisances surrounded the place. Smells from the stockyards and packinghouses penetrated the homes. "Bubbly Creek," an open sewer, formed the area's northern boundary. Some nineteen packinghouses dumped their waste into this slow-moving west fork of the South Branch of the Chicago River. The resulting pollution equaled that of a city of over one million people, and yet the dumping of packinghouse refuse had actually been forbidden by the municipal code. Foul-smelling Bubbly Creek stretched all along the northern part of the district up to Western Avenue until 1910, when the portion west of Ashland Avenue was filled in for industrial purposes. The city closed another section in the

1920s. A large part of the river system remained just east of Ashland Avenue until mid-century.[41]

The western edge of the district faced perhaps the greatest health hazard. For over thirty years along Robey Street, now Damen Avenue, stood the city's garbage dumps. Around 1890 the city had contracted with the owners of that land to dump refuse into the large holes created by the digging of clay for the manufacture of bricks. The city paid 25 cents a load for this. When the residents of the Back of the Yards complained about the problem, a city official simply replied that "one more odor didn't make any difference anyway." Perhaps the municipal government tended to ignore the problem because Tom Carey, the local alderman, owned the brickyards and dumps. The ill-smelling dumps did make a difference: one out of every three infants died

4700 block of South Robey Street (Damen Avenue), early 1920s. These homes on an unpaved section of Robey Street originally fronted on the large open garbage dumps that formed the western boundary of the Back of the Yards at the beginning of the twentieth century. *(Alice May Miller)*

Rooftops in Back of the Yards, early 1920s. Children often played in
the alleys and on the rooftops of the Back of the Yards. This family
lived on the top floor of the wooden tenement. Their closest toilet facility was an outhouse down in the yard. (*Alice May Miller*)

in the area near them. The death rate for the neighborhood as a
whole stood five times higher than in Hyde Park, the fashionable
lakefront district to the east. The garbage dumps were, therefore, one of the first civic problems that mobilized the neighborhood and helped to create a sense of community.[42]

The city government also ignored other problems that plagued
the neighborhood. Scum-covered ditches sometimes proved to
be dangerous to the children of the neighborhood. Houses without sewer connections existed because the city claimed that not
enough buildings stood on the streets to allow a connection with
the water system. Polish women who lived on one block complained that the city constantly ignored their protests. They carried water for home use from hydrants a good distance from
their homes. When settlement house workers investigated conditions, they found six tenements to be without water. The startling
fact was that the population of the block equaled that of many

other blocks with more dwellings on them. Eventually, after social workers became involved, the city responded.

Another difficulty that beset the residents was the pollution
emanating from a glue factory just outside the stockyards. To cut
expenses, the plant used the water necessary for the glue-making
process over and over again. Water stood in an open field next to
the plant and was pumped back into it when necessary. After
much protest, the company gave up the practice. Even when residents dealt with problems, the changes were often as bad as the
original situation. After closing the garbage dumps along Robey
Street, the city dumped cinders and other garbage along 49th
Street as filler for the railroad viaducts being constructed there.
Such actions would never have been allowed in other parts of the
city such as Hyde Park.[43]

The railroads too presented a problem. They ran through the
district at street level and created a constant threat to life and limb.
Between Ashland Avenue and State Street to the east lay forty-
two unprotected tracks. When the railroads that surrounded the
neighborhood were constructed, they did not present much of a
problem, but once the area became residential, they presented a
real danger to residents. Still, the city tended to ignore the pleas
of the Stock Yard District until hundreds had lost their lives.
Eventually, the municipal government demanded elevation and
the problem disappeared.[44]

Besides such outrageous disregard of the basic needs of the
people of the Back of the Yards, there existed the usual disadvan-
tages of living in a place that seemed of no concern to the city as a
whole. The original government of the Town of Lake, and, after
annexation in 1889, the City of Chicago, did not provide adequate sewers or sidewalks. At certain times of the year, the streets
resembled canals. In the words of an early settler:

They was big ditches then, along all the streets, deep enough to drown
in and wide enough for two boats to pass, an' many's the night I fell
into them ditches coming home from Peter Damm's place. Rowin' in
the ditches, tho, was safer than walkin'. They wasn't many sidewalks,
and what they was, was wooden, built over the ditches, an' you was just
as likely to hit a loose board or a rotten one as not an' go all the way

thro; an' one man's sidewalk would be three feet higher than his next
door neighbor's.[45]

Around 1910 matters improved, although many of the streets
remained unpaved. The city connected most of the homes with
the sewer system and built the first cement sidewalks. Some electric lights had even been installed on street corners. The neighborhood, however, was still considered "extraordinary" in character. The uncovered, water-filled ditches, Bubbly Creek, the
garbage dumps, the uncovered stock pens, the hair fields where
hides and hog hairs dried, and the garbage-filled alleys all attracted a plague of flies. The alleys were so littered that often a
pathway through them was impossible, and refuse collection was
so infrequent that garbage became alive with bluebottle flies and
worms. Most of the houses did not have screens on the windows,
and flies and mosquitoes entered at will. An unbearably hot and
stuffy apartment provided the only alternative to an insect in-
vasion. Homes with doors that opened on an alley were especially bad.[46]

These conditions led to terrible health problems. The Back of
the Yards suffered from a high rate of disease, especially among
its children. In 1900 Charles Bushnell of the University of Chicago took a survey of the entire Stock Yard District. He considered the area from State Street on the east to Western Avenue on
the west and from 39th Street (now Pershing Road) to 55th Street
(Garfield Boulevard) as the area affected by the Union Stock
Yards and packing plants. The statistics he gathered relate to this
larger area, but they still show the general trends in the neighborhood southwest of the yards. Bushnell also compared the figures to data concerning Hyde Park, just to the east of State Street.
The results revealed dramatically the price of poverty in a nineteenth-century city.

The investigation showed that the number of children in the
Stock Yard District was much greater than in Hyde Park: 18,094
in the Packinghouse District, compared with 5,339 children in
Hyde Park. The death rate per 1,000, the real test of conditions,
averaged 38.7 in the Stock Yard District, while in Hyde Park it
was 25.7. By 1900 infant mortality had fallen to 20 per 1,000 east

Alley in Back of the Yards, early 1920s. Residents often used mosquito netting for screens in the city's working-class districts. Investigators found these alley tenements to be among the worst housing in the neighborhood. *(Alice May Miller)*

of State Street, while it remained at 39.79 to the west. In addition, the death rate for the entire population stood higher in Back of the Yards than in Hyde Park: it averaged 14.21 per 1,000 as compared to 10.65. The Packingtown average, however, listed lower than the city's as a whole, which was 15.73 during the same period.[47] The Chicago total reflected the densely populated and poorly maintained river wards of the West and Northwest sides as well as the near South Side. The Thirtieth Ward, a large part of which lay in the Back of the Yards, led the city in deaths from consumption (pulmonary tuberculosis) throughout the period 1894–1900, although it was not the most densely populated ward of the city. It also accounted for a very high number of deaths from pneumonia; it ranked first among the city's wards in five out of the seven years examined.[48]

Conditions did not change much with the new century, though the death and illness rates fell somewhat. The Back of the Yards was not the worst area of the city, but its residents continued to suffer, like those on the Polish Northwest Side, which bordered the north branch of the Chicago River, from various forms of diarrhea, which especially affected children. In the summer of 1908 a survey of the area just northeast of the corner of 47th Street and Ashland Avenue found 127 cases of diarrhea, all in children under the age of five. On the 4500 block between Laflin and Justine streets there were 45 cases among a population of 825. One feature noted was the length of the illness. "Many of the babies were badly emaciated and the pallor and sunken eyes were common features." The investigator pointed out that the cause was almost always improper feeding. She stated that the Slavs seemed to have a prejudice against giving the babies water to drink and that the mothers fed them the same food that adults ate. Although this might be an example of cultural clash between the middle-class doctor and the immigrant mothers, the other factors that affected the block proved perhaps of a more serious nature. Both Laflin and Justine were unpaved streets and dust from them covered and entered the home. Alleys stood in deplorable condition and the number of flies reached tremendous proportions.[49]

Such conditions worked against the maintenance of health within the home, and, although reformers tried to blame the nutritional habits of the immigrants, poverty was the real problem. That the Back of the Yards was a most unpleasant place to live was not the fault of the Polish or other immigrant communities. Insufficient incomes provided the key to the host of problems associated with life in what Upton Sinclair referred to as the Jungle.

Various factors affected wages. The great army of unemployed kept them depressed. Work remained unsteady because it depended upon the supply of livestock and the demand for meat. Before the changes due to World War I, the daily amount of hours worked fluctuated greatly. On leaving home in the morning, a worker had no way of knowing when he would return. The hours worked depended on the availability of livestock and on the amount of time needed to purchase and process the animals in the yards. As a rule, the livestock arrived in larger numbers in the early part of the week, for the packers wanted them slaughtered, dressed, and shipped east for sale by the end of the week. Thus the workday in the early part of the week might last twelve or more hours. Foremen did not allow the men to leave the plant until they processed all the livestock. The Union Stock Yard and Transit Company charged 50 cents a head for any animals left in their pens overnight. The packers claimed that this presented too great a financial burden, so the slaughter went on until they emptied the pens.[50]

The start of the workday was just as uncertain. All the employees had to report to the plant at 7:00 A.M. even though there might be no work for them. At times management forced them to wait for hours before the stream of livestock began to flow over the ramps. This was at the workers' expense. The companies did not pay until the actual killing began, which could be as late as noon. The men in the sheep kill suffered the most from this situation because there were twelve different styles of dressing mutton, according to the market to be served. The packers had to wait until the morning for the order of meat cut in "Allegheny," "Boston," "New York," or other styles. The men, therefore, waited at times until two o'clock in the afternoon and then worked late into the night.[51]

The fluctuations in the provision of livestock affected not only daily work but also the yearly cycle of employment. Cattle runs peaked at two times in the year. Farmers marketed the greatest number of animals during the fall-winter cycle, which ran from October through January. The second cycle took place in the spring with the high point in May. A smaller number of livestock arrived in May than in December, the month of lowest receipts for the fall-winter season. These cycles resulted from the way that producers fed cattle. The grass-fed animals that had been on the range during the spring and summer were ready for the market in the fall along with cows that had been milked since spring. The grain-fed cattle stood ready for shipment after the winter. February witnessed the smallest runs and provided the slack period between the two seasons. These cycles varied somewhat

from year to year, as is evident from the records of the Union
Stock Yard and Transit Company.[52]

The processing of other types of livestock followed different
market patterns. Hogs came to the yards in greatest numbers in
January and sheep in September with the same net effect on the
labor force. A study of one of the major slaughterhouses in the
fall of 1909 and through 1910 showed clearly that hiring practices reflected irregularity of receipts of stock. In October the
greatest number of workers were needed (7,046), but by June
only 5,641. The number rose to 7,046 by the following October, a
fluctuation of nearly 20 percent. The seasonal irregularity affected not only the killing department but the entire industry.
Over 50 percent of the women employed in Packingtown in 1911,
few of whom worked in the killing departments, were out of
work from one to twenty weeks per year.[53]

This fluctuation severely curtailed the yearly incomes of families. A 1910 survey of the payrolls of two of the largest packinghouses, reports furnished by timekeepers and officials of four
large packers, and a personal canvass of 350 employees permit a
fairly accurate estimate of income in the Back of the Yards. However, because canvassers grouped adult men and women with mi-
nors on the payrolls, and unskilled labor shifted often from one
department and even from one plant to another, it proved impossible to determine the exact annual wage. Records of the two
major companies showed an average yearly wage for 250 employees of $634.80, or $12.20 per week. The second packer gave
the wages of 100 employees. The average hourly rate was slightly
above 19 cents while that of the plant as a whole was 18.9 cents.
The average earnings were slightly lower in this plant than in the
first. The majority earned between $350.00 and $600.00 a year,
an average of $10.02 per week.

These figures, however, did not tell the whole story. Records
of the second company, showing wages paid for two weeks in
March and April and two weeks in October 1910, revealed that a
considerable group within the plant earned $4.00 or less per
week. It is not to be inferred that there was a definite group earning these wages. Except for a few office boys and some female

employees who averaged that wage for the year, an employee might be paid at one rate one week and at a much higher one the next. This was because of the irregularity of work in certain departments. A substantial number of employees were forced to work at a lower wage than usual during the slack period of their department. Weekly earnings rose significantly higher in October because the number of work hours increased due to the market conditions. Those unfortunate enough to be laid off in the slack season, instead of being transferred to another department, suffered the most. This fate affected mainly the unskilled workers, including the majority of Poles. In some departments the workers were unemployed as much as one-third of the year. Most work, however, was much steadier.

On the basis of the available data, the average packinghouse worker earned from $8.50 to $12.50 per week in 1910. The common wage in the neighborhood stood between $10.00 and $11.00. After 1904, when the Amalgamated Meat Cutters Union disappeared from the yards, the wages showed very little movement. Before that, union activity and the decrease of child labor had brought a general increase in wages from 1896 to 1903. In 1896, for example, 60.1 percent of male workers received less than 16.5 cents per hour, while by 1903 only 14.3 percent fell into this category. The number receiving 21 cents and more per hour in 1896 increased from 15.7 percent to 23 percent by 1903. After this date, the lowest paid groups tended to disappear, the highest groups increased slightly, whereas the middle group of workers found their pay lowered by about 1–1 1/2 cents per hour. According to the statement made by Company Number One, the average wage of the entire plant increased four mills per hour between 1903 and 1910. By 1913 some increases had taken place. The company in question showed an increase of over 5 percent in wage rates and a still greater increase was made possible by the decision to guarantee a 40-hour work week. From 1903 to 1915, the chief investigator of this report claimed that there had been a 10 percent increase throughout the Chicago stockyards; but he claimed this was still inadequate.[54]

The years 1903 to 1910 saw not only stable or slightly reduced

Table 2. Sources of Income and Average Income

Ethnic group	Husband	Children 14–15	Other family member	Lodgers	Other sources	Total
Polish	$486.14	$185.57	$559.00	$159.01	$174.88	$869.39
Lithuanian	511.06	240.60	475.08	191.43	205.69	804.60
Miscellaneous	541.71	207.83	564.19	189.53	138.69	926.46
All families	503.15	200.14	552.02	183.44	145.23	854.13

Source: J. C. Kennedy et al., *Wages and Family Budgets in the Chicago Stockyards District* (Chicago: University of Chicago Press, 1914).

wages but also a constant rise in the cost of living. A comparison of prices of 100 commodities in 1903 with those in 1910 showed a cumulative increase of 16.5 percent. The rise in the cost of living equaled or surpassed the rise of wages paid between 1910 and 1913. By 1916 living expenses had spiraled and left the working families in the Back of the Yards under even worse economic stress.

A survey of 184 families in the year following April 1, 1909, showed the relation between wages and living costs. Eighty-eight of the families were Polish, sixty-eight Lithuanian, and twenty-eight were listed as miscellaneous. Table 2 gives the source and amount of the income of these groups.

It must be remembered that the average total in each column is for those families who actually derived an income from that source. Among the Polish families only thirty-two out of eighty-eight had working children under sixteen. The average family income, on the other hand, was derived from the data for all families, thus the discrepancies in the total.

If a Polish family had derived its income from all the sources listed, it would have averaged $1,564.60 per year. The Polish husband would have contributed only 31.0 percent of the total; other family members (including children under sixteen), a full 47.6 percent. Lodgers, whose pay reflected part of the wife's contribution to the family income, accounted for 10.1 percent. Obviously, no Polish family had such an economic base. The figures show clearly how difficult it was for a family to break even economically in the Back of the Yards. This was especially true if only the husband's wages could be relied upon; if something happened to him, the family was deprived of his weekly pay, which averaged a mere $9.34.

The total expenditures for the 184 families amounted to 96.5 percent of their incomes. For the Polish group the average annual rental was $91.55, that is, 10.9 percent of their expenses. This was the lowest amount paid by the renting families; the average outlay was $107.83, or 13.2 percent of the income. The investigators pointed out that the percentage of income spent on rents did not seem excessive when compared to the city as a whole. Poles spent 51.82 percent of their incomes for food, which also stood as the lowest of the three groups. Of this, they spent 14.78 percent on meat, 11.44 percent on flour or bakery goods. Poles spent less for fruit and vegetables than for beer or liquor. Clothing consumed 13.35 percent of the yearly income, heating and lighting costs 4.08 percent.

Families had to meet other costs. Expenditures for transportation, recreation, health, and education were a necessity. Although public schools stood in the district, most families felt obliged to send their children to parochial schools for at least part of their education. This generally cost 50 cents per month, or about $5.00 a year. Also, the church had to be supported; on the average, $11.44 was given in annual offerings. The 3.5 percent of the income left over proved barely sufficient to cover the cost of a wedding, baptism, or funeral, or for unexpected medical costs. Savings seemed nearly impossible, especially since most families spent their money freely on festive occasions. The expenses for two Polish weddings, for instance, came to $196.38 and $212.58, great amounts for a family with a yearly income of $870.00. But perhaps sickness provided the most common drain on the family income. It reduced the yearly income and demanded expensive medical attention. And, if it ended in death, it could mean disaster. Fifty-six of the 184 families showed deficits during the year surveyed.

After all the expenditures were listed and tabulated, the minimum amount necessary to support a family of five in the Stock Yard District in 1910 was put at $800.00 per year, or $15.40 per

The wake of Mary Prochot, ca. 1920. Mary Prochot died at the age of sixteen. This photograph shows her coffin in the living room of her family's home at 47th Street and Loomis Boulevard. Young adults and children died at an alarming rate in both South Side Polish neighborhoods. A death, like a birth or marriage, represented both an important rite of passage and a large expense for Polish working-class immigrant families. These occasions played significant roles in creating a sense of community in Polish neighborhoods. *(Courtesy of Mr. and Mrs. Theodore S. Swigon)*

week. Of the 184 families, the income of 110 was less than this amount, although many of them had more than five members. With the average annual wage for the husband at only $486.14 for the Poles and $503.15 for all the families of the district, it is not surprising that many of the children of the neighborhood went to work at an early age and that working wives and lodgers played a decisive part in bringing the family income to a level that took care of at least minimal needs.[55]

Living and working in Back of the Yards before World War I presented many problems to the Polish immigrant family. The income was often inadequate, caused a severe strain on the standard of living, and limited the opportunities available to the children. Working and living conditions seemed bleak; and management defined the Polish, like other immigrants and their children, as cheap, unskilled labor. This resulted in what seemed to be a permanent proletariat on Chicago's South Side.

CHAPTER THREE

Working and Living in Steel City: South Chicago, 1890–1914

The Poles in South Chicago faced problems similar to those in Back of the Yards. The steel industry dominated the district in the same manner as the packinghouses did the neighborhood near 47th Street and Ashland Avenue. And, while conditions in the plants near the Calumet River differed because of the nature of the steel-making process, the Polish workers here too found themselves defined as unskilled labor. By the end of the first decade of the twentieth century, they made up the largest immigrant group in the South Chicago mills, comprising 24.2 percent of all steelworkers in the Midwest. Nationally, they were outnumbered by another Slavic group, the Slovaks, but only the native born, who made up 28.5 percent of the men in the works of the Midwest, outnumbered them on the South Side. Also by 1910 many of these native born were in all probability the children and grandchildren of Polish immigrants.

The entry of workers into America's most awesome industry occurred in one of two ways. Companies hired skilled workers such as puddlers through a personnel department that kept detailed records. However, foremen chose most of the unskilled labor from among the unemployed who gathered at the mill gates in the morning and afternoon. Usually no records of employment were kept except lists of names of those chosen and the rate of their pay. Because many immigrants were in desperate need of work, they were willing to bribe the foremen, mostly with the help of a relative or countryman who had already found employment. The secret fee ran customarily from $5 to $10; at times a foreman received a gift, or the workers "treated" him in a nearby saloon or "lent" him some money that he then "forgot" to pay back, or a prospective worker had to agree to live in a boarding-house owned by his benefactor.

Around 1910 the steel industry had achieved a great degree of centralization. The modern steelworks, such as the plant of the Illinois Steel Company in South Chicago, were huge complexes that dealt with all processes of steel-making. As the workmen approached the plant at the beginning of their shift, they saw a high board fence encircling several large buildings over which hung the pall of reddish-tinted smoke from the huge stacks of the blast furnace. Occasionally, the sparks from the Bessemer converter or the blast furnaces lit up the sky. When the engines that drove the blooming and plate mills went into reverse, they threw huge rings of smoke into the air above the mill. Many sounds filled the plant—the whistles that shrieked in all directions, the puffing sound of the locomotives, or the great clanging noises of the steel-making process. Once through the mill gate, the worker crossed the rail yards that serviced the works. Here, many narrow and standard gauge railroads carried ladles of hot metal or cars filled with material and products. By the time that the men reached the blast furnaces, the huge mountains of ore and the great buildings came into view in all their immensity. In this atmosphere, the Polish steelworker met the American industrial order.[1]

Operations could not begin without the efficient handling of ore. South Chicago plants depended on Lake Superior mines. The area's rise as a steel center coincided with the exploitation of these mines. Much of this came from the rich Mesabi Range in Minnesota, which supplied about 85 percent of the ore for Illinois Steel. Also, after 1904, the Baraboo Range provided much of the ore, especially for the Wisconsin Steel Division of the International Harvester Company (which operated mines there). Steel companies tended to own their ore fields, and the Chicago plants were no exception. By 1900, the Federal Steel Company had been created through the merger of the Illinois Steel Company and the Minnesota Iron Company. This made available to the South Chicago firm the huge reserves on the Menominee and Marquette ranges. After the creation of United States Steel in

Employment office, Illinois Steel Company, South Chicago, ca. 1915. The notice on the wall is printed in six languages, including Polish, and warns prospective workers that they must be careful on the job. This was part of the industry-wide safety program put into effect before World War I. *(Courtesy of the Southeast Chicago Project/Columbia College—Chicago)*

1900, the South Works, part of the new enterprise, could take advantage of the huge reserves operated by the Oliver Iron Mining Company of the Mesabi Range. The new corporation united the major ore concerns in the Mesabi district and gave its subsidiaries an advantage over other producers.[2]

Coking coal usually arrived from the east via the Great Lakes. All the companies in the Calumet area owned coal mines in either West Virginia or eastern Kentucky. The Illinois Steel Company and the Inland Steel Company also operated mines in western Pennsylvania. The development of these areas allowed the Chicago plants to obtain a coking coal equal to that supplied in the Pittsburgh district. Coal came by rail to Toledo, Sandusky, or Ashtabula and sailed on lake freighters to South Chicago. During the winter, when the lake could not be utilized, the companies used an all-rail route. The Illinois Steel Company, however, left the transportation of coal totally to the railroads. It owned the Elgin, Joliet, and Eastern Railroad, which tapped some of the mines. The coal used for steam production came mostly from Illinois and Indiana, areas that did not produce adequate coking coal.[3]

The huge lake vessels docked near the plants where unloading was carried out. As the hatches were removed, all parts of the ship were easily reached. Around 1900, large freighters, like the *John W. Gates*, unloaded an average of 7,000 gross tons. By 1910 these ships averaged 600 feet in length and delivered a cargo of 10,000 tons. Within three years another 3,000 tons were added to the average delivery at South Chicago. Mechanical devices that had been pioneered by Illinois Steel at its South Works unloaded the ore. These proved to be very successful, and in 1907 these devices unloaded 12,067 tons at the company's docks in eight hours. The machines facilitated the movement of ore and could even transfer it to hoppers from which it could be fed into the furnaces. By such methods, the great quantities of ore needed in the Calumet District could be handled with ease.

Once the materials were delivered to the steelworks, they had to be fed into the furnaces without interruption. The mills kept large supplies in stockhouses, where ore bridges and transfer cars deposited them in huge piles. The former were huge bridge-like cranes that towered above the plant, scooped up several tons of material with buckets, and emptied the ore into cars that carried the material to the storage areas. From the bins, chutes led to the "larries," the small, electrically driven, hopper-bottomed cars that took ore to the furnaces. This unending procession of ore seemingly occurred without the help of human hands, as the machines carried the great amount of materials from the lake freighters to the ore piles and stockhouses and finally into the huge furnaces that were the heart of the steelworks.

Workmen first appeared on the casting floor of the blast furnace. Prior to this, hands hidden from view guided the machinery. Just before a cast was to be made, about half a dozen men busily prepared the troughs through which the hot metal flowed from the tapholes of the furnace to the ladles. They finished

Noon hour, Illinois Steel, ca. 1910. This postcard shows the day shift breaking for lunch at the South Works. In the nineteenth and early twentieth centuries Chicago's manufacturing plants rarely included cafeterias. These men are off to Greenbay Avenue to eat lunch, probably in one of the many saloons that lined the street. *(Courtesy of the Southeast Chicago Historical Project/Columbia College—Chicago)*

their work within the first hour of a cast, one of which occurred about every six hours; thus, the company provided benches for the men to sit or even sleep on between casts. Just before the cast was made, the activity of the workers increased. They brought out tools for drilling out the taphole and laid boards across troughs on which men would stand while drilling either by hand or with a pneumatic drill. The machinery was quicker, but it was also more dangerous because it worked so rapidly that the hot molten iron poured out rapidly and endangered the workers. Once the iron and the slag ceased to flow, the keeper and one or two of his helpers closed up the hole with the "mud gun," a long cylinder with a steam piston inside. It fired balls of wet clay until it filled the taphole. Workers performed these tasks under very hot and exhausting conditions.

While the workers repaired the taphole, the rest of the keeper's helpers and the cinder snappers cleaned the floor. The iron and slag left in the troughs had to be loosened with bars and broken into small pieces to be taken away by a small electric crane. This had to be done quickly before the iron cooled and hardened. Formerly, men had carried away this waste, but by 1913 electric cranes cut out some of the hardest work in the plant. At the end of a half hour or so, the floor was cleaned and workers were allowed about an hour and a half before they would have to deal with the process again. In most cases, they could not leave the plant. Instead, they stayed in the "bunk house," which was frequently made out of corrugated iron and protected the men from the weather. The Polish immigrants generally found themselves among the unskilled workers in the blast furnace department. The steel companies often attempted to mix the nationalities in the plant, but this proved impossible, and ethnic groups tended to monopolize certain departments. The Poles were concentrated here and in the rolling mills, and other groups filled skilled and unskilled positions in different parts of the plant.[4]

The entire product of the blast furnace went either to the open hearth or to the Bessemer converter in the form of molten iron in ladles or in the shape of solid "pigs," which came out of the pig casting machine. In these two departments the iron was refined into steel and cast into ingots. Then the ingot stripper received the products and removed the holds, sending the ingots either to the blooming, or slabbing, mills, where they were reduced to a manageable size. The slabbing mills rolled them into large slabs, which the plate mills further rolled down into plates of various sizes. The blooming mills changed the ingots into "blooms" and "billets." These two forms provided the basis for all later rolling mill work. The finishing mills consisted of two types: the large mills rolled the heavy finished products, and the small mills the lighter ones. Besides these production departments, the mills included support units that employed a great many men. These divisions included the boiler, yard, water, and mechanical departments.[5]

Steelworkers labored under difficult conditions. Intense heat, a natural by-product of the steel-making process, went largely uncontrolled in the early years of industrial development. The heat loss resulted in a waste of energy and diminished the working efficiency of the men. The blast furnace department provided the most glaring example of this. Workers filled the old-style furnaces by hand and used sand beds for casting. These tasks required three groups of men: top fillers, the casting crew, and iron breakers and carriers. The top fillers worked under especially dangerous conditions; they had to dump charges into the furnace under unbearable heat. The threat of being severely burned by a rush of flame through the furnace top or by the force of an explosion constantly presented itself. The casting crew, who made the tap, were exposed to extreme temperatures for periods of varying length. The metal flowing from the blast furnace generated a great amount of heat. The crew had to work in temperatures that ranged from 110 to 150 degrees, so they worked rapidly to escape that condition as fast as possible. After they drained the metal, the cast house had to be cleaned; here too the workers labored under temperatures of from 110 to 130 degrees. Iron breakers and carriers worked under the greatest heat and under almost continuous stress. They also had to operate "constantly in a cloud of moist vapor of high temperature, which itself proved decidedly debilitating."

Technological advancements improved conditions in the blast furnace department. In 1913, in the modernized plant, only the casting crew remained, and they labored under more tolerable conditions. By 1913 machines filled the furnaces of the larger and newer plants. The introduction of ladles (to carry the metal from the blast furnaces) and of casting machines had done away with the need for iron breakers and carriers. These improvements brought not only more efficient steel-making but better working conditions. There were even greater changes in the fundamental ways of making steel, and these too made the worker's lot lighter. In the puddling mills every man performed heavy manual labor. The introduction of the Bessemer process, which superseded the older type of mill, also helped. The open hearth, which in the first two decades of the century began to replace the Bessemer converter, reduced dramatically the number of men exposed to heat. Use of water-cooled doors on furnaces and

Blast furnaces, North Chicago Rolling Mill Company (later Illinois Steel), South Works, 1885. These blast furnaces provided the heart of the steelmaking process at the South Chicago plant. *(Courtesy of the Southeast Chicago Historical Project/Columbia College—Chicago)*

mechanization of the rolling mills also helped to relieve the heat problem.[6]

Other factors affected the health of the employees. Particles of ore and dust filled the air of the mills and caused catarrh or increased the chances of tuberculosis. Silicosis, a lung disease, became common among steelworkers. Great physical activity under bad conditions led to exhaustion. The noises of the production process led to deafness and nervous disorders, as well as accidents, because warnings could often not be heard above the clamor. Skin diseases also plagued the men, especially those who had to deal with grease-coated steel bars and shafting. Such ailments, although not fatal, impaired a worker's earning power. In one plant the average worker lost one and a half weeks per year due to sickness.[7]

Frequent accidents were an even greater problem. In January 1900, for instance, at the Illinois Steel Foundry at 33rd Street and Ashland Avenue, three Poles were taking metal up in an elevator. Near the top the line broke and the men plummeted to the bottom of the shaft. One survived the fall but died soon afterward in

the hospital. On March 1 of the same year, Marcin Smorgorzew-
ski died while cleaning a switch in the yard of the South Works
of the same company. A passing locomotive snatched him up,
dragged him 150 feet, and killed him. Neither of these events
was unusual in an industry that, before World War I, was known
as a consumer of men.[8]

In 1906, forty-one accidents killed forty-six men in the South
Works alone. In no one incident did more than four die; only
twice did two men die; the remaining thirty-eight men perished
alone. During that time, coroner's juries censured the Illinois
Steel Company six times. When an accident injured ten workers
in the pig casting department, the Building Department of the
City of Chicago intervened and reprimanded the company: "A
little diligent thought and precaution on your part would mini-
mize the occurrence of such accidents." Doctors employed at the
plant hospital claimed that at least 2,000 accidents occurred each
year. The causes of forty-three of the deaths were listed as follows:

12 died in the neighborhood of the blast furnace;
 1 died in a dynamite accident;
 3 were electrocuted;
 3 fell from a high place;
 4 were struck by a falling object;
 4 were killed by hot metal in the Bessemer department;
 3 were crushed to death;
 1 was suffocated by gas;
 1 was thrown from a high place by the wind;
 1 was scorched to death by hot slag;
10 were killed by railroad cars or locomotives.

Only the blast furnace department accounted for more deaths
than the railroads at the Illinois Steel plant.

The very nature of the industry, especially during boom periods, led to a basic disregard for the safety of the employees. The
company neglected repairs that might have assured the safety of
the workers because of a desire to keep up production. At ten
o'clock in the evening of October 10, 1907, for instance, Walter
Stelmaszyk went to one of the blast furnaces at the South Works
to pick up an iron ore sample and stopped to get a good look at

the scene. Suddenly, an explosion and a rush of molten lead shook the blast furnace. When it ended, four men lay dead on the casting floor. The reason for the explosion was simple: hot metal had come into contact with water. Two months prior to this, the keeper of the furnace had found some water trickling near the taphole. He immediately reported this to his foreman, who in turn spoke to his superior. Patches of fireclay were then substituted for the firebrick that had fallen out. This was not adequate, because the clay wore out quickly and had to be constantly replaced. On the night that Stelmaszyk hesitated at the entrance to the platform, the molten iron had eaten through the fireclay and had come into contact with water, ending in disaster.[9] The desire for a high production rate had led to the deaths of the cast-house-gang members.

The companies in general, and Illinois Steel in particular, covered fatal accidents in a cloak of secrecy. This aggravated the situation, leading to rumors and legends that residents passed around South Chicago. The few details that did make their way out of the mill gates were often enlarged upon by the reporters of such local papers as the *Calumet Record*. Factual information was hard, if not impossible, to get, especially in the early years of the century. The consul for Austria-Hungary complained in 1902 that he and the Italian and Russian consuls could not get information on their nationals who had been hurt in the South Works. They finally went through the federal government for permission to speak with injured workers. The family of a deceased employee might never know how he died; if he had been injured, the company frequently denied them access to the company hospital.[10]

Public outcries against the Illinois Steel Company reached a high point in 1907. This resulted in a law requiring that all accidents ending in death or in the loss of thirty or more workdays had to be reported to the Illinois State Bureau of Labor Statistics. The agency then published an annual record and analysis. It was with good reason that the complaints increased sharply during 1907; rising demand in this boom year for the industry led to a very high accident rate. Before 1910, liability for accidents was extremely hard to prove. Injured men could sue, but this re-

Table 3. Accident Rates for Principal Accident Causes in the Iron and Steel Industry, 1905–1914 Combined[1]

Causes	Frequency Rates[2]	Severity Rates
Falling objects	36.3	2.23
Handling	35.6	.92
Miscellaneous	29.2	2.03
Hot substances	20.9	3.27
Cranes and hoists	16.5	3.30
Working machines	15.3	1.40
Falls of worker	12.5	1.71
Power vehicles	6.6	2.44
Engines, etc.	.8	.17
Boilers, etc.	.5	.02
Transmission	.1	.10
Not reported	6.0	.17

1. Based upon an exposure of 191,846 300-day workers.
2. Frequency rate means number of accidents per 1,000 300-day workers; severity rate means number of days lost per 300-day worker.
Source: Lucien W. Chaney and Hugh S. Hanna, *The Safety Movement in the Iron and Steel Industry, 1907–1917*, U.S. Department of Labor, Bureau of Labor Statistics Report No. 234 (Washington, D.C.: Government Printing Office, 1918).

sulted in a lengthy process and the courts tended to favor the companies. From 1906 to 1912 the United States Steel Corporation, of which South Chicago's Illinois Steel was a part, lost only six such cases. The worker had to prove the employer's responsibility in order for compensation to be granted. A lawyer for the U.S. Steel Corporation stated: "Under our common law the employee has not a chance of recovery in two cases out of a hundred." Therefore, the men who manned the great steel mills were virtually left alone in trying to deal with the massive accident rates prevalent in the industry. If and when the companies did try to settle with their employees, management generally forced the men to accept whatever it offered. The firms did not have a reputation of being overly generous.[11]

A chart published in 1918 by the U.S. Department of Labor listed eleven major causes of accidents and established their frequency and severity rates. Table 3 shows clearly that the production of power for the mills had very little to do with accident rates. Work with engines, boilers, and the transmission of electricity had lower frequency and severity rates than other departments. Falling objects caused most accidents. This did not result from unusual hazards but simply from the dropping of tools or materials being used or loaded. The falling of stored and piled materials also played an important role in this problem, but the company eventually solved most difficulties related to this type of occurrence.

In the group "cranes and hoists," falling loads provided the most serious cause of injury. Defective chains and cables led to most accidents. Studies showed that much of this resulted from overloading. Many of the older cranes were subjected to stress far beyond their capacities. Hot flying substances provided another source of serious accidents, but those connected with the handling of tools and objects were, although frequent, generally not severe. A large number of mishaps resulted in injuries to the eyes from objects flying off tools. The increased use of goggles and greater care on the part of the workers diminished this problem.[12]

In the early years of the twentieth century, many accidents at the South Works occurred in the blast furnace department and in the railroad yard. A maze of tracks surrounded the plant, and many of the workers who did not speak English could not understand the warning signs. This led to frequent injury as the locomotives moved quickly from point to point. Illness from asphyxia was most common in the blast furnace department. The frequency was relatively low, but the severity was high. Leakage of gas also contributed to such accidents as falls, but these were not listed under the category of asphyxiating gas. The hazard nearly disappeared when the companies replaced furnaces that had to be filled by hand with mechanically filled structures. But falling objects, sparks and splashes, furnace slips, breakouts of fire, and the wrong handling of tools continued to cause serious accidents in blast furnace divisions.

In the fabricating shops many deaths were caused by crushing; in the sheet and plate mills, workers frequently succumbed to heat. The many fatal accidents prompted morticians to move closer to the plants because the company brought victims unclaimed by their families to the nearest undertaker. By 1907, the public outcry against the high accident rate had reached a peak, and measures had to be taken to change the industry's image as a mass murderer.[13]

In 1905 Robert J. Young of U.S. Steel undertook the first successful effort to deal with the safety problem. The following year the South Works established a safety committee that initiated more than 3,000 changes in the operation of the plant. Two years later, the United States Steel Corporation developed a safety program for all its plants. A Central Committee of Safety, chaired by an officer of the firm and consisting of five members who represented the largest plants and mills, dealt with the safety of some 200,000 workers. They held monthly meetings and considered about 6,000 recommendations made by the inspectors. Because conditions varied from plant to plant, no uniform plan could be developed, but each received attention through local committees. One of them was the foremen's committee, the other the workmen's committee. Their work made superintendents, as well as the workmen, more safety conscious. The company took necessary precautions, which included repairing broken equipment and replacing dangerous instruments.[14]

Table 4. Accident Rate of a Large Steel Plant, 1905–1917

Year	Number of 300-day workers	Accident frequency rates (per 1,000 300-day workers)	Accident severity rates (days lost per 300-day worker)
1905	6,406	300	34.5
1906	7,494	214	61.3
1907	7,585	189	38.1
1908	4,575	150	29.0
1909	6,215	174	23.7
1910	7,612	134	10.9
1911	5,774	113	18.6
1912	7,396	153	14.3
1913	7,562	115	21.3
1914	4,741	74	12.2
1915	5,599	48	20.6
1916	10,034	06	13.4
1917	10,802	83	12.9

Source: Lucien W. Chaney and Hugh S. Hanna, *The Safety Movement in the Iron and Steel Industry, 1907–1917*, U.S. Department of Labor, Bureau of Labor Statistics Report No. 234 (Washington, D.C.: Government Printing Office, 1918).

These efforts led to a decline in the accident rate from 1907 to 1917. This was of special importance during World War I, when military orders demanded a high rate of production and workers had become scarce. Table 4 illustrates the dramatic improvement in the safety of working conditions.

A similar change is indicated by data for several plants combined. In 1907, 2.2 deaths were reported per thousand 300-day workers; in 1917, 0.8. Permanent disability rates declined less dramatically in the same time span, from 3.8 to 3.2, but the temporary disability rate dropped from 236.3 to 77 per thousand employees. In the blast furnace department the decline was also very striking. From 1907 to 1916 the frequency dropped 66 percent, the severity rate 71 percent. In 1917 several fatal accidents reversed the severity rate, but the frequency rate continued to decline.[15]

Concepts of responsibility also changed with the safety movement. The president of the National Tube Company, a subsidiary of U.S. Steel, spoke out against the old common-law concept of liability and proposed that the industry should come to the aid of

the injured workman. On May 1, 1910, the U.S. Steel Corporation issued its compensation plan, which granted all employees
benefits regardless of the type of accident if they did not sue the
company. The program cost U.S. Steel about $2 million per year
and was, in historian David Brody's view, quite generous. By the
time U.S. Steel put this plan into effect, many states were consid-
ering legislation to protect the workers. Only a few plans, however, equaled the Steel Corporation's. Having begun to deal
effectively with the problem of safety, the industry changed its
image.[16]

The safety program was the core of a larger welfare program
that the steel companies developed. In the Calumet area they
subsidized local hospitals. Illinois Steel donated $5,000 to the
South Chicago Hospital in 1909, while the Iroquois Iron Company gave $1,000. Almost every firm in the district also supplied
visiting nurses to the community; Illinois Steel established this
service in 1912. After setting up various charitable organizations
among the workforce, the nurse became a sort of middle-person
between them and the community. During the 1914 depression
many of the plants started Good Fellow Clubs to help deal with
the problems faced by needy members. In December 1913 the
Illinois Steel Company club, which had been organized in 1912 as
one of the first in the industry, distributed Christmas baskets with
the help of the nurse and her assistants. The plant's large and
small motor drays, as well as several cars, were needed to distribute the gifts. The South Works Good Fellow Club gave a Christmas tree and basket to a Polish family with five children whose
father could not find steady work. At this point the club's membership numbered 368. During the summer of 1914 the organization opened a playground on Green Bay Avenue just around the
corner from the 89th Street gate of the South Works. The popularity of the club grew over the years; in 1920 its membership
reached 3,937.[17]

Illinois Steel began a monthly magazine for its workers in
1913. The publication not only gave local plant information to
the steelworkers but also promoted its safety and welfare programs and instilled loyalty and good behavior in the workers. Although it generally ignored ethnic differences, the magazine con-

tained in a back section a message printed in nine languages: "Take this magazine home with you and have someone read it for you if you cannot read it yourself." The *South Works Review* contained stories and sermons that extolled the work ethic. In May 1914 it stated: "The successful men are they who have worked while their neighbors' minds were vacant or occupied with passing trivialities, who have been acting while others have been wrestling with indecision." The monthly also warned that since the machines had been improved, men must improve their minds. It also discouraged alcohol consumption. "The last man to be promoted and the first man to be laid off was the drinking man," the magazine proclaimed. The *South Works Review* also gave information on safety hazards and issued multilingual warnings from the plant's chief surgeon regarding heat stroke. It recounted the life stories of such loyal men as Frank Guzman, who had retired, as well as Tony Piotrowski and Michael Oliniczak, who had taken the advice of the monthly and had gone to night school. Features included news of the Good Fellow Club and of company sports teams. The magazine provided a way of influencing employees at a time when the company claimed labor agitators were "insulting working men."[18]

The safety and welfare programs of the steel companies were also an economic success. The workforce became more stable and efficient. A slightly better relationship developed between the mills and their neighborhoods. The firms also offered pension and profit-sharing plans and stock subscription opportunities. These, however, could be manipulated as management wished. There was little security against dismissal of an older employee on the verge of retirement, and management alone settled disputes. Although the workers had found their lot to be improved, especially in regard to safety, the measures mostly benefited management.[19]

South Chicago sat on a low plain resting about six feet above the level of Lake Michigan, which bordered it to the east. The landscape was rather unattractive, and the mills cut off any view of the lake. Like the Stock Yard District, the area was dominated by one industry. While the packing industry had a degrading effect on the Back of the Yards, the steel-making process created a terrifying atmosphere that filled the skies of the Steel District. An investigator put it in 1911: "Near the Steel Mills there is the sound of gigantic processes suggesting peril to life and limb, and mysterious accidents of which the public never learns. Here the pall of heavy smoke darkens the sky by day, while by night the lurid glare from the furnaces tells of unceasing toil."[20]

The Thirty-third Ward, which contained the neighborhood in 1900, covered more than 13,000 acres, but the bulk of the population lived on less than one-fourth the area. The homes of the Polish workers stood crowded close to the mill gate of the Illinois Steel Company. An 1890 survey found 3,558 dwellings in the neighborhood, with an average of 7.26 people per unit. Many houses contained more than one family and flats were numerous. Although quite a few single family homes stood along the streets, the majority of structures contained two stories. In the area between 85th and 93rd streets, the mills and Exchange Avenue, the city raised the grade of the streets a few inches on some blocks and as much as six or eight feet on others. This caused some of the homes to rest several feet below street level, and many of the first-floor apartments became basement flats. Lots were now even harder to drain properly, and pools of stagnant water developed in the area. Many homes stood in or over them, and typhoid fever became frequent in these districts. Observers considered the area bounded by 81st Street on the north to the Calumet River and from the mills on the east to Muskegon Avenue as one of the most unsanitary in Chicago. No sewer system existed in large parts of South Chicago in 1900, and outdoor vaults and indoor water closets emptied into cesspools that endangered the general health.

The mills and other industries of the Calumet region polluted the water supply. In 1901 the refuse going into Lake Michigan from the Calumet River was estimated to equal that of a city of 700,000. The wind carried it out to the 68th Street pumping station, which supplied water to not only South Chicago but also most of the South Side below 39th Street. The city tried to diminish this danger by forbidding sewer construction south of 95th

Bush neighborhood housing, ca. 1920. The noise, grime, and smoke-stacks of the steel mills dominated all of South Chicago but had the strongest impact in the Polish Bush neighborhood. *(Mary Faith Adams, "Present Housing Conditions in South Chicago." Master's thesis, University of Chicago, 1926)*

Street because sewage would empty into the river. This prohibition only increased the health hazards in that area.

Sidewalks and streets posed another problem. They were in good condition in the business district and middle-class sections of the community, but north of 89th Street both the east and west, they were poor or even missing altogether. When sidewalks did exist, they often varied in height, as in the Stock Yard District. Streets also lay in deplorable condition. In the Polish quarter all but one or two went unpaved, and they turned into mud or slush during rainy weather. This, the oldest residential section of South Chicago, served as a receiving area for newer immigrant groups.[21]

Many Poles settled in the part of South Chicago known as the Bush. Mills and railroads surrounded the district. According to a 1911 survey of six blocks in the Bush and one outside it, the Poles made up 52.1 percent of the households. If canvassers had looked at only the blocks in the Bush, the Poles would have made up 56.9 percent, by far the largest ethnic group in the neighborhood. This section was representative of conditions faced by Polish immigrants in South Chicago.[22]

In the early 1880s the Bush was a strip of beach with a small wooded area. By 1885 a lakefront pavilion had been built there. The business did not do well and eventually the Illinois Steel Company purchased part of the land. Developers constructed workers' housing on the remaining section. The district ran from 83rd Street on the north to 86th on the south and Commercial Avenue on the west. The Illinois Steel Company mill that extended along the lakefront from 79th Street provided the eastern boundary. Russell Square, a small community park on 83rd Street between Houston Avenue and South Shore Drive, stood in this community. The six blocks canvassed in 1911 lay closest to the mill gate and seemed typical for the neighborhood.

The streets were wide, and 20-foot alleys divided the blocks. Lots in South Chicago had the same shoestring shape as in other parts of the city: 25 feet wide and 125 feet long. This resulted in narrow passageways between the buildings and dark, poorly ventilated rooms. Vacant lots offset this in part. Buildings, furthermore, did not cover a large part of the land. Sixty-one percent of houses surveyed in 1911 covered less than half the lot on which they stood, as compared to 43 percent in the Stock Yard District and 15 percent on the Polish Northwest Side. Table 5 gives the percentage of the lot covered by buildings in South Chicago as compared to the two other neighborhoods. Thus, large tenements were even scarcer in the Steel District than in Packingtown; the contrast with the Polish Northwest Side was even more striking.

South Chicago contained a less dense population than the other districts. Density averaged 129 persons per acre on the seven blocks in South Chicago as compared to 208 in the Back of the Yards, which observers did not consider overpopulated. The neighborhood was not a lodging house district, as was commonly believed, even though lodgers did play an important role in the workers' homes. Families with children presented the real prob-

Table 5. Percentage of Lot Covered by Buildings in Three Districts

	South Chicago, 7 blocks		Back of the Yards, 13 blocks		Polish Northwest Side, 10 blocks	
	Number	Percent	Number	Percent	Number	Percent
Less than 50	134	61	248	43	67	15
50 and less than 60	12	6	65	11	54	12
60 and less than 70	28	12	92	16	117	25
70 and less than 80	15	7	75	13	131	29
80 and less than 90	12	6	56	10	55	13
90 or more	4	2	25	4	25	5
No report	13	6	21	3	6	1
Total	218	100	582	100	455	100

Source: Sophónisba Breckinridge and Edith Abbott, "Chicago Housing Conditions, V: South Chicago at the Gates of the Steel Mills," *American Journal of Sociology* 17 (September 1911).

lem. The boarders simply added to congestion. The typical build-ing stood two to three stories high and had been built before 1900. Wooden frame houses made up 95 percent of the struc-tures; 40 percent stood only one story high, 50 percent contained two stories, and 10 percent three stories. Thirty-eight percent contained only one apartment, but these often suffered the most crowding because housing regulations did not affect single-family dwellings, and lodgers helped pay off mortgages. The four-room apartment was as typical of the Steel District as of Packingtown, and cellar dwellings were rare; a survey of 545 units counted only twenty-six basement flats. Also, rear tenements did not appear numerous; they represented only 16 percent of the houses in 1911. Therefore, like the Stock Yard District, the Bush gave the outward appearance of a neighborhood that did not suffer from overcrowding. The reality proved, however, quite different.

The condition of toilet facilities reveals the true amount of crowding. Table 6 gives the number of families dependent on the various types of accommodations. The yard closet provided the typical toilet facility available in 1911 in the Bush. Only 25 per-cent of the apartments surveyed had indoor plumbing; 1,730 persons used a yard closet; 207, basement or cellar closets; and 280 persons used those in public halls. These conditions pre-sented a particular problem in an area noted for many small chil-

Wooden frame tenement in South Chicago, ca. 1920. This building is typical of the larger balloon-frame structures that filled Chicago's industrial districts. *(Mary Faith Adams)*

dren. Still, much improvement occurred after 1901, when the outlawed privy vault prevailed in the district. Ten years later, twenty-six vaults survived in one two-block area, but residents no longer used fifteen. Because they had not been removed, they remained an offensive nuisance. "On one lot two of these unused vaults were still standing open in a most shocking condition,

Table 6. Number of Families Dependent on Specified
Toilet Arrangements

Provision	Number	Percentage
Privy vault	9	2
Yard closet	302	55
Basement or cellar closet	41	8
Hall closet	8	9
Private (in apartment)	135	25
No report	8	1
Total	503	100

Source: Sophonisba Breckinridge and Edith Abbott, "Chicago Housing
Conditions, V: South Chicago at the Gates of the Steel Mills," *American
Journal of Sociology* 17 (September 1911).

overflowing, and the wood rotting." Four families used two dirty
hall closets built to replace them.

Although South Chicago had the lowest population density
per acre, it suffered from the severest case of overcrowding found
in the city in 1911. Investigators found 72 percent of the 1,148
sleeping rooms in the Bush too small for the number of occupants. This was considered to be a conservative count because it
was obvious that some of the families surveyed did not reliably
report the number of individuals occupying the premises. When
compared to the Back of the Yards with 53 percent of the sleeping
quarters overcrowded and the Polish Northwest Side with 69 percent, the effect of this problem on the Steel District was obvious.
Building owners ignored the legal requirement of a minimum
space of 400 cubic feet for each adult and 200 cubic feet for each
child. As in the Back of the Yards, investigators witnessed startling examples of too many people in too small a space.

In one case, the father, the mother, and five children were crowded
into a room containing only 744 cubic feet, although the law required
1,800; in another case, a lodger slept with the father, mother, and two
children in a room containing only 800 cubic feet, although 1,600 cubic feet were required; in another case, a room containing only 841
cubic feet was occupied at night by a man and his wife, their one child,
and three lodgers, while four lodgers occupied the same room during the day.

The South Chicago tradition of keeping animals worsened the overcrowding. One family who lived in an overcrowded flat kept two pigs and fifteen chickens in their basement. Another had seven pigeons. In the latter, six families, along with twelve lodgers and six children under twelve, all lived under one roof. Two filthy yard closets provided the only toilet accommodations.

A survey of 2,318 rooms found 375, of which all but 10 were bedrooms, containing less than 70 square feet; 449 rooms had ceilings that were lower than 8.5 feet, the minimum legal height after 1902. Investigators considered 20 percent of all rooms to be dark or gloomy, but found only 6 windowless. Of the 462 that were dark, 388 were interior rooms whose windows opened on the gangways between two buildings. Those that did open on these passageways suffered from poor ventilation because the space between two parallel buildings was usually too narrow for the air to move.

Rents presented an important part of the housing problem in South Chicago. When compared to other neighborhoods in 1911, the median rent appeared to be higher than in any other white working-class district. Whereas half the people in the Back of the Yards paid $8.00 or less, and the median rent on the Polish Northwest side stood at $7.50, in South Chicago it reached $9.00. It is here that the lodger problem had its most serious effect on living conditions. Although it was often said that boarders were taken in to help pay the rent, investigators pointed out that they actually increased rents. This was true for the Stock Yard District, but in South Chicago investigators found a unique system of adding 50 cents to the rent for each lodger. As in Packingtown, the lodger problem was more than simply economic. In industrial areas large groups of unmarried men, or those who had left their wives and children behind in Europe, gathered to look for work. They often moved in with families of their own nationality who felt that they had to help their relatives and compatriots. Lodgers in South Chicago and in the Back of the Yards made up 27 percent of the population surveyed.

Whether lodger, renter, home owner, or investigator, the experience of life in South Chicago was mesmerizing. Shut off from the lake by the huge steel plants and from the sky by the dense masses of smoke belching out of the chimneys, the neighborhood stood as a creation of the industry that dominated it. As an observer wrote in 1911:

One cannot walk these streets without a weird impression of the fulfillment of an old prophecy that here men are the slaves of machines and that machinery has ceased to be the servant of its makers. The stranger within the gates of South Chicago is overwhelmed by the fact that the world is made for industry, not for men and women and little children; that with magnificent enterprise on the one hand, there is a hideous waste of human life on the other.

The Polish worker who made his home in the Bush before World War I was daily reminded of his role in American society as cheap labor to be used by the great industrial plant that had grown on the banks of Lake Michigan.

Ward statistics showed people in South Chicago to be healthier than the city average and much better off than the Back of the Yards residents. The lower population density contributed to this. In 1900, the Thirty-third Ward had 13.37 deaths per 1,000; the rate for Chicago stood at 14.42. This did not, however, distinguish the poorer, more unhealthy parts of the neighborhood like the Bush from sections farther from the mill gate. In the areas where the Poles settled, the health inspector claimed a higher death rate prevailed, especially for children. Consumption, pneumonia, typhoid fever, and diseases of the heart and nervous system were the standard diseases. To these had to be added the high rate of industrial accidents.[23]

Spot maps produced by the Chicago Health Department show that ward statistics did not accurately portray conditions in such local areas as the Bush. The maps demonstrate that residents of small apartments near the mills suffered more health problems than in other parts of the city. In January 1910, sixteen deaths from pneumonia, a relatively high concentration, occurred just outside the Illinois Steel plant. During the summer of 1910, the health department reported cases of typhoid fever more often for South Chicago than for Packingtown. Once again, the disease prevailed in the Bush. Poor drainage provided the major cause. The summer of 1909 witnessed a heavy outbreak of diarrheal diseases, again concentrated in the Polish quarter. The death rate of children under two reached 22 per 1,000 in the Eighth Ward, which included South Chicago, and 34 in the Twenty-ninth, containing the Back of the Yards.[24]

Steelworkers suffered not only from problems of safety at work and bad sanitary conditions at home but also from low wages and long workdays. As in meatpacking, the market demand fluctuated, the supply of labor remained great, and the loss of work time due to accidents was often significant. These factors combined to keep wages low and to depress the standard of living for the Polish people of the Bush.[25]

A 1910 national study of the hours of labor revealed that of 173,000 employees, 50,000, or 29 percent, labored seven days per week and twelve hours per day. This work schedule prevailed not only in the blast furnace department, where a need for constant operation existed, but also in other departments. In the blast furnace department 88 percent of the men had to work the eighty-four-hour shift. Changes of shifts made their lot worse. The switch from days to nights every two weeks forced them to work an eighteen- or twenty-four-hour day to accommodate the change. During this "long turn" one of the shifts received a day off. Workers in the early years of the twentieth century considered this schedule a necessary evil. But they did protest the practice of the Illinois Steel Company, which paid the night shift workers at three o'clock in the afternoon and further deprived them of sleep and the company of their families. In 1904 the men also demanded a change in the scheduled lunchtime for the night crew since saloons closed at midnight and the men could not purchase a hot meal.[26]

During the boom years of 1906–7 the practice of the seven-day, eighty-four-hour week became so widespread that it even concerned management. In April 1907 the finance committee of the United States Steel Corporation called for an end of the seven-day week and of Sunday labor wherever feasible. When an industry-wide depression set in during the fall of 1907, none of the steelworks and rolling mills operated on the seven-day week except for the blast furnaces. By the second half of 1909 the demand for steel products had revived, and management forgot

the seven-day resolution. On March 21, 1910, a telegram from
E. H. Gary, president of the United States Steel Corporation, reinstated the ban on the seven-day week in most departments. By
February 1912, conditions had improved for 42.5 percent of all
blast furnace employees nationwide, and the number of seven-
day workers in the industry had fallen from 30 percent in May
1910 to 15 percent in August 1912.

The workforce as a whole, however, did not rejoice over the
elimination of the seven-day week; for them, it resulted mainly in
a cut in pay, not the end to an inconvenience. In most of the plans
adopted, the men in the blast furnace department did not regu-
larly get Sunday off. They felt that a day off in the middle of the
week did not benefit them because everyone else remained at
work, the children went to school, and they had nothing to do
except to go to one of the neighborhood saloons. The reduction
to a six-day week meant a financial loss that the worker found
difficult to bear. Because of this 14 percent cut in income, many
of the plants reported that blast furnace men had quit rather
than work at the reduced rate. The end of the long turn provided the only advantage to the new schedule. Nevertheless, the
elimination of the seven-day week continued. By 1911, Illinois
Steel reported that less than 5 percent of their labor force of
10,470 worked the eighty-four-hour week. Before the telegram
from Gary, 1 out of every 5 had worked the long week. In November 1913 management announced that no employee would
be allowed to work the seven-day week at the South Works. It was
hoped that work could be more evenly distributed this way during slack time. But the company maintained the twelve-hour day
as the norm in 1911 for 60 percent of its workers.[27]

The twelve-hour day remained the major problem for workers
during periods of steady work. Shorter shifts had appeared before 1900, especially in the Carnegie Steel plants, but they disappeared with the new century. In 1902 the South Works put most
of their employees on the half-day shift with the excuse that
many of the plants were mechanized and that men did not have
to work as hard as they had when the ten- and eight-hour days
prevailed. Where heavy manual labor remained, so did the shorter
hours. In 1910 over half the pouring crews in the Bessemer de-

partment had eight-hour days. By this time the technology of steelmaking had advanced so that nearly 75 percent of the steel-workers, except in the sheet and tin mills, worked the twelve-hour day. Employees who maintained the plant, supplied electricity, and provided other services—about half of all workers—were evenly split between the twelve- and ten-hour shifts.[28]

The negative effect of pure exhaustion on the lives of the steel-workers proved considerable. The shifts ran either from 6:00 A.M. or 6:00 P.M., leaving the exhausted worker little time for family or friends. He went home, ate, and went to sleep. After he woke up, he ate again, then went to the plant. When the long turn was still common, the following day was usually given over completely to rest. The families of the men became, in effect, fatherless. Workers had little time left for the self-improvement that they were supposed to undertake for becoming "good" Americans, as the *South Works Review* recommended, nor had they time left for recreation and leisure. Many also felt that the twelve-hour day led to an inefficient workforce, but for the most part the steel companies dismissed such views. An investigation committee of the U.S. Steel Corporation itself condemned the practice as inefficient in 1912 with no result.[29]

International Harvester's Wisconsin Steel Division, which implemented a three-shift program during the latter part of 1913, was the first company in South Chicago to institute a shorter workday. The U.S. Steel Corporation, represented by Illinois Steel's South Works, did not adopt the eight-hour day until 1918. At that point the company used the shorter shift to combat union organizers. Long workdays remained, but workers received overtime pay for labor over the eight-hour limit. The elimination of the twelve-hour day remained throughout the war period a goal of workers in the plants of South Chicago.[30]

The hourly wages of steelworkers were, of course, of great concern. In the period between 1900 and 1910 wages, except for the most skilled workers, on the whole increased. The same leveling trend that marked the meatpacking industry occurred in steel. The skilled force experienced a decline in their pay, while common laborers saw an increase. In 1904 the skilled men at Wisconsin Steel and at the South Works received a 10 percent wage reduction, in part due to a depression in the industry but mainly as an attempt to level wages. For example, at Illinois Steel men who had received from $5.00 to $8.00 a day dropped to $3.00–$5.00. At the same time, those who had got $1.40 to $1.60 per day saw their pay increased to $1.85 and $2.15. In 1900 the general hourly wage in steel-producing departments stood at 21 cents per hour, dropping in 1905 to 20.2 cents and rising again in 1910 to 23.7 cents per hour. In real wages the steelworkers' pay increased approximately 40 percent. Mechanization brought more unskilled immigrant labor to the steel mills as it had to the packinghouses and with it a general leveling off in wages.

Although the hourly rates of pay seemed high, the problem of irregular employment hurt the financial security of the men. In 1909, steelworks and rolling mills had the largest turnover in the labor force for any of the great industries. Employment fluctuated yearly at a rate of nearly 25 percent. This did not take into account time lost because of illness or as a result of an accident. If an employee in 1910 worked an impossible 365 days a year at an average rate of 17.16 cents per hour in a U.S. Steel Corporation mill, he would still end up with less than the subsistence income estimated for that year. In 1910 the average wage of $556.00 for the industry fell $73.48, which the Charity Organization Society of Chicago estimated to be below the $629.48 minimum needed for a family of five in the Steel District. The report made no mention of sickness or other expenses; this provided only a bare subsistence budget. The occasions listed as extras in the Back of the Yards certainly applied in the Bush. A funeral, christening, or wedding in South Chicago could wipe out any meager savings that a family might acquire. As in Packingtown, women and children were expected to help out. This had the same negative effect on the education of the young and the stability of the family as elsewhere.[31]

The hazardous conditions and exhausting labor in the mills combined with long hours to prevent the steelworkers from spending much time either in self-improvement or with their families. Conditions in the Bush were as bad as could be expected in an American urban industrial community early in the century, and wages proved to be inadequate for a decent standard of living. These factors combined to place the Poles in South Chicago in the same relative position as their compatriots in Back of the Yards. But there was one exception! The steel mill presented a much more dangerous place of work than the packinghouse. In either case, management defined steelworkers in much the same way as cheap, unskilled labor and their proletarianization remained a fact even if the men they served in the plant never admitted it.

CHAPTER FOUR

Remaking the Polish Village:
The Communal Response

In the last half of the nineteenth and well into the twentieth
century the Polish peasant lived in a world based on the
church, the community, and the family. These three institutions marked, within the rhythms of the seasons, the frontiers of
rural society and formed the folk's worldview. Polish peasants
lived through much of the nineteenth century in self-contained
villages, but slowly outside influences affected them, especially
after the abolition of serfdom. Still, traditional society did not
give way easily and the old ways stubbornly persisted. Immigrants transplanted many of these practices to new settlements in
America. Of course, the new milieu influenced these cultural patterns and modified them to meet a new reality. A similar process
occurred in Poland as that country underwent industrialization
and became more fully absorbed into the developing Western
economic order.

Unlike in the United States, the Roman Catholic church in Poland was organized along strictly geographic lines. There was
little need for ethnic congregations except in some eastern sections of the old commonwealth. The parish embraced the core
village and the outlying farms. People in the district knew one another and one another's families for generations. An entire system of obligations evolved on the basis of the permanence of the
community and the stability of family life. The parish played a
central role in this system. It provided a meeting place and a symbol of local solidarity.[1] The priest served as a leader, and the community treated him with a good deal of respect. He presided over

divine liturgy and therefore served as an important link between the people and their God. This was his major role, but not his only one. As the most formally educated member of the community, he became its intellectual leader, at least in affairs that dealt with matters outside the farm. And, of course, the priest kept the moral and religious traditions of Polish Roman Catholic society.[2]

Church celebrations expressed the continuity of peasant life. The traditions surrounding All Souls' Day in November perhaps best exemplified this unbrokenness. Many believed that deceased parishioners returned on that day to gather up the prayers of the living for the repose of souls. The congregation asked the priest to pray for the departed members of their families and for friends. This followed a small donation. Mass on that day took on an especially solemn character. Villagers crowded the church for the calling out of the names of the deceased in front of the catafalque. Also, although the church condemned the practice as pagan, peasants spread food among the graves to nourish wandering ghosts. A similar tradition, which also predated Christianity among the Slavs, had peasants place leftovers from the evening meal on the doorstep for the hungry spirits.[3] This unity with past generations that surpassed even the intrusion of time and death is what the peasant saw in the church. Because of this, many emigrants hoped to return to die under the bells of their native parish.[4]

Roman Catholic festivities and sacraments covered all the various stages of life, not only death, and celebrated them with traditional rites of passage. Baptism, communion, confirmation, marriage, and finally death were all interconnected in the cycle of life that the peasant understood. The church year, too, followed a continuing cycle that paralleled the natural year. Christmas celebrated not only the birth of Christ but family and community as well. On Christmas Eve families held the traditional meal, the *Wigilia*, and then attended the Shepherds' Mass, or *pasterka*, at midnight. The evening's festivities began with the sighting of the first star. At this time the family shared the wafer, or *opłatek*, wishing each other health and happiness throughout the coming year. The mother of the house set an additional place at the table. Originally this was reserved for the dead who might visit on that magical night, but later Poles set the place for any who might be traveling and could not have Wigilia with their own family. The meal included semimagical rites dedicated to bringing a good harvest in the next year. The Midnight Mass and the singing of *kolędy* (carols) gave further expression of communal unity.[5]

Easter provided another communal event. On Holy Saturday the priest blessed food for the traditional Easter meal, or *święconka*. In smaller parishes he visited homes to perform the ceremony; in the larger ones the villagers went to the church. Blessed food usually consisted of eggs, sausage, bread, ham, and horseradish. The family ate the meal on Easter Sunday after the celebration of Mass. Family and friends shared eggs in the same manner as they shared the wafer on Christmas. The usual blessing and wish for health accompanied this. Above all, the Easter meal was a family affair and signaled the coming of Spring.

Other traditions filled the church calendar, and days often took on the name of their patron saint rather than the calendar date. February 2 became the feast of *Matka Boska Gromniczna*, or Candlemas Day. On that feast believers came to church to have tapers blessed. The folk believed that the candles would ward off lightning during a storm, and placed them in the hands of the dying when they received the sacrament of Extreme Unction. The faithful also used the tapers for numerous Catholic rites including those associated with the feast of Saint Blaze. Another important feast was that of the Assumption on August 15. The Poles referred to it as *Matka Boska Żielna*, or Our Lady of the Herbs; parishioners brought flowers and herbs to the church for the priest's blessing on that day. The parish's patron saint's day was also an important local feast. Local youth primarily attended the celebrations, which provided a chance to meet new acquaintances, especially those of the opposite sex.[6]

Seasons marked different periods in the life of both the farm and the church. Because of this, Roman Catholicism never completely destroyed the peasant relationship with nature but modified and took advantage of folk ties with a natural religion that predated Christianity among the Slavs. Peasants relied on nature to provide for them and felt, in turn, that they had a duty to preserve nature. Because in the Christian tradition all of nature

glorified God, the church reaffirmed peasant ties with their surroundings. Nature was indeed part of the community and, as in
regard to family and neighbors, certain obligations had to be met.

Animals deserved respect and care. Peasants treated the need-
less killing of wild creatures as a grievous sin. In the peasant's
mind each animal had its purpose and place in the world. For this
reason the folk avoided those who killed for profit.[7] One should
take only what was needed for survival. Peasants treated domestic
animals especially well. During the Christmas Eve celebration the
family shared the wafer first with the livestock. A cow was of special importance. It provided food, and when bad times necessitated its sale, the peasant grieved as at the death of a kinsman.[8]

Nature thus had to be treated like a very temperamental friend.
It provided for the community and expected to be granted respect. The peasant became a careful observer of its many moods.
A common belief held that certain birds predicted the future by
their actions. The relationship between people and nature was so
special that upon a death, friends gathered to ask the land's for-
giveness for any wrongs committed against it by the deceased.[9]

The church could not do away with the pagan spirits that
roamed the Polish countryside before conversion in A.D. 966. Instead, it turned them into devils and lesser demons. The peasant
relied on these spirits and developed a whole system of magic
and ritual that persisted outside official Catholicism. Individuals
who understood the naturalistic order were referred to as the
wróz, or *wiedzący* (wise ones). His or her task was to give advice
and help in different matters outside the realm of the priest.
These individuals were not witches or magicians, for they never
profaned religious articles, like those who belonged to the community of the damned. Rather, they were intermediaries between nature and the community. Wiedzący worked within the
Christian framework. Peasants regarded them as holy men and
women. Other types of individuals who understood natural law
were the *bacy*, or the head shepherds of the Podhale region.
Their secrets often passed to the next generation only on the
deathbed.[10]

This system thrived in a society that relied on an oral tradition
and had not yet felt the full impact of industrialization. Slowly, by

the end of the nineteenth century, however, the older patterns eroded as villages in different parts of Poland opened up to outside influences. Still, many of the old beliefs lived on and controlled the rate of change. Much protest greeted the introduction of the iron plow in Galicia. Farmers feared that the earth would be upset and not give up its produce. The Polish mountaineers believed that certain practices connected with dairy farming had to be performed the same way each time or nature would revolt and harm the milk or livestock. The mountaineers even regarded the introduction of tin buckets with mistrust. Peasants held those who knew the magical and natural ways in great esteem. Old community leaders like the wróz retained their power by frightening their fellow peasants and helped to maintain the traditional social system of the village.[11]

Communal relations involved everyone, touched all the families, and entailed a mingling of a social character that provided entertainment and served a practical communal purpose. On the simplest level this took the form of visiting. Homes were always open to neighbors who gossiped over food and drink. Only those branded for some misdeed did not have a regular flow of guests. Another more formal gathering occurred when women met to spin yarn or the community came together for the shredding of cabbage after harvest. This latter event supplied an especially festive occasion. Peasants gathered at the home where it took place. Women came dressed in their finest clothing, and the men brought in the harvest to be divided up among them. Local gossip and news of the "wide world" accompanied the work. Talk took the place of newspapers and books. The meeting provided a means of preserving the local folk culture through its oral tradition. Participants told tales and legends with moral and religious themes. In this manner the truths of the community passed from one generation to another. Often one of the roaming *dziady* visited. These beggars traveled from one part of the country to another bringing news from areas far from the village. Many of these pilgrims visited holy shrines in Poland, the rest of Europe, and even the Holy Land. The folk prized them as religious instructors and interpreters of cultural traditions. Fables and legends told by the dziady were a key factor in maintaining the mystical-magical outlook. They, like the wróz, helped to preserve the old beliefs by decorating them in Christian garb.[12]

Although the oral tradition gave the community a rather limited historical vision, the meetings did help to form a strong bond of communal solidarity. Despite class differences among peasants, the gatherings held the communities together and provided a great sense of unity. Local desires and frustrations stood out in traditional songs and stories. The Polish mountaineers, who lived on very poor land, told stories of highwaymen. Bandits supplied many of the folk heroes of southern Poland; these Robin Hood characters helped the peasants, who were always vulnerable to the whims of the gentry. They were also peasants and provided an outlet for the struggle for independence and emancipation even after the abolition of serfdom. The traditions of that system took a long time to disappear and molded much of the psychological makeup of the Polish peasant.[13]

The stereotypical peasant was humble and quick to bow before authority in the form of the village priest or the local gentry (szlachta). This vestige of serfdom survived, but there was a more violent reminder, which revolved around the long-established hatred between the peasants and the szlachta. Many folk songs condemned the manor house and its life-style. Those peasants who had gone to school or served in the military and had wider experiences became the leaders of political or ideological revolts and even the rare, but much feared, jacqueries, as in Galicia in 1846.[14] The landowners—not the Prussians, Austrians, or Russians—became the immediate enemy. In a social system that was top heavy this was to be expected. The unity of the community and the concern for its survival were of paramount interest to the peasants. They could look forward to their own deaths as the natural order of things, but when the entire village seemed threatened, they would almost be driven mad with fear. This led to group action during which the folk stood together to protect their rights.[15]

Mutual obligation and reliance typified the people's attitude toward the community. The welfare of the entire village came first in relations with the outside world. This was especially true in dealings with the manor house, in which it was necessary to

protect peasant rights to forest and pastureland. Violence seemed
sometimes unavoidable. Whole villages, including women and
children, turned out to defend what they considered to be their
inherited rights. Much of the distrust was a holdover from serfdom, but often the threat was real. Economic life was precarious
enough without the loss of valuable land and privileges to the
upper classes.[16]

Peasants observed utmost fairness in relations with one another. Precapitalistic attitudes dominated peasant life both before and for sometime after emancipation. Peasants strove to
provide food and shelter for their families by their labor. They
talked little of the accumulation of money. Land was the only
meaningful form of wealth, and until the last quarter of the nineteenth century, increases in this commodity most likely occurred
through marriage, not purchase. Trade, while permissible, was
rare among neighbors except at yearly fairs in the autumn. The
general view held that among their own kind there could be no
bargaining. Only an honest price could be asked for or offered.
At the fair, however, by tradition even a neighbor became a
stranger.[17]

Polish Jews served the peasant's trading and banking needs.
Living in towns and villages, they offered a number of business
services to the local Christian community. Jews operated most of
the taverns and inns. In the Polish countryside these places became neighborhood centers where men and women gathered to
discuss important communal issues and take part in large celebrations. Officials often held town meetings there and at times
some of the inns served as a type of local jail. In some parts of
Poland the innkeeper kept those who had broken the law prisoner until the fines bought the villagers drinks. The owner could
keep the prisoner's goods in pawn until he paid his bar bill. Jewish merchants made goods from distant markets available to the
peasant households. They also dominated the purchase and selling of animals for slaughter. Much of this trading was done in the
time-honored tradition of bargaining. Although the Jews stood
outside the Gentile community, they did play an important role
in its structure. Even toward the end of the nineteenth century,
when Christians began to provide many of the same services, the

peasants preferred to trade with Jews. Their manner and place in the community were understood whereas the role of the new entrepreneurs was often misunderstood. This led to nationalistic and antisemitic agitation on the part of the new Polish-Christian middle class, but it had little success until after World War I.[18]

The parish and community, as interconnected social systems, shared many celebrations. The parish also brought several villages together and provided a wider experience for the local peasantry.

The wedding combined elements of both religious and secular celebrations. On the three Sundays prior to the actual event the priest announced the wedding banns from the parish pulpit. Most marriages occurred in the fall, after harvest and during the carnival season between Lent and Advent. The celebration was open to the community. After the church ceremony the bride's family held the *wesele*, or wedding party, usually in their home, or in the case of a large reception, in the local inn. As the newly married couple entered, the bride's parents greeted them with bread and salt. The celebration lasted three days or longer, with music, food, and drink in great quantities. During the wesele participants took up a collection and used it to pay for the party and to help the couple get a good start in life. At midnight on the first night the capping ceremony, *oczepiny*, took place. In parts of Poland the new bride's hair was cut to symbolize her new state.[19] Thus, the wedding served as a communal rejoicing that ushered the man and woman into the life of the marriage group. The church sanctified it, and it worked toward the preservation of the most important institution in the peasant's life, the family.

The Polish family consisted of both blood and law relatives. Generally it was an association of related marriage groups living close to one another. Up to three generations might reside within one household, but this was probably not as frequent as previously supposed because of limited life expectancy. A whole set of social obligations depended on this most important social institution. The family, as a unit, and its status were paramount. The needs and wants of the individual fell subservient to this. Family solidarity meant both assistance rendered to individual members by the group and control over their actions. The relationships among family members allowed no gradation as friendship or love did. Parents were normally obliged to provide for their children, as the children in turn were expected to care for their parents in their old age. Group pressure on the individual to fulfill his or her duty could even result in court action. For this reason, as well as because of the traditions concerning the distribution of land, children tended to be closer to their parents than to their siblings. It was not until after the parents' death that the relationship between siblings became stronger. When this occurred, the older children assumed responsibility for the family. Always, however, every member felt answerable for every other member. This sense of duty often transcended time and place. Two immigrants meeting each other and realizing they were in one way or another related normally became close friends bound by a sense of mutual obligation. The standing of the family was based on the ownership of land, from which a whole class system had developed in peasant society. The family, rather than the individual, owned the land. The head of the household simply held title to the land in the name of the family. A familial form of communism thus prevailed across the Polish countryside. Morally, land could not be sold without the consent of the whole family, which was only rarely given. Peasant society looked down on those with no land. Near the bottom of the scale lay the *komorniki*, who worked other men's land in order to provide for themselves. Landless peasants who traveled from farm to farm stood below the komorniki in the agricultural class system.[20] As the agricultural crisis deepened in Poland these groups grew in number.

Because land determined status, it provided a primary consideration in social exchanges, especially in the choice of a marriage partner. As a result respect prevailed over love in marriage relations. Family members were expected to marry—except in the case of the occasional aspirant to the religious life. The family reserved the right to choose the partner. Careful selection of the spouse guarded against the lowering of the standing of the family and meant the addition of a person who could be easily assimilated into the family group. The choice could not, therefore, be too far above or below the partner's social status. The *swaty*, or matchmaker, took all these things into consideration. Once the family made a selection, representatives of the would-be bride-groom visited the home of the future bride to toast her with vodka. If she accepted and drank along, the banns would be an-nounced; if not, her suitor had been turned down.[21]

The marriage was in many ways a business arrangement be-cause of the dowry that both partners received. This was espe-cially important for the woman, whose family tried to provide for her in case she should be widowed. Both families made these arrangements before the church declaration. The community looked down upon a family that did not give sufficient dowry. However, peasant society also scorned a marriage that simply in-volved money.[22]

The traditional peasant family could exist in its perfect state only in an agricultural setting. It was, to a large extent, based on traditions resulting from feudalism. Once the old economic system began to disintegrate, social change came to the Polish countryside. Since this happened in the different partitions at different times, the change for the nation as a whole was uneven. In Galicia, in the Hapsburg Empire, the Austrians abolished serfdom in 1848, but many of the vestiges of the old society re-mained well past the turn of the century. This precisely graded social hierarchy, with the family at its core and the landless peas-ant at the bottom, endured for many years in all of Poland.[23]

Even after peasant emancipation in Prussian and Russian Po-land, the struggle for the national culture was difficult. Under the constant cultural attack of the occupying powers, the peasant could not even attend Polish language schools. In the Congress Kingdom the government allowed only Russian schools, but peas-ants would have little to do with them. For this reason illiteracy rates remained high even at the turn of the century.[24] Faced with defeat in the insurrection of 1863 and the possibility of losing the loyalty of the peasantry forever, the Polish intelligentsia in the Russian partition attempted a new approach. During the last third of the nineteenth century, as part of a movement known as "organic work," the intellectuals tried to reach the folk by the es-tablishment of underground schools. These aided the growth of Polish national identity among the peasantry. When attacked in both Protestant Prussia and Orthodox Russia, the Roman Catholic church identified itself with the Polish nation and played an important role in the spread of national consciousness. This was especially true in Prussian Poland, where Otto von Bismarck persecuted the Church under his policy of *Kulturkampf*. It became one of the few institutions that had loyal adherents in all three partitions; thus Poles identified Catholicism with nationalism.[25]

Poles had more cultural autonomy in Austria. The Hapsburgs, Catholic like their Polish subjects, allowed parish schools, which had existed for centuries but not extensively before emancipation. Often the schools included rectors and teachers of peasant origin who understood the needs of the local community. As a consequence of the reorganization of the Austro-Hungarian Empire after 1867, the Poles controlled the Galician educational system. Polish schools and even universities appeared. By the late 1890s some peasants took advantage of these opportunities and endowed them with an important cultural role in the region. Jacob Bojko, a poet who also became a prominent political figure, was one of them. The *Stronictwo Ludowe* (Peasants' party) represented the folk in both the Galician Sejm at Lwów and in the Imperial Diet in Vienna. Local priests, whose authority peasants seldom challenged, found themselves ignored when they spoke out against the party and in the interests of the landed classes. Bojko explained that the peasantry could no longer be bullied by the clergy.[26]

These changes, slow in coming, faced opposition. The conflict between the gentry and the peasants was especially intense in Galicia. Vienna allowed much local control, and the szlachta played a major role in the political structure of the province. They often exercised this power at the expense of their former serfs. The gentry did not feel the obligation to upgrade the educational level of the countryside. The Provincial School Council ran the primary and secondary school system in the Austrian partition, which fell under the influence of the Polish gentry. The latter saw the pedagogical question only in terms of its impact on the relationship between themselves and the folk. Thus, the upper class lost a unique chance to win the rural people over to the national cause through the Galician schools. The situation remained unchanged until the appointment of Michał Bobrzynski, a historian of the Kraków School, to head the council in 1890. He helped develop primary education and made a serious effort to bring formal schooling to the peasantry. The spread of literacy had a great impact, especially in regard to the role of the press. Written in Polish, well distributed, and cheaply priced, newspapers and various types of almanacs became a sort of window to the world. Often a village would subscribe to a journal, which would be read aloud to large gatherings.[27]

Though the Roman Catholic clergy could generally be counted on to support the gentry's dominance of the social system, a priest initiated the peasant movement. Reverend Stanisław Stojalowski purchased and edited two weeklies in 1875. He changed their pro-manor-house stance to a populist position. Stojalowski urged the peasantry to improve themselves through thrift and cooperative farming. A dynamic and ambitious priest, he soon came into conflict with both political and ecclesiastical leaders. When rebuffed by the heads of Galician society, he became a "radical and demagogic tribune of the people."[28]

Over the next twenty years the peasant question continued to fester in both Austrian- and Russian-occupied Poland. In 1862 peasant leaders established "agricultural circles" in Prussian Poland, and a Peasants' Diet convened in Torun five years later, but the first peasant political organization originated in the Hapsburg Empire. The Polish gentry controlled the peasant groups in Prussia, which were reformist rather than radical in outlook. The Galician party, on the other hand, assumed the characteristics of a class movement. An intellectual circle in Lwów effected this change under the leadership of Bolesław Wysłouch, who took refuge in Galicia after imprisonment in Russia. Wysłouch and his followers founded the journal *Przegląd Spoleczny* in 1886 to further the cause of populism among the Polish peasants.[29]

At this same time, the political situation in Galicia quickly deteriorated. Conservative Polish politicians knew that Stojalowski and the socialists were beginning to politicize the peasantry. In 1888 Count Kazimierz Badeni, a believer in strong government, became viceroy of Galicia. He fought against the peasant movement with police repression and imprisoned Stojalowski, who in turn mounted a fierce campaign against the gentry. In the end,

Badeni's attempts to destroy the populists hastened their radicalization. In 1895 in Rzeszów a radical peasant agitator, Jan Stapinski, led a group that founded the Peasant party. He and Wysłouch edited the periodical *Przyjaciel Ludu*, which waged an untiring war against the upper classes.[30]

That same year the emperor called Count Badeni to Vienna to form a new cabinet. Supported by Austrian conservatives and the Czechs, he introduced the universal fifth curia. This measure provided that all males of age had the right to vote and elect representatives to the imperial parliament. Its purpose was to perpetuate the status quo while giving some political voice to the masses. Instead of quieting the Polish peasants, however, it led to their further involvement in Hapsburg politics. Martial law had to be declared during the stormy elections of 1897. That year for the first time Polish deputies appeared in parliament who refused to join the Polish Club, a group of Galician representatives who voted as a block. These rebels included socialists and members of Stapinski's party.[31]

Much of this happened because the Austrian sector suffered most from an imbalance of land and population size that occurred throughout the Polish lands. The "Galician misery" was to a large extent a long-term effect of the partitions. The province had been cut off from Gdańsk (Danzig) on the Baltic Sea, the natural outlet for its farm products. It could not effectively compete with Hungarian and Czech agriculture for Hapsburg markets. As a result, the area's economy collapsed. Thus, from 1899 to 1914, some 600,000 emigrants left Galicia.[32]

Emigration, whether seasonal or permanent, had a profound impact on peasant life. While it lessened the rural population, it also supplied sorely needed financial support for the Polish provinces. For example, remittances from Polish colonies in America to Prussian Poland were negligible at the turn of the century, but in 1901 Polish workers in the interior of Germany sent roughly five million marks to the province of Poznań alone. Galicia proved very dependent on the earnings of Poles abroad. One assessment set the total at twenty-four to thirty million American dollars annually. Emigrant wages in America and elsewhere were a crucial factor in the fiscal solvency of the Polish countryside.

The influx of money from the outside also enabled peasants to purchase land in Poland. The large estates, which suffered under the same economic pressures as the small farms, had to be divided up as improvements in agriculture and industrialization expanded east of the Oder River. Between 1873 and 1914 peasants acquired 2-1/2 million morgs through estate parcellization in Russian Poland alone. In Galicia the process continued despite inflated land prices. This in turn increased emigration and further fueled the peasants' land hunger.[33]

A different attitude toward work and saving spread throughout the countryside. Whereas the peasant family in its traditional setting had regarded work as simply a means to obtain food and shelter, it now provided a possible means of social advancement. The old world had been shaken to its roots, and attitudes quickly changed. The cultural world of the peasantry widened. The possibility of social mobility became an important factor in the peasants' life for the first time. Land meant wealth and it could be gained through work overseas. The position of the gentry, in turn, fell. When this combined with the traditional peasant mistrust of the gentry, clergy, and older intelligentsia, it resulted in a new political assertiveness across the countryside.[34]

Events transformed Eastern Europe, and what happened in one sector had repercussions in the others, especially true in 1905, when an abortive Russian revolution rocked the area. This and internal political difficulties brought more electoral reform to Austria-Hungary. The new law of 1907 introduced secret, equal, and direct suffrage for the Austrian *Reichsrat* in Vienna and weakened the power base of the Galician conservatives, resulting in a quick change in provincial politics. The Peasant party, led by Stapinski, gained seventeen seats in the new parliament. Eventually the party split into two factions, and in 1913 Wincenty Witos became the leader of a new organization, the Polish Peasant party, or Piast. Although divided, the peasant movement remained an important factor in the Austrian partition until World War I.[35]

During the last quarter of the nineteenth century the Polish peasant started to feel the effects of emancipation. The new capitalist order, emigration, and mass political movements transformed the old society. In Austrian Poland even the Church loosened its grip. It remained a strong rural institution, but it could no longer count on political domination. The parish remained the oldest and chief institution in the social life of the village, but because of its traditional support of the gentry's political interests, the clergy could no longer control the folks' political views. A permanent change had come to Poland. Industrialization and an agricultural revolution opened new worlds to the peasantry.[36]

Emigrants leaving Poland during the last half of the nineteenth century acted as catalysts in this process. Inexplicable forces did not move peasants about the world. Rather, the peasants understood them and acted in what they perceived to be their own best interests. The end of serfdom, the advent of capitalism, and a market system based on international exchange presented challenges and opportunities to the Polish peasantry. Neither conservative nor radical in the traditional sense, the peasantry attempted to deal positively with the upheavals. Emigration and politics provided two ways to do this. Although the peasant held on steadfastly to his religious beliefs, his sense of communal solidarity and, eventually, class consciousness led him to ignore the clergy and gentry in both the political and economic spheres. The lower clergy, many of whom were of peasant origin, often came to the aid of the folk and thus preserved Catholicism's broad base in Poland. A community that believed in the teachings of Rome could still act in a very nontraditional manner when faced with a threat to either what it perceived as inherent rights or an obstacle to further social advancement. The Polish peasant in Europe and America faced change with a determination based on values that had developed over centuries. Church, community, and family remained important realities for Poles at home and abroad.

The realities of life in industrial America faced the Poles as they settled in Chicago. Their initial response was a communal one. Instead of attempting the impossible task of melting into the dominant society, they strove to build their separate community and continued to preserve or adapt their own culture. Polish Chicagoans developed an intricate communal system based on primary relationships. The family-neighbor support system, which had been so successful in helping to ease the problems of passage and initial settlement, also became a basis for the creation of a community as Polonia's population grew. Polish immigrants sought to create a society similar to the one they left behind. It was never to be an exact replica; the smokestacks symbolized circumstances very different from those of the Tatra Mountains or the fertile fields of central Poland. Polish peasants entered into a new social, economic, and political order. The emerging communities reflected those realities while still harboring the traditions of a rural past. The communal response of the Chicago Poles would both be shaped by, and in turn shape, the city in which they found themselves.

The Chicago Poles originally settled in five distinct parts of the city: West Town on the Northwest Side, Pilsen on the West Side, Bridgeport and Back of the Yards in the Stock Yard District, and South Chicago, adjacent to the steel mills on the Southeast Side. West Town was the oldest of these neighborhoods. Polish settlers established Chicago's first Polish Roman Catholic parish, St. Stanislaus Kostka Church, there in 1867. Most major Polish American organizations eventually located their national headquarters in this district, often referred to as Stanisłowowo-Trojcowo after the two oldest parishes in the community. By World War I, West Town stood, in many respects, as the capital of Polish America.[37]

Other Polish communities followed the pattern set down by the Northwest Side Poles. The local parish provided more than a focus for the religious beliefs of the community. It served as the social, economic, and often political center of the neighborhood. Because of its historical roots and the milieu in which it found itself, it could hardly have developed otherwise. The church steeples of Polonia symbolized the sense of community to its members as well as to the outside world.[38]

Church steeples, of course, dominated the medieval city even more than they did nineteenth-century Chicago. The Polish American parish system had its roots in these cities as well as in the peasant villages. Chicago's Polish neighborhoods contained a strange mixture of the old and the new. Out of this blending, Polish peasants, now Polish American workers, had to create for themselves a sense of belonging or community. The Roman Catholic church could serve as a guide, but only one of many that presented themselves.

Despite the upheavals of the modern period, medieval Catholicism still dominated the Polish countryside during the periods of the great migrations. While economic change and ideological revolts undermined the leadership of the church, the parish priest held on to his role in the community. During the uncertainties of the migration process clerical influence regained its importance in the new colonies. To whom could one turn for advice if not the parish priest?

Moreover, the parish served as a community center in rural Europe. It seemed natural that this institution would serve the same purpose among European peasants as they migrated to the American city. Medieval European cities also apparently developed neighborhoods with the parish church as their center. Cities like Venice included districts named after their local parish churches, much like Chicago's neighborhoods with popular sobriquets hundreds of years later. Catholic popular traditions died hard.[39]

Anthony Smarzewski-Shermann is considered by most to be the founder of Chicago's Polonia. He was not the first Pole to settle in Chicago, but his family did establish the core around which the West Town settlement developed. He came to the Northwest Side from Prussian-occupied Poland in 1851. Thirteen years later some five hundred of his countrymen also lived in the city, the great majority from the German partition. In 1864 they organized the St. Stanislaus Kostka Benevolent Society as the first Polish organization in Chicago. The new group hoped to eventually establish a Polish parish. In 1867 the society agreed on definite plans to form a Polish congregation. Three years later Rev. Adolph Bakanowski, a Resurrectionist priest, came to Chicago to serve as pastor to the Poles. In 1871 the original combination school and church building were completed. Over the next fifteen years the other four Polish core neighborhoods developed in various parts of the metropolitan area.[40]

It is significant that a Resurrectionist priest came to St. Stanislaus Kostka. This order of priests dominated both the local Chicago community and national Polonia. The priests provided leadership for the vast community building process that took place over the next sixty years. Chief among the Resurrectionists in Chicago was Rev. Vincent Barzynski. As the pastor of St. Stanislaus Kostka he provided a solid base for the expansion of the Polish community all over Chicago. The long string of Polish parishes paralleling Milwaukee Avenue owes much of its existence to Barzynski's leadership, as does the growth of the Polish parish system throughout the city.[41]

The parochial system developed rapidly as a major factor in Polonia. Diverse community elements combined to build the churches. Such a task naturally involved a good deal of disagreement and strained peaceful relations in the Polish community. As others have pointed out, this sometimes led to violence, as in the Holy Trinity confrontation in Chicago's West Town or the Kolasinski affair in Detroit.[42] In general, however, the parish system developed quickly and peacefully in Polish Chicago. The neighborhoods far from the large and prestigious West Town settlement developed their institutions in allegiance to and imitation of those on the Northwest Side. One of these, South Chicago, is an early example of this trend.

Although the parish provided the visible symbol for Polonia, it was not the first institution to develop. Because of the manner in which immigrants established their churches in Chicago, they had to create other organizations before they could demonstrate to the bishop their need for separate congregations. Although the Poles of South Chicago had settled within the territorial boundaries of the parish of St. Patrick, they came technically under the care of the priests of St. Stanislaus Kostka in West Town. In 1880, Chicago contained only three Polish parishes, and all stood far from the emerging steel-mill district in the then far south suburbs.

As a response to this problem the South Chicago Poles organized the St. Vincent Benevolent Society in the summer of 1881. This group apparently took the initial steps toward the creation of the first parish for Poles in South Chicago. On December 19,

1881, the association's trustee, Archbishop Patrick A. Feehan, purchased six lots on the corner of 88th Street and Houston Avenue. One week later the Reverend John Radziejewski, an assistant at St. Stanislaus Kostka's, celebrated mass for the Polish community at St. Patrick's. Soon afterward, a storefront church opened on 92nd Street, and in early 1882 the bishop named Radziejewski pastor. The St. Vincent Society sold its lots and, on June 26, 1882, it brought a new parcel of land on 88th Street and Commercial Avenue. This became the permanent site of the church.

No undertaking of this social, economic, and symbolic importance could take place without controversy. Parishioners established another society, St. Josephat, to aid the parish. This second organization, although younger, had a large membership. Both groups wanted the new church to be named after their respective patrons. Finally, after much deliberation, Father Radziejewski and the parish committee proposed a compromise that no Pole could refuse. They placed the community under the patronage of the Blessed Virgin Mary and called it the Parish of the Immaculate Conception.

Disaster struck the parish almost immediately. Late in 1882 fire destroyed the original storefront location and forced the parish to seek shelter in the nearby German parish of S.S. Peter and Paul. Early the following year a windstorm damaged the new church and school while still under construction and further delayed the erection of a new home for the South Chicago Polish congregation. Soon, however, the Poles held services in the basement of the still incomplete structure, and the parish continued to grow rapidly.

The working-class community responded with enthusiasm and developed a variety of parochial institutions. On May 6, 1884, the various societies organized the first Polish Constitution Day celebration in South Chicago to commemorate the May 3, 1791, reform designed to revive the failing Polish state. This demonstration provided both a public protest against the foreign powers occupying Poland and, more important, a showing of *Polskość*, or Polishness.

Shortly after the celebration, the pastor, Father Radziejewski, was transferred to St. Adalbert's on the city's West Side. Reverend Michael Columban Pyplacz replaced him in South Chicago. At that time the parish owed over $24,000, while the treasury contained only $220.50. This was not surprising since the parish consisted mainly of poorly paid steelworkers who had large obligations to their families both in Chicago and in Poland. The debt signaled not weakness but growth. The church had to administer to the ever-growing population of the mill district. In 1882, when the original thirty families banded together, the Polish community was small. Eight years later some 1,100 families attended Immaculate Conception, giving evidence of the permanence of the Polish presence in South Chicago.

Naturally this tremendous growth caused difficulties. The Sisters of Charity, who had arrived in 1884 to run the school, could not meet the growing need for Polish-speaking nuns. Furthermore, students filled all the school's seats. As a result of the need for more teachers, a new teaching order arrived, the Felician Sisters of Detroit. Also, the school basement was subdivided into classrooms. Father Pyplacz ordered a new convent to be built for the Felicians on Commercial Avenue. This order stayed at Immaculate Conception until 1894, when the School Sisters of St. Francis took their place. Meanwhile, more and more Polish immigrants arrived in South Chicago, which Chicago had annexed to the city proper in 1889.

The Polish district quickly expanded to the northeast past 83rd Street into the Bush. In 1891 a group of Poles from Immaculate Conception saw the need for another Polish parish and purchased the block bounded by South Shore Drive and Brandon Avenue, between 82nd and 83rd streets. On February 2, 1892, the bishop named Reverend A. Nowicki the pastor of the new parish to be named St. Michael the Archangel. About three hundred families belonged to the congregation. Owing to the startling growth of the local Polish population, the archdiocese eventually partitioned the original parish of the Immaculate Conception three times.

The Reverend Michael Pyplacz continued as pastor at Immaculate Conception until 1894, when the bishop transferred him to St. Joseph's in the Back of the Yards. Reverend Victor Zaleski suc-

Saint Michael the Archangel Roman Catholic Church, 83rd Street and
South Shore Drive, ca. 1917. Polish American steelworkers built this
massive neo-Gothic structure just down the street from the gates of the
huge Illinois Steel South Works. Construction of the building began in
1907 under the leadership of Rev. Paul Rhode, who the following year
became the first Polish Roman Catholic bishop in the United States.
*(Courtesy of the Southeast Chicago Historical Project/Columbia College—
Chicago)*

ceeded him and stayed until September 1895. During this period disaster again struck the parish. A fire destroyed the wooden church on May 6, 1894, following a celebration of the 100th anniversary of the Kosciuszko insurrection. Zaleski took on the task of rebuilding, but it proved too much for him. He soon left for a parish in Calumet City, where he died shortly afterward at the age of thirty-six.

His replacement, Rev. Francis M. Wojtalewicz, stayed in South Chicago until his death in 1942. The new pastor was the "builder priest" of South Chicago, a role he had already begun to play when he founded the parish of St. Andrew in Calumet City in 1892. The parish he inherited from Zaleski had a debt of $15,000 and no church or school building. An architect had drawn up plans for a new structure and the basement had been built, but little progress was made after that. The future did not seem bright when Wojtalewicz arrived on the scene, but the new pastor showed an uncanny ability to rally the parishioners, and within fifteen months the parish paid off its debt. By the end of 1897, he could announce that the treasury contained enough money to build a new church, but the outbreak of the Spanish-American War hampered construction because of a shortage of materials. The congregation and its pastor finally celebrated Mass in the new edifice on Christmas Day 1898. By the end of 1905 Wojtalewicz's leadership provided the community with a new school, rectory, convent, and lavishly decorated church as a permanent religious center for the South Chicago Poles.[43]

The Poles of the Stock Yard District also quickly established parishes in the Back of the Yards. Polish Catholics founded the parish of St. Mary of Perpetual Help in Bridgeport northeast of the stockyards in 1882. The Polish parish of St. Adalbert north of the Back of the Yards on 17th and Paulina streets organized this church as a mission. In turn the Bridgeport parish established a Polish mission in Back of the Yards in the mid-1880s. While Polish Catholics dedicated the church of St. Joseph on December 19, 1886, the parish remained a mission until 1889, when Rev. Stanislaus Nawrocki arrived as the first permanent pastor. The parish and the parochial school grew rapidly. In 1895 419 students attended the Polish parochial school. Eight years later the number

Saint Joseph's Roman Catholic Church, 48th and Hermitage streets, ca. 1916. The parish of St. Joseph was organized in 1889 as the first Polish church in the Back of the Yards. The building was constructed in 1914 with a seating capacity of 1,200. Headquarters for the Amalgamated Meat Cutters Polish Local 554 stood across the street in Columbia Hall during World War I. (*Courtesy of the* New World, *formerly the* Chicago Catholic)

rose to 710. In 1912 the number of students totaled 1,212. In 1913 under the leadership of Rev. Stanislaus Cholewinski the parish broke ground for its third church, a huge Romanesque structure designed by Joseph Molitor and built at the cost of $200,000. Archbishop James E. Quigley dedicated the new church the following year.[44]

The swift growth of Packingtown Polonia resulted in the creation of two other Polish churches in Back of the Yards. In 1906 Polish Catholics founded St. John of God Parish at 52nd and Throop streets. The first pastor, Father John Jendrzejek, was a native-born Chicagoan who had been raised on the North Side. Father Jendrzejek earlier served as an assistant pastor at St. Joseph's Church and thus knew the Stock Yard District. The young priest purchased thirty-six lots, an entire square block, across the street from the newly landscaped Sherman Park. On April 10, 1907, construction began of the first church building, school, rectory, and convent according to the plan of architect William Brinkman. Archbishop Quigley dedicated the church on October 27, 1908. Father Jendrzejek died less than a year later of tuberculosis, a disease that threatened many of his parishioners. At the time of his death St. John's counted three hundred families and large numbers of single men and women as its parishioners.

The Reverend Francis J. Karabasz then served as temporary administrator of the parish until 1909. In June 1909 Father Louis Grudzinski arrived as the pastor of the young parish. Grudzinski's appearance came at a crucial time in the history of the Polish congregation. He dealt with various factions that had risen during the illness of the first pastor and went on to build a dynamic parish. On October 13, 1918, the cornerstone of a new church was blessed. The new edifice cost $250,000 and opened in 1920.[45]

The parish grew fast. In 1915, St. John's priests performed 171 marriages in the church. By 1922, 2,400 families belonged to the parish and 2,506 students attended the parochial school. Over six hundred baptisms were performed in 1918. The parish included many different Polish and Catholic organizations that increased the vitality of Stockyard Polonia.[46]

The third Polish congregation to be organized in Back of the Yards was the Parish of the Sacred Heart of Jesus. In July 1910

Archbishop Quigley requested Rev. Francis J. Karabasz to organize a new Polish parish out of the territory of St. Joseph's north
of 47th Street. Karabasz was born in 1881 in Lemont, Illinois. He
attended the Polish seminary of S.S. Cyril and Methodius in
Michigan, and Archbishop Quigley ordained him a priest in
1904. Karabasz served first at St. Joseph's in Back of the Yards,
then at Immaculate Conception in South Chicago. In 1909 he returned to the Stock Yard District to serve at St. John's and then
moved to S.S. Peter and Paul Church just north of the Back of
the Yards in the McKinley Park neighborhood.[47] The priest's
background fitted him well for the task of organizing a church in
one of the poorest parts of the Back of the Yards. Karabasz had
already spent much time among the Stockyard Poles, and his own
upbringing among Polish workers in Lemont made him familiar
with the problems of Polish workers in industrial America.

Karabasz organized the purchase of several lots on the 4600
block of South Lincoln Street (Wolcott Avenue) for $26,187.50.
He purchased all but one of the lots from Poles. The largest
grouping belonged to Andrew Musial, who owned thirteen par-
cels near the corner of 46th Street and Lincoln (Wolcott) and sold
them for $11,375. Bronisław F. Kowalewski, a real estate agent
from St. John's and a community leader, aided Karabasz in this
venture. The new parish was almost an entirely Polish affair.
Karabasz hired John Flizikowski to design the multiuse building he planned to erect. The building's iron came from John
Rybarczyk of South Chicago. John Paczkowski provided the carpenters, and Albert Sikorski organized the masons.

Like the other two Polish parishes in Back of the Yards, Sacred
Heart grew quickly. By 1925, 1,400 families called Sacred Heart
home. In that same year 1,519 children enrolled in the parochial
school staffed by the Felician Sisters. Many of the parishioners of
Sacred Heart came from the Podhale region of southern Poland.
These *Gorale*, or mountaineers, became the backbone of the congregation through much of its history.[48]

The creation and maintenance of a parish provided an extremely important and symbolic act for the immigrant community. Church steeples, rising high above the wooden tenements
and challenging the smokestacks (symbols of industrial might),

gave the workers and their families a sense of security and accomplishment. No longer drifters, they could make peace with their God as their ancestors had. Angelus bells brought back memories of Poland as they signaled morning, noon, and evening prayers. The parish represented everything that had been good in the fatherland. Immaculate Conception, St. John of God, Sacred Heart, and the other Polish parishes of the South Side provided anchors for communal life in the new urban setting. The Roman Catholic rites provided continuity. They furnished a medium for the transmittal of Polish peasant culture to America and to future generations who might never see Europe. The parish also served as a temporary home for those who felt they would one day go back to the fields or mountains of the Polish lands.[49]

The religious practices in America replicated those of Poland. Besides the uniformity and familiarity of the Latin Tridentine Mass and the major holy days, immigrants brought Polish variations in church practice with them in their cultural baggage. The church calendar closely resembled that of the East European countryside. Festivals still marked the seasons for those now separated from the natural cycle by the urban and industrial world in which they lived.

Parishioners celebrated Christmas with the same enthusiasm in Chicago as in Mazowia, Kujawia, or any of the other sections of Poland. The Wigilia remained an important part of the season. Here, however, the new setting meant a change in some aspects of the customs. No longer living in the country, Poles found it difficult to carry out the old traditions. Sheaves from the four different types of grain could not be easily found in Chicago and therefore could not be placed in the corners of the house. And although festivities still began with the sighting of the first star, few families kept livestock with which to share the wafer. The odd number of dishes remained part of the rites, but the tradition of having them represent the field, garden, orchard, water, and wood disappeared. Polish Americans kept the practice of attending Midnight Mass and the singing of carols from Christmas to Epiphany, as well as the custom of avoiding dancing throughout Advent until the Feast of the Three Kings. The latter day marked the end of the season, and Poles observed it by the blessing of fake gold, chalk, and incense to be distributed throughout the congregation. Parishioners used the chalk to mark their home entranceways with the year and the letters K, M, and B separated by crosses. These were the initials of the traditional names of the wise men and were thought to protect the household throughout the year.[50]

Chicago Easters resembled those in Poland. Beginning with Ash Wednesday, Lent provided a period of penance and contemplation. In Polish neighborhoods parishioners had to register with the priest to perform their Easter duty. Catholic tradition obligated all believers to attend confession and receive Holy Communion at least once a year during the Easter season. Parishioners came to the rectory to give a small offering and pick up tickets for each member of the family who had received First Communion.[51] Parishioners dropped the cards off at the confessional or at the communion rail when partaking of the sacraments. By this practice the size of the congregation could be ascertained and those less active in the rites of the Catholic church forced to make at least a nominal appearance. This practice had also been customary in Poland.[52] Priests distributed Communion at five in the morning for those who worked and could not attend the regular Mass. All families practiced *Swiećonka*, or the blessing of food for the Easter meal. The priest prayed over the baskets in the church or, upon request, visited parish homes to perform the rite.[53]

Polish Americans also celebrated Candlemas and the Feast of the Assumption but made no attempt to keep the tapers lit on the way home from church. Also, flowers increasingly replaced herbs during the blessings on August 15.[54] The Mass on All Souls' Day remained solemn, but, because of the size of the American parishes, the priests did not call all the names out at the catafalque on that day. The pre-Christian tradition of leaving food for the dead also disappeared, in part because parishioners believed that the spirits returned to the old parishes back in the native villages rather than to the new settlements.[55] As in Poland, the pastor and

his assistants visited families and blessed homes for a small donation.[56] Once a parish was established, the religious celebrations
were constant events in the life of the immigrant community.

The new American setting forced a change of traditions with
regard to weddings as well. Living in an urban milieu, where the
timeclock, not the seasons, ruled, the Poles could no longer celebrate for three days or more.[57] Also, the family no longer dictated
the choice of a partner. Far from the confines of the old system,
immigrants could choose a mate in the tradition of the Western
"love marriage."[58] Still, choices made on the basis of compatibility
resembled those that would have been made under familial scrutiny. The new partner held more promise if he or she could blend
successfully into the life-style of the spouse. Therefore, Poles generally married other Poles, often from the same district or even
village.[59] If intermarriage did occur, it was usually with someone
from another Slavic group, especially the Catholic Slovaks and
Czechs. But this was rare. In America, the matchmaker also virtually disappeared.[60]

Most of the saloons in the neighborhood had halls behind or
above them where guests for the wedding party assembled after
the church service. These gatherings often attracted over two
hundred people. A policeman was hired to sit at the door and
maintain order. One Irish cop remarked in 1910 that there were
"only two drunks and we fired 'em both downstairs. These people
ain't here for that kind of time." Meanwhile, the band played constantly, and the foot-stomping that accompanied the polkas and
obiereks shook the floor as Poles took part in their favorite pas-
time—dancing. The couples whirled about late into the night as
they did in Poland.[61] The men of the community approached the
bride and paid to dance with her. Each of them threw a silver
dollar on a plate placed on the floor. Tradition had it that if he
broke it the coin could be retrieved and the dance was free, but if
it did not shatter, the money remained as a gift for the couple. In
this way, the community helped with the cost of the wesele and
gave a financial start to the newlyweds. The ritual eventually
changed to simple gift-giving, but the traditional practice remained popular during the first third of the twentieth century.[62]

Dorula/Walkosz wedding, January 17, 1915. Both Marysia Dorula and Stanisław Walkosz emigrated from the town of Szaflary in the Tatra mountains of southern Poland before World War I. Walkosz first settled in Pennsylvania, where he worked as a coal miner. Dorula came directly to the Back of the Yards sometime later. They met while Walkosz was visiting his brother and were married in the parish of the Sacred Heart. *(Courtesy of Rita Walkosz Hurley)*

The community attempted to keep the three days of amusement. Because of the necessity of conforming to an industrial work schedule, this occurred over a period of two weekends. The practice did not last very long, however, because of its expense for the working-class communities. Still, the wesele remained as important a community event in American Polonia as it had been in Poland. This is evident from the cost of the celebrations.[63] Polish weddings offered the packinghouse and steel-mill workers much needed entertainment away from the workplace.

Besides the rites of passage and daily Mass, the church provided different forms of religious and communal services. The pastor, in his role as mediator between God and his people, officiated at vespers and other types of worship. In May and October the parish held special devotions and rosary hours in the evening

South Chicago charivari, ca. 1922. The charivari or *Kocia Muzyka* was a well-established European tradition. Merrymakers blew horns, beat drums, and followed the wedding party down the streets of the neighborhood, often presenting the bride with a baby carriage. This Kocia Muzyka honored the wedding of Josephine Nowak and Edmund Czosnowski at Immaculate Conception Church, whose spire appears in the background. *(Courtesy of the Southeast Chicago Historical Project/ Columbia College—Chicago)*

and in the mornings after Mass in honor of the Blessed Virgin. During the Lenten season the priest led the community in saying the Stations of the Cross and in the prayer service known as *Gorzkie Żale*.[64] The chances for divine worship were many, and services held in honor of the Mother of God easily filled the church. The gentry had handed down these Marian practices to the peasantry, who in turn faithfully carried them to America.[65]

The role of the parish was not limited to worship. As in Poland, it provided a social institution that went far beyond that function. One aspect of its organization was the creation of parochial societies, both for the purpose of prayer and for other more mundane matters such as life insurance and cultural development. Nineteen such groups are listed as having been organized in the history of Immaculate Conception parish alone.[66] One of these, the St. Vincent Society, even predated the official establishment of the parish. Whatever their purpose, societies, sodalities, and clubs multiplied rapidly in the Polish parishes of Chicago.

The religious organizations adopted the name of a patron saint. Besides serving purposes of worship, they also contributed toward the upkeep of the parish church and school and provided social interaction. The self-help and insurance organizations, while frequently of a local character, became increasingly associated with large fraternal organizations such as the Polish Roman Catholic Union and the Polish National Alliance. Finally, every parish had its dramatic, literary, and singing circles organized to maintain the cultural life of the immigrant group. In South Chicago's Immaculate Conception parish, for instance, the first of these was the St. Stanislaus Dramatic Circle, founded in 1911 as

Towarzystwo Potęga Kosynierów pod Dowodztwemu Tadeusz Kosciuszko (PNA Group 1983), 1913. This Polish National Alliance affiliate included many of the more influential men of the parish of St. John of God in the Back of the Yards. It took its name from the peasant warriors who fought against the Russians at the side of Thaddeus Kosciuszko in the eighteenth century. Fraternal organizations provided an important organizational backbone for the Polish community in the United States. *(Courtesy of Mr. and Mrs. Theodore S. Swigon)*

the drama club of the Federation of Polish Catholics in America. The group staged two major plays annually and sponsored picnics, socials, and a baseball team.[67]

Parishioners founded the Casimer Brodzinski Circle in the parish of St. John of God in the Back of the Yards in 1917. During its active years, it presented as many as four major plays a year. At nearby St. Joseph's, the three choral societies of the Alliance of Polish Singers of America staged plays as well. These took place at Słowacki Hall across the street from the parish church and school. At Sacred Heart, the last Polish parish organized in the Stock Yard District, parishioners organized a drama circle in 1922. Similar groups appeared in parishes throughout Polonia.

At St. Mary Magdalene's in South Chicago two drama clubs thrived, and although a separate thespian group was not established at St. Michael's, the various societies collaborated two or three times a year to put on plays.[68] The various organizations presented plays on Polish themes. *Królowa Jadwiga*, *Dwie Sieroty*, and *Racławice* opened to standing room only crowds.[69]

Other types of entertainment drew people to the parish hall. The Immaculate Conception choir, for example, offered benefit concerts and, at least on one such occasion in February 1900, the choir attracted Poles from Bridgeport, the Back of the Yards, and the West Side as well as many other Americans. The program also featured the choir of the parishes of St. Stanislaus Kostka and Holy Trinity from the North Side.[70] Magic shows also drew donations for the benefit of the church.[71] The proceeds from raffles went to the church or to secular organizations like the Kosciuszko Society Library.[72]

Libraries, established by both parishes and secular organizations, played a major role in the cultural life of Polish Chicago. In South Chicago, Father Wojtalewicz opened a lending library at Immaculate Conception in 1897.[73] It charged 10 cents for its catalog and levied a fine of one or two dollars for overdue books.[74] This library joined the older Kosciuszko Society Library.[75] Similar book collections appeared in the Back of the Yards. The most important of these was the Julius Słowacki Library, organized in 1902 by sixteen Polish societies. It began with only thirty books but grew rapidly to become one of the largest on the South Side. These libraries filled a need that the Chicago Public Library did not meet. They provided amusement and entertainment for the working-class families and helped to maintain a viable Polish culture.

The neighborhood societies, whether connected with the parish or secular in nature, generally held their meetings in the same halls that served the wedding parties. Słowacki Hall, on the northwest corner of 48th and Paulina streets, provided a favorite Back of the Yards meeting place. Originally called the Columbia Hotel or Hall, the building had its name changed when it was purchased to house the Słowacki Library. It was renamed Columbia Hall at a later date. During one month in 1918 alone, no fewer than eighteen Polish organizations met there.

Pulaski Hall on 48th and Throop streets, just four blocks to the east, listed five organizations, and Czajkowski Hall on 49th and Loomis streets listed three. The fieldhouse at Sherman Park, across the street from St. John of God, had two groups meeting, for a total of twenty-three different gatherings in one month.[76] There were probably others, meeting at Kosciuszko Hall and local saloon halls, that were not listed in the Polish newspapers. Organizations sprouted everywhere in Polish neighborhoods. Most allied themselves with parishes and large fraternal groups such as the Polish National Alliance, the Polish Roman Catholic Union, the Polish Women's Alliance, or the Polish Sokol.[77]

By World War I, the Polish communities developed a complex pattern of group activities that gave a sense of unity to the Poles living in the ethnically mixed neighborhoods. The clubs gave the immigrants an opportunity to involve themselves in local affairs and to assume leadership roles. In America, the organizations enabled a much larger group to participate and take control. That the great number of clubs also led to fragmentation cannot be denied. At times, as in the case of the Polish National Alliance and the Polish Roman Catholic Union, there was even bitter rivalry. Still, they provided an avenue for voicing opinions and practicing community action. They established a means of socialization and thus made a great contribution to Polish American society.[78]

Although the various parish groups and the large fraternal organizations struggled to organize Polonia and preserve its culture, a constant fear of losing the next generation existed. The lament of Złotopolski, in Sienkiewicz's novel *Za Chlebem*, that "the people who come here are lost to the old country," seemed very real to the immigrants.[79] Therefore, the Polish peasant, who resented the establishment of Russian or German schools in the Polish countryside, now also rebelled against the American public school. Each Polish parish established a parochial grammar school. The Poles would not entrust their children to either the Protestant-dominated public school or the local Irish Catholic school.[80]

The creation of a school was thus one of the earliest concerns of the immigrant community. As soon as Poles founded the parish of Immaculate Conception, a parochial school opened in a frame building on the corner of 88th Street and Commercial Avenue. In 1889 the church hall was turned into a school as the student population of the parish outgrew the cramped quarters in the basement of the church. Children crowded the classrooms, and the sisters often taught classes of ninety to one hundred students. In 1901 the parish moved the frame building that housed the school to 88th and Escanaba streets, and construction of a new building began. On May 26, 1901, Bishop Muldoon blessed the cornerstone and, in November, returned to bless the new school.[81] The same basic story repeated itself in the other parishes. The Poles found their desire to operate a school expensive, but they continued to meet the challenge. They saw primary schools as a way of maintaining cultural continuity in the new land over generations.

This view was clearly expressed by the newspaper *Polonia*, which was published in South Chicago by people closely associated with Father Wojtalewicz and Immaculate Conception. In an editorial the paper called for the raising of children in the Polish spirit. It reminded parents that the schools could not perform the task alone:

Polish parents should remember that they ought to tie their children to Poland . . . they should stand by the fatherland and remember to do their duty to the younger generation. . . . The Polish schools cannot do the whole job. If it is left only to the schools after the children leave, they will lose not only their memory of Poland, but even the Polish language.

A Pole born in America should honor his American homeland, but must also realize that he has another fatherland . . . Poland. This is the land of his parents and grandparents. The child should be ready to honor Poland as he honors America. . . .

Polonia further encouraged the parents of South Chicago to continue using the Polish language in the home and to encourage the American born to read Polish books, especially those concerned with history.[82] The Polish newspapers also urged the community to foster a good working knowledge of English. The *Chicagoski*, published by the Resurrectionist Order, pointed out in 1900 the importance of both tongues to the Poles. In reporting about an English-language play performed by the students of the College at St. Stanislaus Kostka, the newspaper observed that Americans did not think highly of the Polish schools but that such programs would prove their quality to the outside world. The *Chicagoski* stressed that because the immigrants lived in the United States, it was essential for them and their children to speak English.[83]

Polish schools became immediate successes, in part because they fit well into the tradition of Catholic Chicago. The church had long fostered the development of separate ethnic schools to parallel the establishment of national parishes. The Poles simply followed the lead of Irish and German Catholics before them, who also looked upon their cultural traditions as sacred and had created schools to safeguard these traditions for future generations. The Catholic school provided a place where "ethnic truths" could be taught without the contamination of Protestant, Anglo-Saxon, or Celtic influences. The system certainly did not make economic sense as parishes just down the street from each other duplicated schools throughout the same neighborhood. In the Back of the Yards, twelve parochial schools served over 12,000 children by 1915. At that date, however, the once large student body of the Irish parish of St. Rose of Lima had dwindled, whereas the Polish schools were overcrowded. Although the system may not have been logical, if cost was taken into account, it was necessary psychologically, culturally, and communally.[84] By 1920, 3,557 children attended the Polish schools of South Chicago, where they made up 92 percent of the Catholic student body. In the Back of the Yards, a more ethnically diverse area, they made up 42 percent. English was taught in the Stock Yard District as an "ornamental language," that is, merely secondary, and 92 percent of the immigrant-ethnic families sent their children to parochial school for at least part of their education in 1912.[85] The sisters taught children four hours a day in the language of their forebears. These classes embraced religion, the Polish language, and Polish history. The sisters taught other classes in English, but only after the hierarchy and the state forced the issue.[86] In fact, many schools originally used texts adopted from the Galician school system.[87] Later, the Felician Sisters developed special textbooks to be used in the Polish American schools.[88]

The impetus behind these developments was not just ethnic pride; it was also practical in nature. The Polish peasant found that an industrial milieu offered at least some degree of mobility for himself and his children. The key to this, however, seemed to be education. The greenhorn who could not speak English was felt to be looked upon with scorn by the dominant society.[89] The inability to read English or Polish, furthermore, proved dangerous in industrial America, where companies posted hazard warnings in the factories.[90] It became increasingly obvious that formal education was necessary to enhance the social mobility of the children and the family.[91]

The Poles' aim to use education to further mobility did not surface immediately. At first, the Polish Catholic school provided a way of preserving the religious and cultural values brought from Europe. The peasant, who had been exploited by the class system in Poland, often regarded formal education as a waste of time. In the early years of immigration, the typical Polish child attended parochial school until he or she received the sacraments of the Catholic church and then transferred to public schools until old enough to join the workforce. In the typical life cycle of the family, the older children left school at an early age in order to work to help the family accumulate enough money to purchase their own home. Younger children frequently stayed in school

Ann Zon's first Holy Communion, 1926. The reception of the sacraments in the Roman Catholic church marked basic turning points in
the lives of Polish American children. Families celebrated the various
sacramental events in Chicago as they did in Poland. Ann Zon received
her first Holy Communion in the parish of St. John of God. *(Courtesy of
Mr. and Mrs. Theodore S. Swigon)*

longer, and after a while, Polish American children even began to attend secondary schools and colleges.[92] In the years before World War I, however, higher education was still the great exception. In 1911 only thirty-eight men and six women of Polish descent studied in the seventy-seven institutions of higher learning in the United States.[93]

While the community endeavored to develop formal institutions, other types of social interaction also thrived. In the adult world the saloon offered the most important of them. Looked upon with scorn by reformers, the tavern played a principal role in communal life as a social center where information as well as companionship could be had. The bartender not only entertained but also gave advice and lent money.[94] In this way the American saloon played much the same role that the village tavern did in Poland; however, women frequented the saloons less often.[95]

Bars proliferated in Polish Chicago. In 1901 a report from the University of Chicago Settlement House near the stockyards stated: "There is a saloon for about every forty voters. These saloons are political and social centers, the saloonkeeper and the ward politician being the interpreters of American institutions. The saloon is often an employment bureau and the bank where checks are cashed. It is the only place near the 'yards' which offers a comfortable seat at the lunch hour."[96]

A survey of the Back of the Yards in 1911 found thirty saloons on ten typical blocks. While this averaged out to three per block, one block had seven. Most of these saloons stood on corner lots, and those on the ten blocks were probably of the neighborhood variety. The study, however, also looked at another part of the area, so-called Whiskey Row. On this section of Ashland Avenue, which stretched on both sides of the street from 42nd to 45th streets, stood forty-six barrooms. These were located along the western border of the packinghouses and served the workers, especially during the noon lunch hour.[97] In some cases, workers drank in these establishments in order to take advantage of the free lunch, but young boys also brought beer out to the men in the packinghouses. One man said in 1921:

I used to work in the yards as a machinist 26 years ago. The cheapest beer was given in a can and was almost near beer. Every man from the packinghouses drank. Beer men went out before the rush at 12:00 a.m. with forty empty cans on sticks. The faucets on the beer barrels were never stopped at noon and every other door was a saloon. (When the men came out at 12:00 the "beer men" were ready with their 40 cans full). Beer sold at 2 quarts for a nickel.[98]

These taverns, which also served as lunchrooms, were not patronized only by neighborhood people but by anyone who worked in the yards. Those off the main streets acted as neighborhood and ethnic institutions.

Taverns contributed much to the life of the community. Although owners and patrons welcomed neighborhood people, strangers often found these places hostile. In 1918 when one man stumbled into a Back of the Yards bar on West 47th Street and became involved in a brawl, a customer hit him on the head with a bottle. The perpetrators simply left and could not, of course, be identified. The victim had a German name and hailed from Bridgeport, while the bartender and the patrons were Polish.[99] Customers respected ethnic divisions in the neighborhood bars, whereas anyone could drink on Whiskey Row.

Drinking had a traditional place in Polish peasant society. The community sanctioned drunkenness on certain occasions. It was part of celebrating and also a matter of peasant hospitality. Neighbors greeted each other with vodka, and each social occasion had its prescribed toasts.[100] In America, immigrants maintained this practice, as a visiting nurse pointed out in an interview: "I attended a wedding recently with a young Polish woman. There, something very splendid was offered me, but I took soup with a half-inch of grease on it instead. It is a breach of etiquette for a Pole not to partake, so my friend was obliged to. It would have been an insult to them if she had refused their hospitality. The next day she was sick."[101]

But, while a tradition, drinking often became a vice. The packinghouse employees and steelworkers, who labored hard under harsh conditions before World War I, often turned to the bottle for comfort. The result could be unfortunate, as when one Pole came home drunk to his Back of the Yards flat and got into an argument with his wife. He "staggered" into a knife held by his wife and was rushed to the hospital with a wound in his arm.[102] The problems surrounding the abuse of alcohol were extensive. The saloon, however, was not primarily to be blamed for this; moreover, it played an important function as a community meeting place and working man's club.[103] Labor unions and political organizations often held their first meetings in taverns.

While the saloon provided a gathering place for adults, the street corners served the same purpose for children. Young boys and girls were everywhere. They crowded the streets and, even after the introduction of parks, the alleys and sidewalks remained their playgrounds. Children fell into natural play groups. These, in turn, sometimes developed into gangs and even delinquent factions. Although there was often no real ethnic identification among members, they were ethnically segregated because of residential and parochial separateness.[104] Observers identified Polish neighborhoods with gang activities.

Children who lived on the same block and attended the same schools consorted with one another. These play groups were innocent, but some evolved toward delinquent behavior, often under the tutelage of older children. The quest for excitement lay at the root of much of this conduct, be it vandalism, shoplifting, or more serious crime. The community did not consider some of the acts—such as stealing wood or coal from the mills and yards for fuel—delinquent, but they were so regarded by the dominant society. Other behaviors were simply mischievous and made up a large percentage of the so-called offenses.

The typical child who turned to serious crime began his career prowling the streets in quest of adventure. This led to outings to the downtown and bright-lights districts. Boys and girls went shoplifting and "junking." Stores were well aware of the tactics used by the children.[105] The junking expeditions began usually with groups of children looking through garbage dumps and alleys for salable material such as copper. They often ended, however, with gangs stealing pipes and fixtures from buildings. Junk dealers were guilty of not only buying "hot" material but also of encouraging the gangs to go out and find more.[106]

South Chicago alley, 1918. Working-class districts in Chicago often suffered from a lack of city services. Homes lined garbage-strewn alleys where children often played. *(Courtesy of the Southeast Chicago Historical Project/Columbia College—Chicago)*

Gangs practiced "jack-rolling," or mugging, on dark streets, and many workers lost their pay before returning from work. Often the gangs waited in an alley until one of the men passed by—a little tipsy from cashing his paycheck at a local saloon— and then jumped out and surprised him, taking his earnings.[107]

Violence between children happened frequently. The streets were crowded, and a good fight often broke up a dull afternoon. Such events were common in the immigrant quarters.[108] Gang fights as a whole were rarely large but were important in protecting turf. Gangs provided the defensive arm of the neighborhoods and adults sometimes supported them. This type of behavior also appeared in Poland, where gangs of children from competing communities clashed at village borders.[109]

Delinquent behavior, or at least the type of actions deemed delinquent by the outside world, centered in the poorest sections of

John and Anna Dudzik family, ca. 1925. The Dudzik family lived at
4737 S. Loomis Boulevard in the parish of St. John of God. John
Dudzik worked as a laborer in the stockyards. This posed photograph
speaks to the middle-class aspirations of this Polish American family.
(Courtesy of Mr. and Mrs. Theodore S. Swigon)

the neighborhoods that stood closest to the two great industries
that dominated them. In South Chicago, the Bush, and the Back
of the Yards, the original settlement, just southwest of the slaughterhouses, contained the most recorded activity. Serious overcrowding also occurred here.[110] Foreign- and American-born
generations clashed here most frequently.

The Polish family found itself in an entirely new milieu in Chicago. Support systems that had developed in rural Poland seemed
weak or nonexistent, and conflicts between generations broke out
more often than in Europe. Neighborhoods went through many
unsettling changes. The constant arrival of new immigrants put
pressure on the newly developed institutions as well as the family.[111] In addition, children born or raised in America saw the
world through an American rather than a Polish perspective. Because of this, they frequently disagreed with their parents. Children of all ages united against their parents, whereas in Poland
the older children generally sided with the elders.[112] This re-

Majorgczyk house, 1915. This home at 8355 S. Baltimore Ave. in South Chicago stood directly in front of one of the railroads that serviced the South Works. Homeownership was important among Polish immigrants. They enjoyed one of the highest rates of homeownership among ethnic groups in Chicago after World War I. *(Courtesy of the Southeast Chicago Historical Project/Columbia College—Chicago)*

sulted in cultural, as well as generational, conflict within the community and the loss of a great deal of control by parents over their offspring.

Because of their familiarity with American ways, children often felt superior and questioned parental authority.[113] For example, a young woman who worked in a packinghouse and lived in Back of the Yards regarded her mother as too "old country" in outlook. The disagreement came to a head over the purchase of a living room rug. The mother had bought an "old-fashioned one" with the picture of a dog woven in the center. The girl felt embarrassed and refused to bring home friends. Although such examples might seem petty, they do reflect a disintegration of parental authority. The Americanization of younger members of the family hurt the stability of the family unit.[114]

In part the instability occurred because economic independence could be attained earlier in the United States than had been possible in preindustrial Poland. As in the traditional peasant family, parents required children to work for and contribute to the family income. Parents disposed of money put into the common account as they saw fit.[115] Children who often worked at adult jobs felt that they should have more to say about the use of the family's finances. This developed into a source of serious generational conflict.[116]

The Poles also found themselves in a polyglot community made up of many different peoples at various stages of assimilation. Some of the groups had been familiar with one another in Europe. The Prussian Poles knew the Germans well, and while there was much hostility between them in Europe, they often sought out the latter's neighborhoods.[117] This was true because Poles from the German Empire were among the first to come to the city.

Relationships with other former European neighbors were not always cordial. Conflict between Poles and Lithuanians was evident in the neighborhoods where they lived together in large numbers. Although a recent study of the immigration of these two groups has played down this hostility, it did exist.[118] In Europe there is much evidence of this conflict, especially after the rise of Lithuanian nationalism at the turn of the century.[119] In the

Back of the Yards, Polish women often would not even talk to Lithuanian men, much less date them.[120]

Other groups less familiar to the Poles also settled in these neighborhoods. When the first Italians moved into the Back of the Yards, they found their windows broken by a mob of Poles. Later, Mexicans and Poles fought in the streets. The Poles blamed the newcomers for cuts in packinghouse wages.[121]

Polish relationships with blacks were at the outset less violent and more complicated, in part because few blacks lived in the immediate areas of Polish concentration and Poles did not assimilate traditional American racial beliefs until after World War I. The first blacks to move into the Stock Yard District arrived after the 1904 strike. The Poles accepted these union members into the neighborhood.[122] Evidence of blacks living in the Back of the Yards even after the 1919 race riot shows that the color line had not been completely drawn by the Polish community, even at that late date.[123]

Jews played much the same role in the immigrant settlements in Chicago as they did in Polish villages. Jewish-run stores stood along commercial strips. Although, as in the homeland, Polish merchants tried to raise the banner of nationalism and anti-semitism, the general community continued to patronize the Jewish-run stores.[124]

Polish Americans responded to both the conditions and the role definitions with which they had to contend. The dominant society characterized them as cheap, unskilled labor. Their neighborhoods remained poor working-class districts with few amenities and populated by various ethnic and racial groups. These circumstances initially proved disorienting for social institutions like the family and the Church. The Poles reacted by creating a new order, a new social system that, although based on old Slavic peasant traditions, was really neither Polish nor American. Even the language spoken on the streets became a mixture of the worker's native tongue and English. Sometimes children answered their parents in English while their elders spoke in Polish.[125]

The European village could not be reestablished, but a new urban village, which dealt to a degree with a new set of problems, might be created. Ethnic institutions like the parish, the parochial

Frank and Lottie Dolatowski store, ca. 1921. The Dolatowskis opened
this cigar and candy store at 8409 S. Burley Ave. in South Chicago's
Bush neighborhood in 1918. Pictured here are Frank Dolatowski with
his godfather, Frank Mularski. Polish neighborhoods quickly developed small businesses to serve the immigrant community. *(Courtesy of
the Southeast Chicago Historical Project/Columbia College—Chicago)*

schools, the fraternal societies, and even the saloons and youth
gangs provided a way of making sense out of the new milieu, as
well as of maintaining some connection with the past. Folk beliefs
brought from Poland also had their place in the new settlements.
The belief in *wrózy* or *wiedzący* (wise ones) who knew the secrets of
nature and of healing, as well as superstitions like the widespread
credence in the evil eye, helped to reinforce mores and even
morals that had lost their basic support system in the migration.[126] All these factors were important in setting up a stable society in a constantly fluctuating world. Polish immigrants were
hardly lost or uprooted. They brought their roots with them and
planted them in the alien soil. Once here, they could evolve a new
system that might or might not mean success but that certainly
revealed that they actively participated in American society.

Once the community reached some sense of stability—and this came fairly quickly—they joined with others in the same basic situation. The communal response was insufficient to deal with all the problems that life in Chicago presented for the Polish immigrant. The next step was cooperating with other ethnic groups to deal with problems of a much larger scale. The Chicago working class, in the years after the Civil War, established a viable movement that included cooperation among various ethnic and racial groups as well as with reformers. That cooperation, combined with communalism, gave one answer to conditions and role definitions imposed by the industrial elite that controlled Chicago.

CHAPTER FIVE

Defending the Polish Village: The Extracommunal Response

While the Poles in Back of the Yards and South Chicago struggled to build their parishes and intricate community institutions, individuals from outside the neighborhoods attempted to find the meaning of the developments in the two South Side areas for a quickly changing America. Even the definition of work in a society that cherished the ideal of labor was in question as the factory system altered the relationship between man and the product of his toil.[1] The great labor strikes after the Civil War brought attention to the new realities of the workplace. And whereas some simply scoffed at the "radicals," other Americans were deeply moved and disturbed by the plight of the urban industrial worker. College-trained women and men came to the slums to look for solutions to the problem. These middle-class reformers who founded the settlement movement in Chicago, and across the country, became the unlikely allies of working-class organizers who had been trying to establish unions in the packinghouses and factories.[2] With the unions also came outsiders who hoped to develop an effective means for workers to defend themselves in the new industrial milieu. The immigrant communities thus found allies as they built their villages. These new friends would not always understand nor would they be understood by the foreign born, but they played an important role in the response to conditions on Chicago's South Side.

The University of Chicago opened its doors for instruction on October 1, 1892; during its second academic year the faculty and students began to look for a way to get involved in the life of the city. The University of Chicago Settlement House in the Stock Yard District supplied one answer. The university's Christian Union organized the project. Jane Addams, who had opened Hull House in 1889 on Chicago's West Side, and Professor J. Laurence Laughlin addressed a fund-raising meeting of the Christian Union in December 1893. As a result, five rooms were rented in a tenement in Back of the Yards on January 1, 1894, and the university opened its "laboratory of social service." Five residents and ten other workers came to the apartment at 4655 South Gross Avenue in the heart of the immigrant district.[3]

The first of the new "neighbors" to arrive were members of the Day Nursery Association and a group from the Chicago Kindergarten Institute Training School of the South Side. The Gertrude House Kindergarten Association established an infant school. The University of Chicago hoped to expand operations in Back of the Yards to that of a full-scale settlement house and asked Jane Addams to recommend a head resident. She suggested Mary E. McDowell, then in residency at Hull House.[4]

Mary Eliza McDowell was born in Cincinnati on November 30, 1854. Just after the Civil War her family moved to Chicago, where her father established a steel-rolling mill. She witnessed the Chicago Fire in 1871 and took part in the relief activities following it. The McDowells moved to Evanston shortly afterward, and Mary joined the Women's Christian Temperance Union. In 1894 the Pullman strike shook first the city and then the nation. Mary McDowell met the Reverend William Cawardine, the pastor of the Methodist Church in Pullman, and he helped her to begin to understand the problems faced by the urban working class. As a result, she went to work in the kindergarten at Hull House, where she came under the influence of Jane Addams. Finally, on September 17, 1894, she found herself in Back of the Yards in the middle of a stockyard strike in support of the Pullman workers. The U.S. Army set up camp down the street, and blood had been shed in the neighborhood. Crowds set railroad cars on fire just a few blocks away in the yards. Amid this chaos Mary McDowell settled in to be a "neighbor" of the packinghouse workers.[5]

Mary McDowell's living quarters consisted of four small rooms behind a larger one that served as a meeting place on the second floor of the tenement on Gross Avenue. She hoped to unite the diverse elements in the community to act upon the various social problems besetting the district by establishing a neighborhood guild. The guild stayed in operation for only one year. It did, however, set a precedent for neighborhood organization.[6]

McDowell's arrival in the Back of the Yards was greeted with suspicion, not only by her new neighbors but also by the Chicago newspapers, which were not quite sure why this middle-class woman had come to the Stock Yard District. The University of Chicago, also unsure of the definition of a settlement, gave McDowell free rein to define the institution. Caroline Blynn and others joined her as permanent residents of the settlement. Soon the university took another floor in the tenement, but even this proved to be too small. In 1896 the university rented four small flats above a feed store located at 4638 South Ashland Avenue and a nearby storeroom.[7]

McDowell faced a district that seemed to be in constant flux. She arrived in the midst of an immigration movement that changed the neighborhood from Irish and German to Slavic. Not only cultural change but technological change as well threatened to transform the area. The initial problems of the University of Chicago Settlement House would be, first, to deal with the cultural diversity of the populace and gain their trust, then to help them to see their options in the industrial and political world of the South Side.[8]

McDowell had been involved in both the kindergarten and the women's club at Hull House, and these two provided the first and most lasting features of the university settlement. The kindergarten predated McDowell's arrival, but she fashioned the women's club to fit the needs of the women as she saw them. She recognized the ethnic diversity of the neighborhood from the outset. Members elected McDowell the first president of the University Settlement Women's Club in 1896, with Mrs. F. H. Montgomery as vice-president. Eight other vice-presidents represented Polish, Russian, Norwegian, Irish, English, French, and Bohemian members. In addition, Czechs established a separate Bohemian section of the club with Mrs. Vanasek as president.

Meetings of the women's club began with the singing of various national hymns: Members sang "America" followed by the Polish anthem and Irish, Welsh, German, Swedish, and Finnish songs. The club emphasized the need for cooperation among the different nationality groups. In 1901, for example, Mrs. Humphrey spoke on the sisterhood of all nationalities. The club's discussions did not center on the nationality problem but rather covered a wide range of subjects of interest to the feminist and labor movements in the United States. The list of topics for the fall of 1897 indicates the concerns that Mary McDowell hoped to bring before the women of the Stock Yard District:

October 7	Public Baths and Playgrounds
October 14	Postal Savings Banks
October 21	Child Labor
October 28	Social
November 4	Cycling trip in the Black Forest
November 11	Women's Place in the Labor World
November 18	Our Grandmothers—Social
December 2	Christians in Art
December 9	Women in Art
December 16	Children in Art
December 30	Christmas Party

The list shows the basic reformist orientation of the settlement and also the middle-class interests of Miss McDowell.[9]

Not only a discussion group, the club became actively involved in the life of the community, and McDowell used it to raise the consciousness of its members. The club provided a tool to help the neighborhood deal with its social, economic, and political problems. Throughout the history of the settlement house most of the people who came to it lived within one square mile of the intersection of 47th Street and Ashland Avenue. This resulted in a tight group that shared common interests and problems despite different ethnic and religious backgrounds. The women were very interested in the health of the district, and various members reported on different health hazards and problems. For example, when the city elevated the railroad right-of-way on 49th

Street, members scrutinized the type of landfill being used. Two members, Mrs. Neckerman and Mrs. O'Brien, investigated the site and found garbage being dumped. The women's club promptly complained to the Health Commission.[10]

McDowell and a group of local women led a long crusade against the city's manner of refuse disposal. The city had placed the largest dumps in Chicago in the Back of the Yards, and they presented a serious problem for the health of the community. The refuse, lying exposed over several acres on the western edge of the neighborhood, created an ideal breeding ground for all kinds of vermin. Immigrants along Lincoln Street approached McDowell as someone who would know the ways of city hall and asked her aid. Her involvement in the long struggle, which eventually closed the dumps and led to the filling in of Bubbly Creek, gained her the title of "Garbage Lady."[11]

Mary McDowell saw political activism to bring change as only part of the mission of the settlement. She and the other residents wanted to be good neighbors to the working-class residents of the Back of the Yards. They believed this responsibility to include the broadening of the educational vistas of the community. Through discussion groups she introduced art and culture to the women of the community, but she also hoped to reach other residents of the neighborhood. At a meeting of immigrants who might be interested in an educational program, a vote was taken on the subjects preferred by the group. The immigrants chose American history and constitutional history, followed by Polish literature and history.

Doctor and Mrs. Kodis, a Polish-Lithuanian couple, planned the lecture series, and at the beginning of one of the early meetings they asked Mary McDowell to greet the participants. She had been warned beforehand not to do this as she would probably be misunderstood. McDowell approached the group a little nervously, remarking that she was sorry that there was no Polish flag. She went on to say that any Pole who loved Poland would also make a good American. McDowell barely uttered the last word of her greeting when a hissing sound rose from the Polish crowd. McDowell was mystified because the crowd seemed to be smiling. She turned to her interpreter, who, clapping his hands, remarked to her, "You have said what they did not believe any American would say and they are showing their appreciation." McDowell later learned that the crowd had been saying the Polish word for "bravo." [12]

The university settlement established many clubs and classes, which the residents of Back of the Yards attended in considerable numbers. In 1911 sixty-eight clubs and classes met at the settlement with an average weekly attendance of 1,035. All together, between 1,200 and 1,500 local people came to the house each week. This great amount of activity obviously required a huge staff. Besides the residents who lived at the settlement, men and women from outside the neighborhood came to help on Gross Avenue. Twenty-three of these volunteers came from the University of Chicago and twenty-one arrived from other parts of the city. Staff members had to be able to deal with various language groups. A Lithuanian woman who spoke Polish and Russian as well as her native tongue joined the permanent residents. Another resident could also speak the "Slavic language." [13]

McDowell's interest in education extended beyond the programs of the settlement house. The problem of public education was paramount among the concerns of the settlement house movement. McDowell soon began to agree with some of the immigrants that the schools offered little to the working class. Teaching children traditional subjects when they would find themselves working in the factories surrounding the Back of the Yards seemed futile. In 1897, McDowell, with the help of Mrs. Emmons Blaine and Mrs. George Sturgis, who donated the money, set up a "vacation school" in the neighborhood. Seward Public School on 46th and Hermitage streets, a few blocks west of the settlement and the packinghouses, provided a site for the classes. Instructors based the curriculum on nature study and handwork. Several hundred students enrolled. With the close of the six-week session, a meeting was held in Polish, Czech, and German to explain what had been accomplished. At the same time, settlement workers passed a petition among the parents to help establish a manual training school in the district. The following fall, Seward School became such a center. Edward Tilden, president of Libby, McNeil, and Libby, then one of the major packers, and also president of the school board, helped to pass the measure. Tilden later gave his name to Tilden Technical High School, which the city established in the Stock Yard District to carry on the idea of training in manual skills.[14]

Recreation also played an important role in the life of the university settlement. Many of those involved in the settlement movement saw the environment of the city as basically debilitating. Their ideas of an ideal childhood dealt with open spaces and fresh air, both of which seemed to be missing from the tenement districts of the industrial South Side. Because of this, one of the first projects of the university settlement that attracted attention was the establishment of small parks in the neighborhoods near the mills and packinghouses. Chicago had a long tradition of planned parks, but these, such as the huge South Park system that graced Hyde Park along the lakefront, provided recreation primarily for the middle-class districts at the edge of the city. Jane Addams and Mary McDowell advocated the extension of the parks to the industrial districts. In 1904, the efforts of the University of Chicago Settlement House came to fruition with the establishment of Davis Square Park on the block bounded by 44th, 45th, Paulina, and Marshfield streets, just to the west of the packinghouses. The small ten-acre park quickly became a community center. The fieldhouse eventually contained both a men's and women's gym and a branch of the public library that replaced the one at the settlement. Meeting rooms were also available in the building. After 1906, the packers paid for a nurse who cared for the sick in the community and was based at the settlement but also spent time in the park. When Davis Square opened, the president of the park commission described the fieldhouse and the playgrounds as the settlement ideal applied to parks. Shortly afterward, another small park opened to the south of Davis Square. The South Park Commission also dedicated a large park on the edge of the Back of the Yards and connected with the original South Park system along Garfield Boulevard. Community organizations used all of them. Davis Square in particular played an important role because of its location close to the stockyard gates.[15]

Originally, the University of Chicago hoped the settlement

Boys' shower house, Davis Square Park, ca. 1907. Chicago began to develop a series of small parks in working-class districts shortly after the turn of the century. The fieldhouse of this park in the Stock Yard District included bathing facilities and a swimming pool. *(Courtesy of the Chicago Park District Special Collections)*

house would provide it with a type of social laboratory. McDowell, however, felt that the institution should be well established before it allowed researchers to flood the district. She held off the academic mission of the settlement until 1911, when she allowed Professor John C. Kennedy of the University of Chicago and his associates to have the aid of the settlement in making a study of Back of the Yards. Earlier, McDowell had allowed Upton Sinclair to stay at the complex on Gross Avenue while he did the research for his investigation of the packing industry that resulted in *The Jungle*. He had announced to McDowell that he planned to write the *Uncle Tom's Cabin* of the working class.

To an extent, McDowell was sorry that she had aided both these studies. Sinclair's dramatic discussion of the conditions prevalent in the neighborhood and the industry upset her. McDowell maintained that the young socialist had gathered the legends and gossip of forty years and put them into his book. She agreed with the packers that conditions were not as bad as Sinclair painted them. As for Kennedy, pressure from the packers on the settlement house forced him to remove from his study recommendations concerning labor unions in the stockyards. While testifying before a U.S. Senate investigation, Kennedy later pointed out that the University of Chicago Settlement House was too dependent on contributions from the packers to be an effective instrument of social change in the community. Kennedy brought out the basic fact that the community had a very weak economic base. Although McDowell agreed, she had to walk a very thin line because of the source of her financial support. The packers contributed heavily to the settlement, especially after the 1904 strike and the 1905 publication of *The Jungle*. Additional funding came from conservative middle-class sources. Many of the settlement's benefactors believed that its task was simply to help assimilate immigrants into American society—to teach them to be good, honest, loyal workers. Professor Kennedy, who later became the secretary of the Socialist party of Illinois and the alderman of Chicago's Twenty-second Ward, located to the west of the Stock Yard District, obviously did not agree with this kind of middle-class reformist thinking.

After the Kennedy report, few studies came directly out of the university settlement until the Great Depression, when the settlement once again allowed students to use the institution to help gather information about social problems. By this time, Mary McDowell was playing almost no role in the daily life of the settlement. McDowell retired as the active head resident early in the 1920s but remained the force behind the settlement throughout the decade. (McDowell passed away on October 14, 1936.)[16]

What exactly was the purpose of the University of Chicago settlement? Even residents found this question difficult to answer. McDowell often spoke of its mission as a religious one. The settlement was to bring a religious revival without directly proselytizing. One observer stated that no one seemed to be able to come up with a working definition, and while neighborliness provided the dominant interest of the residents, they spent the greatest amount of energy on organizing all types of social and athletic activities. Residents explained that they gave the people of the

neighborhood what they wanted, but in reality they followed pre-
conceived notions of what they thought the people of Back of the
Yards should want. The middle-class background of the settlement residents presented the formative impetus behind the programs of the University of Chicago Settlement House.[17]

At times the community felt uneasy about the settlement house
and its work. After a while, the people began to expect certain
things from the institution, such as the athletic program, English
language classes, and political activism, but some friction between
the Catholic East European population and the white Anglo-
Saxon Protestant organization was bound to take place. In 1915
the three Polish parishes led by the Reverend Louis Grudzinski
of St. John of God and the Reverend Francis Karabasz of Sacred
Heart created the Guardian Angel Nursery and Home for Working Women at the intersection of 46th Street and Gross Avenue,
just one door down the street from the university settlement. The
corner where Guardian Angel stood had long been given the
neighborhood nickname of Whiskey Point. Before the arrival of
the Polish settlement, saloons occupied each of the six corners
created by the crossroads of Gross Avenue and 46th and Laflin
streets. Guardian Angel's facilities included a dispensary operated by both a male and female doctor, a day-care center, and a
hotel for the single working women who came to the Stock Yard
District from Poland in large numbers. Guardian Angel typified
Catholic settlement houses in Chicago, many of which provided
simple responses to Catholic fears that the Protestant and American settlements would lead their children away from their religious and ethnic beliefs. Nevertheless, although the Polish settlement operated effectively in the community, only the University
Settlement offered a full range of activities and organization for
the people of the Back of the Yards.[18]

Although some mistrust existed between the Catholics and the
residents of the settlement house, they often worked with each
other to relieve suffering in the area. During a large fire in 1916,
the settlement, in conjunction with the Polish parishes, gave
many immigrants shelter. Also, during the flu epidemic of 1918,
McDowell turned the gymnasium into a hospital to care for the

sick, especially the children. Whenever a crisis confronted the community, the settlement could be counted on to give aid. Being a good neighbor was perhaps its true mission.

From McDowell's first days in Back of the Yards, it became evident to her and her co-workers that something must be done to alleviate the poverty of the district. The overriding concern of the community had to be economic. Mary McDowell turned to organized labor in the early years of the twentieth century. Increasingly, the discussions held by the University Settlement Women's Club and lectures presented in the meeting rooms dealt with the labor movement in general and with the organizing campaign in the packinghouses in particular. Miss McDowell proved an outspoken supporter of organized labor and helped to establish the first women's local of the Amalgamated Meat Cutters and Butcher Workmen in the yards. She also belonged to the Women's Trade Union League. The settlement played an important role in the early organizing campaigns of the unions in Chicago.[19]

The dominant society defined Polish immigrants, like those who came before and those who would come after, as unskilled casual laborers. Some would look upon them as only parts of an economic equation that bound Chicago with Eastern Europe. Poles served as cogs in the great industrial wheel of the city and the country. Unskilled workers began to predominate in the workforce of the large mass production industries like steel, meatpacking, and the garment trade. The Poles and their fellow workers were faced with the definition of their place in society and they reacted to it. Once again this took the form of an extra-communal response, one that involved uniting with other ethnic and racial groups to bring about change. Out of this came the Chicago labor movement.

Chicago has a long tradition of attempts by workers to organize into effective labor unions. Almost from the beginning the men and women who labored in the packinghouses, factories, and mills tried to exert some control over conditions in the workplace. The city had a reputation for labor violence dating back to the period just after the Civil War. The Haymarket Riot of 1886 and the Pullman strike of eight years later provided outstanding

examples of the tradition of labor radicalism that manifested itself in the history of the city. The struggle for a strong labor
movement was long and drawn out both in Chicago and across
the nation. This was the result not only of management opposition but often of the labor leadership itself, whose petty rivalries
and conservative viewpoints often aborted the development of
successful grass-roots organizations.

The first strike in the Chicago stockyards took place in 1869,
less than five years after the opening of the Union Stock Yards.
Another labor stoppage happened in conjunction with the labor
riots of 1877, but the first organized walkout occurred in 1886. It
was at this point that the packinghouse workers first became affiliated with a national labor organization, the Knights of Labor.
The tragedy of the Haymarket Riot that stained the eight-hour
movement was the result of a series of errors that harmed organized labor not only in Chicago but also across the country. The
1886 strike was not the last to be bungled by inept leadership.

Even after the defeat of the Knights, working-class fervor still
ran high. Small walkouts persisted throughout the next eight
years. The local populace supported labor causes in general and
could be counted on to uphold strikers in other industries. In
1894, when workers at the Pullman plant on the far South Side
walked off the job and the American Railway Union backed them
with a nationwide boycott of Pullman cars and a strike, the people
of the Back of the Yards responded accordingly. Crowds burned
railroad cars in the stockyards; especially hard hit were the refrigerated cars owned by the packers, which had little to do with
the Pullman crisis. Also, crowds looted freight trains in the giant
railyards east of the neighborhood. Few of the residents of the
community supported these extreme actions, but enthusiasm for
the Pullman workers remained high. A real organization of packinghouse workers did not come out of this crisis and, for the most
part, the men and women working in the plants remained unrep-
resented. They also paid dearly for their participation in the riots
as troops occupied their neighborhoods, and the corner of 47th
Street and Ashland resembled an armed camp. The events of
1894 stood out in stark contrast to the relatively peaceful strike
of 1886.[20]

Other small strikes broke out in 1896 and 1899, but at this point the meatpacking industry remained virtually unorganized, and many believed it unorganizable. Considerable obstacles faced any union that might attempt to reach workers in the stockyards. Not only were the packers hostile but, because of past experiences, many of the laborers harbored fear and resentment. Also, the workforce remained ethnically diverse and management made it a point to increase the heterogeneity, thus hampering attempts by union organizers. A plethora of languages could be heard in the slaughterhouses, and many of the nationality groups did not trust one another or the Americans. Bitterness between the Irish, who generally led the labor organizations, and other ethnic groups persisted. All these factors, plus the inherent weakness of craft unionism in a large mass production industry, impeded organization. Still, the American Federation of Labor, which emerged after the decline of the Knights as the largest representative of organized labor in the United States, felt an obligation to revive unionism in the industry.

This task fell to the Amalgamated Meat Cutters and Butcher Workmen, who had been organized in 1897 in Cincinnati. Established as a national union with a constitution that encouraged industrial unionism, it set out to organize the nation's slaughterhouses. President Michael Donnelley, a skilled butcher, led the drive to sign up both the skilled and unskilled in the industry.

As of 1900, about one-third of all employees in meatpacking worked in Chicago. Obviously, there could be no success if the Butcher Workmen did not win in that city. On June 9, 1900, the Cattle Butchers Local 87 received its charter from the International and the union came out of the industrial underground. Workers wanted a union they could trust and saw hope in Donnelley, who convinced many of them to join as he stood on the corner of 47th Street and Ashland Avenue greeting the men while the shifts in the yards changed. In January 1901, Donnelley moved his headquarters from Omaha to Chicago, where the main work of the union had to be done. Membership expanded quickly. By July, the union had established seven locals in the Union Stock Yards. The major packers came to a quick agreement with the Amalgamated despite their turbulent history in dealing with labor groups. They were willing to wait to see what would happen to the new union and, as in 1886, could bide their time to challenge Donnelley's group.

Also, a second generation of packinghouse owners now held power in the yards. These men searched for a new approach to labor relations, one that might not lead to the periodic costly disturbances that hurt production. Donnelley, too, was a rather conservative labor leader whose approach toward management followed the traditional AFL contention that a strong union would give a sense of stability to the industry. What the packers might lose in bettering conditions and raising wages they would gain in a well-settled workforce. By September 1902, it seemed that a working relationship had been established. Homer D. Call, the secretary of the union, stated that it had gained the respect of the majority of the large employers in the stockyards. There was greater resistance from the smaller concerns, who believed that to compete with the Big Six they had to keep labor costs down. But the union had made progress in all the plants.

Although the national organization left the question up to the locals, unskilled workers were at first not welcomed into the Butcher Workmen's union. Michael Donnelley opposed this attitude and stated that there should not be an "aristocracy of labor." Craft unionism had actually long been rendered obsolete in the industry by the development of mass production methods, which made it possible for the packers to operate with great numbers of unskilled laborers who could learn their jobs in a matter of minutes. Management would never be immobilized by a walkout of the skilled as they had been in 1886 and in other strikes. The unskilled provided a major component of industry and their membership proved essential to the Amalgamated.

That East Europeans made up a large percentage also led to problems. Canners Local 191 at first did not grow because many of the canning department workers could not speak English. Once the leadership recognized this problem and overcame their nativism, it made advances with the use of immigrant officials and interpreters. In 1904, the Pork Butchers Local numbered 600 Irish, 600 Germans, and 300 Poles and Lithuanians. The same year they elected a Polish president. East Europeans quickly recognized the advantages of the union and flocked to it, especially since Donnelley and the leadership seemed to be willing to make them feel welcome and give them a voice in the organization. The unions faced greater difficulties with other segments of the workforce.

Women and blacks posed two question marks for the union. While the worker population included only about 500 blacks out of 25,000, they did represent a possible source of strikebreakers should there be a union-management conflict. During the labor problems of 1894, the companies imported African Americans into the yards as strikebreakers, and this nearly precipitated a race war. The same prospect faced the butchers ten years later. Although the union was willing to organize the East Europeans, many members hoped the organization might be a tool to drive the blacks permanently out of the yards. Racism hurt the union.[21]

Sexism also hampered the union movement, but with the aid of Mary McDowell packinghouse women forced organization. When women first went to work in the packinghouses, they filled new positions that had never been occupied by men. They did not use the tools that men in the plants used; above all they did not wield the knife. During the strike of 1894 management brought women in to replace many male strikers, and they began to use the tools of the butcher's trade for the first time. Many of the men saw the new union as a way of pushing women out of the departments in which they had displaced men. It was obvious, however, that women were in the yards to stay. From 1880 on, the two industries that witnessed the greatest increase in the female population of the workforce were meatpacking and the electrical supply and apparatus industry. In fact, in the forty years between 1880 and 1920 meatpacking showed the greatest increase in female workers. In 1900 women made up 5.6 percent of the Chicago packinghouse labor force. The percentage more than doubled over the next five years. Clearly, the emerging Meat Cutters Union had to deal with this group. Women had played an important role in trade union activity in Chicago, which was long a center of their trade union activity. The earliest organizing activity took part among operatives in the garment trades, cigar industry, and the boot and shoe factories. No union for women in meatpacking appeared until 1902.[22]

Mary McDowell, a staunch advocate of unions, threw her support behind the Amalgamated shortly after Donnelley appeared in the Stock Yard District in the spring of 1900. The University Settlement Women's Club scheduled many talks about the progress of the union in the yards. Mrs. Donnelley joined the club, and the settlement allowed the union to use its facilities. McDowell, a feminist, naturally felt an interest in the plight of women in the yards. During an address at a meeting of the Union Label League, an organization to promote the purchase of union-made goods and services, she referred to the packinghouse women. When a Chicago newspaper published her remarks, a group of women who had organized themselves into an unofficial and secret union sometime before approached her. They found her to be helpful, and her friendship with Donnelley led to their recognition by the Amalgamated Meat Cutters.

Women's wages ran generally lower than men's and foremen often cut the pay rates of those who did piecework. Women always worked under the threat of the speed-up. Irish American women in the yards had come to feel that unionization might be the answer to their problems. In March 1900, even before the Amalgamated Meat Cutters began to make their move in Chicago, these women walked out in a spontaneous strike against a wage cut. Hannah O'Day and Maggie Condon, the leaders of the group, tied a red handkerchief to a stick and led their fellow women workers out. The company retaliated by replacing them with Slavic immigrant women and blacklisting the strikers. Nine of the women sued the packers but lost and remained out of work. This event apparently had a positive effect on the workforce's attitude toward the union: the female workers now realized how vulnerable they were. In the meantime, some of the female strikers had been rehired and they formed the Maud Gonne Social Club to take the place of a real labor organization until one could be formed. As the men organized and the university settlement house supported them, the members of the Maud Gonne club turned to Mary McDowell. Gradually the union was formed; in

March 1902, it received the first women's charter from the Amalgamated Meat Cutters. Women in all departments joined Local 183, a strictly female local. Not allowing them to join the respective male locals may have been sexist, but it actually gave them a degree of independent power in the International. They had equal footing with the men at conventions and in the Packing Trades Council, something that would have been impossible if the women had joined the male-dominated locals.

The independent status of women proved important because many of the men still resented the presence of women in the plants and in the union. The representatives of Local 183 at the Meat Cutters convention in 1903 stopped a motion of some of the other locals demanding that immigrant women not be allowed to work in the sausage trimming departments as meat trimmers. The women's union achieved this despite the fact that few East European immigrant women had joined Local 183 at that time. Eventually the Slavic women, especially the Poles, joined in large numbers. African American women were also welcomed into the organization. As members of the International Union they took part in the strike of 1904. From that point on, organized labor had to deal with women on an equal footing with male workers in the packing industry. In fact, the constant demand for equal pay for equal work grew out of the actions of the pioneers of Local 183.[23]

Donnelley steered the union toward accepting the unskilled, immigrants, women, and blacks into its ranks; this alone provided a major victory for the divided stockyard workers. But the organization faced the tremendous problem of bringing the different groups together, especially blacks, who in 1900 formed only a small minority among the packinghouse workers. The higher paying jobs of the North had attracted a sizable population of African Americans to the South Side. The packers themselves saw employment of blacks as one more way to divide the labor force and frustrate unions, which already had to deal with ethnic rivalries. As the union grew in power, the packers began to look more and more toward the possibility of using blacks as a weapon against resurgent unionism. The year 1904 proved to be a crucial test of this tactic.[24]

As the agreement negotiated in 1903 came to an end, the union felt strong enough to gain another from management with added guarantees for unskilled workers. This time, however, the packers believed their position strong enough to test the will of the Amalgamated Meat Cutters. They felt a split between the skilled and unskilled workers and between the South Side's white and growing black population would give them the upper hand. First, management attempted to divide the union ranks by favoring the skilled workers at the expense of their fellow workers. These two groups roughly reflected the white ethnic divisions in the industry, with the so-called old immigration making up the great majority of the skilled butchers and the new immigration employed in the lesser jobs in the slaughterhouses. The favoritism consisted of a contract that would leave out the unskilled. After several conferences, management offered a uniform wage scale of 16 1/2 cents for the unskilled. Donnelley and the other leaders rejected the offer and demanded 18 1/2 cents, and the rank and file decided to stick by their decision. The organized packinghouse workers realized that their organization was doomed if they did not support the unskilled in their demands, even though many unskilled workers still did not belong to their union. Indeed, the decision brought more of the Southern and Eastern Europeans into the union fold. The packers' demand to exclude the unskilled men from the agreement provided a major point of contention. Management continued to mechanize their plants and thus could run them with fewer and fewer skilled workmen. The owners no longer depended on the packinghouse elite of skilled butchers. They had no intention of repeating the mistakes of 1886. Management hoped to keep the two classes of workers divided.[25]

On July 12, 1904, negotiations came to an end and the packinghouse workers stopped kill-floor operations at 11:30 A.M. They cleaned the workplace as if it were the end of the normal workweek and walked out at noon, beginning the first strike in the history of meatpacking called primarily for the interests of the unskilled workers. The shutdown was peaceful; the union ordered livestock handlers to make sure that they fed and watered animals left in the pens. The strike closed the plants of the major packers. Public support ran high for the union. Strikes spread to other packing centers and soon the country's butcher shops felt the impact of the Butcher Workmen's efforts. Nearly 50,000 workers supported the union nationwide with about half that number in Chicago.

The packers immediately began to import strikebreakers, especially blacks whom they believed to be antiunion and loyal to management. Although the Polish newspaper *Dziennik Chicagoski* reported that the strike district remained generally peaceful, violence did break out on occasion. On July 14, 1904, Michael Czahla addressed a crowd of strikers near 46th and Marshfield streets in the Polish and Lithuanian district just west of the packinghouses. The police attempted to arrest Czahla for incitement to riot when the crowd attacked the group of twenty-five policemen with bricks.[26] The police chased the crowd to 44th Street, where once again the workers showered the police with bricks. The police then fired into the crowd. Four days later the *Dziennik Chicagoski* reported more violence in Back of the Yards. The newspaper called both management and the union unreasonable. On July 20 the Polish newspaper described the situation in the yards as critical and claimed that management brought black strikebreakers in at a very high wage of $5 a day. The *Dziennik Chicagoski* reported that many immigrant strikers, especially Poles and Czechs, were leaving Chicago and going back to Europe. The same day as the *Chicagoski* painted this gloomy picture the Amalgamated Meat Cutters announced a back-to-work agreement with the packers after eight days of conflict.[27]

The agreement of July 20 proved to be very difficult to carry out. It specified that workers should return to work in several stages, but the owners demanded that all workers return to their jobs on July 22. Union officials feared that this would cause chaos but agreed since they felt that they had won the strike. Management also consented not to discriminate against any of the strikers who had taken part in the original walkout. On the morning that the workers were to return, all were taken back in three of the Chicago plants, but according to the union, flagrant discrimination prevailed at the other major plants. Other packing centers reported similar violations of the pact, and within hours the

Amalgamated sanctioned another strike, which in fact had already taken place. This time all the trades in the stockyards not associated with the Meat Cutters, such as the teamsters, coopers, carpenters, car workers, and others, walked out in a sympathy strike.[28]

After the second walkout the packers resumed their efforts to fill the empty slaughterhouses with blacks or with bums and tramps. They also began to impress supervisory personnel from their nationwide chain of branch houses into work as skilled butchers in the Chicago plants, sometimes rotating them to other packing centers in order to give the impression that the plants continued to operate at nearly full capacity. The scabs in large part lived in the packinghouses for the duration of the conflict. According to one report, the Chicago police department actually staged prize fights to amuse the "new" workers. In Chicago the packers imported nearly 18,000 African Americans as strikebreakers. They brought them directly into the yards on special trains. Many women also acted as scabs, not even knowing about the strike. Meanwhile the neighborhood became more and more frustrated as the stoppage dragged on. In turn, the public became disenchanted and turned against the union as meat prices soared.[29]

As the conflict dragged on, strikers attacked trainloads of strikebreakers at the points where they entered the yards. On July 22, the day that the first conflict ended, a white mob attacked a group of two hundred blacks leaving the district. On July 27, the police announced that pickets would not be allowed at the stockyard gates, and six hundred scabs, including a large number of blacks brought in directly from Kentucky, entered the yards. The packers played up the racial issue by portraying themselves as friends of the African Americans and the union as their enemy. Management also attempted to get more strikebreakers into Chicago from nearby communities, including Joliet. Blacks were even brought in from the middle-class suburb of Evanston to break the Chicago strike. Meanwhile, the industrial battle had a devastating effect on the already impoverished people of Back of the Yards.[30]

Although a permanent fund and food supply station for striking families had been established by the Allied Trades Council, which included all striking unions, there were not enough funds for a prolonged struggle. On July 28 Donnelley announced that food distribution centers had been opened at 1354 West 38th Street in Bridgeport northeast of the stockyards, in Canaryville at Root and Halsted streets just east of the main gate to the stockyards, and in Back of the Yards at 4705 South Ashland Avenue.[31] On August 1, 1904, the Amalgamated issued a statement to the Chicago newspapers attempting to explain their position and win back public support. Also on that day a group of women and children started what amounted to a bread riot at the union's food distribution center at 47th Street and Ashland Avenue. The problem emerged because of inexperienced organizers and the fact that truckloads of food arrived late. Even when they did arrive, they contained too little food to distribute to the crowd. Strikers seemed to be turning on one another. The packers announced that they had won the strike. Police Chief O'Neil concurred and pointed out that those men who went out in sympathy during the second strike were returning to the yards.[32]

On August 3 a riot took place at the corner of 47th Street and Loomis Boulevard just east of Ashland Avenue. The *Chicagoski* reported that eight Poles were among those beaten and arrested by police. Four days later a crowd chased a Pole accused of strikebreaking down Gross Avenue and attacked his brother's home with bricks when he took refuge there. That same day the unions held a massive parade down Ashland Avenue as a show of solidarity. The *Dziennik Chicagoski* reported rumors of strikebreaking throughout the conflict.[33]

Despite this violence and some obvious ruptures in the solidarity of the packinghouse workers, the Polish community held together in support of the Amalgamated Meat Cutters. The riot on Gross Avenue was perhaps only a more dramatic sign of this unity in the teeth of at least perceived betrayal. The Polish pastor of S.S. Peter and Paul Parish just to the northwest of the stockyards supported the strike, as did the pastor of St. Rose of Lima Church, the Irish Catholic parish at 48th Street and Ashland Avenue. The local Bohemian pastor spoke out against the union, but this did not seem to be very effective. Small businesses in the

Back of the Yards also supported the strike by donating money to the strike fund.[34]

The strike resulted from miscalculations on the part of both the union and the meatpackers. Although the Amalgamated had twice put off calling a strike, it did refuse a last minute call for arbitration before the first walkout. Donnelley simply could not call off the strike again because feelings ran high among the rank and file, who hoped they would be able to defeat the packers.

The packers' reason for forcing a confrontation by cutting the pay of the unskilled probably stemmed less from a desire to cut wages than to deny the union any control of the level of production in the plants. The workers had long suffered under the speed-up system, and the union, once it had gained power, instituted a slowdown in the slaughterhouses. The union did not allow its members to exceed a prescribed number of livestock in each division per hour. The managers felt that the union had overstepped its bounds and wanted to go back to the old days of pacemakers and the speed-up. This was probably the real cause of the 1904 conflict.

Donnelley's refusal to arbitrate mirrored the attitude of his membership. Both pro- and antilabor observers condemned the second strike as a grievous blunder. One writer claimed that the union had already won the strike but by walking out again had destroyed its position in the industry. In fact, however, the strike had been spontaneous and in effect hours before the International sanctioned it. The second walkout was a direct expression of working-class militancy. Nor were the packers blameless. They had agreed not to discriminate in the process of taking the men back, yet many foremen openly treated strike leaders as undesirables.

On September 7, six weeks after the start of the second walkout, Donnelley approached the Allied Trades Council with a proposal to end the strike, but the council, which had been formed to represent all the unions in sympathy with the Butcher Workmen, voted him down. Shortly afterward the executive board of the Amalgamated Meat Cutters and Butcher Workmen of North America announced they would call off the strike. Now the council agreed, and the struggle ended. Many regarded Donnelley as

a traitor. A group of workers beat Donnelley as he walked down
Ashland Avenue. He disappeared, eventually turning up in the
southwestern United States.[35]

As its legacy the strike left an atmosphere of fear and despair
in the Back of the Yards. Wages remained basically frozen until
after the declaration of war in Europe in 1914. Mass immigration
continued, keping the working class divided. Nevertheless, in
1904 the Polish community had undergone its first real test in the
class struggle, and by and large it had stuck by the union. The
increased participation of African Americans as strikebreakers
proved to be significant for the future. It intensified racial antagonism up and down the streets of the South Side. Still, just as
union officials predicted, once the conflict ended, the packers let
go of most of the nonunion blacks. The great migration of the
coming war years brought more African Americans to Chicago
and provided the packers with more recruits in their war against
the union. The dangerous social game that the capitalists continued to play eventually exploded all across the South Side, but
for the time being, the growing black population seemed to be a
tremendous resource for the packers.[36]

After the 1904 debacle, the Amalgamated had been effectively
crushed. Gains achieved during previous years, when the union
had exerted pressure on the packers, disappeared. Slowly the organization attempted to come back, but without much success. In
1913 the Butcher Workmen again tried to organize the yards, but
for the most part the workers shunned them. The memory of
1904 remained too bitter in Back of the Yards. International
events, however, soon changed the fortunes of both the workers
and the union.

The assassination of Austrian Archduke Francis Ferdinand on
June 28, 1914, in Sarajevo set off a chain of events from which
the Western world has perhaps still not recovered. For the mass
of immigrant workers in the United States it proved a watershed
in the development of ethnic communities. As the great European powers moved into battle, migration to the United States
came effectively to a halt. The peasant class of Eastern and Southern Europe, which had supplied much of the manpower for the
continued expansion of Western capitalism, now provided sol-

diers for the carnage of the First World War. Poland, still divided among the three original partitioning powers, found itself the major battlefield of the eastern front. Polish patriots referred to the conflict as the great war for which Adam Mickiewicz, the epic poet of Poland, had prayed, while Polish politicians and soldiers found themselves fighting for both the Allied and Central powers. On August 2 Vienna ordered Pilsudski's legion, nominally loyal to the Hapsburgs, to invade Russian Poland and liberate it. Amid the confusion, Polish communities in America watched in horror as the motherland turned into a battlefield. Organizers formed a Polish army in the United States to fight, under French command, on the western front. The major contribution of the American Poles consisted, however, of aid in the form of relief to those caught in the middle of the fighting. Not until the American entry into the war did members of the Polish community volunteer in large numbers for the front. But even before 1917, the war had a vast impact in both South Chicago and the Back of the Yards.[37]

The fact that immigration had been stopped meant both hardship and opportunity for the working-class families of the Polish South Side. They were, of course, cut off from their relatives and villages, over whose safety they worried as the huge armies clashed on Polish soil. Many of the workers had left spouses there, and the war made communication difficult. On the other hand, the lack of a constant supply of new immigrants gave the community a stability it never had before. Crowds gathering outside the packinghouses looking for work became smaller and smaller. Gearing up for wartime production, the packers needed more and more labor. Slowly, for the first time since the 1904 strike, wages increased, but they did not catch up with inflation pushed higher by the European conflict. The workers now found themselves to be a more important commodity in the equation that made up American industry. Several small, spontaneous, and successful strikes took place, but laborers still did not trust the union. Yet their experiences in the 1904 strike and the fact that they no longer seemed to be expendable to the packers brought back a feeling of working-class militancy below the surface of peacefulness as the United States moved toward war.

When America entered the First World War in April 1917, William Z. Foster was working as a car inspector on the Soo Line in Chicago. He had been involved in the labor movement for a long time and once belonged to the IWW. Although Foster had broken with the anarchosyndicalists, he was still a labor radical and not trusted by many of the old line union leaders. The railway carmen's union, however, got him a job and he went to work on the Soo Line. On July 1, 1917, the idea of trying to organize the Chicago stockyards and the packing industry struck Foster. The American Federation of Labor continued to ignore the yards, and only the Teamsters had an effective organization there. Because of the wartime labor shortage and the cutting off of immigration, it seemed the perfect occasion to unite the workers. While conditions remained good, Foster knew that the international unions would be hesitant to enter the struggle again. He saw as the only hope for a revival the Chicago Federation of Labor led by John Fitzpatrick. The CFL was a progressive institution, one of the most radical of the city federations associated with the AFL. Fitzpatrick had been involved in the 1904 strike and lived in Bridgeport near the stockyards. He knew the conditions in the industry and the problems associated with the huge ethnically and racially diverse workforce.

Foster began to act almost immediately. The Chicago District Council of the Railway Carmen and Local 87 of the Amalgamated Meat Cutters introduced a resolution to the Chicago Federation of Labor on July 15 calling for a campaign to organize all trades involved in the packing industry. The time seemed right, and under the leadership of Foster and other left wing unionists the movement gained momentum quickly. On July 23 the CFL formed the Stock Yard Labor Council (SYLC). This organization included a dozen local unions, including the Meat Cutters, Railway Carmen, Mechanics, Electricians, Coopers, Carpenters, Office Workers, Steam Fitters, Engineers, and Firemen. The unions elected Foster secretary and Martin Murphy, a rank-and-file butcher, president. Joseph Manly and Jack Johnstone, both labor radicals, joined the new organization.

Foster rejected the traditional radical call for one big union. He knew it would bring too much opposition from the AFL organizations themselves. Instead, the plan called for a federation of all the locals. Still, industrial unionism infused the movement. The decision was made early to base the new organization in the ranks of the unskilled. This, of course, meant that the major organizational drive would have to be among the foreign born and black workers.

The immigrants had had some experience in the labor movement because of the 1904 strike, but African Americans remained outside. Although the Amalgamated Meat Cutters accepted blacks, other trade unions banned them. Once again, African American participation would provide an especially thorny problem for the union organizers. The black middle class remained openly hostile to unionism because of previous AFL discrimination. Another problem was the large number of southern migrants who had not yet been assimilated into urban life, much less into the labor movement. The war brought thousands of these potential strikebreakers to the South Side, and the packers moved quickly to take advantage of them.

Black leaders demanded a separate union and the Stock Yard Labor Council gave in to their pressure. This decision prompted charges of discrimination. The SYLC decided to organize along neighborhood lines in order to develop mass unions that, though technically open to all, because of Chicago's segregated housing patterns were divided racially. With support from Samuel Gompers, the Amalgamated Meat Cutters established Local 651 at 4300 South State Street in the Black Belt. Special charters brought blacks into the SYLC, thus bypassing union Jim Crow laws.

Originally, two black organizers from the Illinois miners' union came to help the organizational drive. Capable organizers were hard to come by; several who were hired turned out to be opposed to unionism. Finally, the union obtained the services of I. H. Bratton and George Strather, and John Riley of the AFL also arrived to help. Ninety percent of the black stockyard workers eventually joined the union. The greatest number were northerners, whereas recent southern migrants opposed unionization. Like white ethnics, the black community faced the dichotomy between those who had been in the urban North for a long period and those who were newcomers. Those who had been in Chicago longer seemed likelier to join unions than those who had just arrived.

Still, black leaders opposed the labor movement in the yards, and some became obvious agents of the packers. The organizational drive was fairly successful until the 1919 race riots, when the union collapsed among blacks. By this time about 12,000 blacks worked in the packinghouses.[38]

Women proved to be less of a problem for Foster and Fitzpatrick. The women's labor movement was sluggish at first but it then gained momentum. Once the SYLC agreed on plans for organizing in the yards, a corps of Women's Trade Union League workers began to greet female workers at the stockyard gates. They passed out literature that spoke to the women. At first female workers ignored them, but eventually Polish women responded in large numbers. Although the first women stockyard workers' meeting was held on October 1, 1917, Polish women did not organize a local until the following February. Then the membership drive took off; by April the Polish union numbered some 1,500 members.

The national organization of the Women's Trade Union League sent Mary Anderson from Washington to Chicago to join Mary Haney and others in the campaign. While the union prospered among the foreign born, English-speaking women continued to balk at joining the union. They had memories of the 1904 strike and feared the consequences. Eventually they began to join, and by May two English-speaking locals operated as well as a local for black women workers. Also, many women joined sexually mixed locals that organized workers along ethnic or craft lines.[39]

John Kikulski, an organizer brought in by Fitzpatrick and Foster, sparked the organizational drive among Polish workers. He lived on the Northwest Side of the city and was ideal for the job. A fine orator, he was able to touch the mass of the Polish workers in their native tongue. The SYLC had its headquarters in the heart of the Polish quarter, at 48th and Hermitage streets in Columbia Hall across from St. Joseph's Church. The big Polish local, No. 554, provided a base for Kikulski's activities. He joined the campaign in September 1917, when the SYLC received permission from the AFL to employ a Polish speaker. Foster told Kikulski to report to headquarters in the Back of the Yards, and immediately he became the most important of the foreign-born organizers.[40]

With the advent of a large-scale labor organization in a vital wartime industry, the federal government began to show interest in the plight of the packinghouse workers. Foster and Fitzpatrick knew how important the products of the packinghouse industry were to the war effort and that the Wilson administration would be interested in maintaining peace on the kill floors. Foster aimed the drive at the Big Five packers who supplied both the American and Allied armed forces with meat. At first, many workers came to the meetings, but few signed up. Six weeks after the Chicago Federation of Labor resolution, only about five hundred had joined the SYLC locals. Foster then tried an organizing trick; he announced the possibility of a strike. This caused headlines and workers began to swarm the unions. At its first meeting after the press release, Local 87 of the Amalgamated Meat Cutters alone took in 1,400 members. The locals found it difficult to handle the demands for membership. At the same time, a dozen cooperating packinghouse unions formed a national organization with Foster as secretary and Fitzpatrick as chairman. As thousands of workers entered the organizations, it became difficult to weed out labor spies and agitators for the packers. Later, Foster claimed that two out of three Polish and Lithuanian organizers actually operated as management spies. These were eventually expelled, and the organization established a broad base in the industry.[41]

Only two unions active in the yards had not joined the Stock Yard Labor Council, the Teamsters and the Hair Spinners' Union No. 10399. But by the spring of 1918, the latter also joined the SYLC because of a dispute with the Nelson Morris Company that it could not resolve. After contacting Samuel Gompers, who advised them to contact Fitzpatrick, they joined the new organization. By this time the SYLC had won its case before the public and the federal government.[42]

With the creation of a national organization after a meeting held in Chicago on November 13 that adopted the demands set down by a meeting of the Butcher Workmen in Omaha two days earlier, the packers began to act. They refused to discuss the issues with the union representatives, and Libby, McNeill and

Libby, as if to emphasize their position, fired fifty-two men active in the movement. The reaction of the membership was tremendous: on Thanksgiving eve 75,000 rank-and-file packinghouse workers voted overwhelmingly in a nationwide referendum to call a strike. Notified of the vote, the AFL called on the federal government to mediate the dispute. Foster and Johnstone disapproved of this move, but Gompers and the heads of the international unions forced the issue. The Department of Labor sent in Fred L. Feick to mediate the crisis.

Feick called for a truce between labor and management until the government could investigate the situation. The unions agreed on condition that the men discharged at Libby's be reinstated. Feick tried to get the packers to sit down with the union representatives, but they refused because this might imply recognition of the new organization. The mediator then left for Washington to report to his superiors, and a new crisis appeared for Fitzpatrick and Foster. The union leadership felt that the members might lose courage now that the initial attempt at mediation had failed. Therefore they formed a committee to reestablish negotiations and named Fitzpatrick spokesman.

The union representatives then traveled to Washington, D.C., where they met first with Gompers and Secretary Morrison of the AFL, who suggested a meeting with Secretary of War Newton D. Baker. Baker took the matter under advisement and two days later wired the president's mediation commission in Minneapolis to go to Chicago to seek a settlement.

The packers refused to meet directly with the union, so the commission met with each separately and exchanged written testimony between the two. Finally, a separate agreement was worked out between the commission and the packers and another one between the commission and the unions. The unions signed at three o'clock on Christmas morning. The major point of the settlement was that there should be no strikes or lockouts during wartime. All differences that labor and management could not settle among themselves would be referred to a federal arbitrator, whose decision would be final. The federal government named John E. Williams as administrator.

E. N. Nockels of the Illinois Federation of Labor then invited Frank P. Walsh to represent the unions in the coming arbitration. Walsh, a well-known friend of labor, had in 1916 headed the Industrial Relations Commission, which had investigated labor conditions in various industries, including the Chicago packing industry, for Congress.

Williams took office on January 2, 1918, and was faced with the stubborn opposition of the packers. Once again, they refused to sit down with Walsh and Fitzpatrick. It became apparent that management had no intention of living up to the agreement and once again fired union men. At that point, Williams resigned because of bad health. The whole process seemed a failure. Union members became restless and a crisis in morale once again seemed imminent. The group of union representatives that had visited the secretary of war now left for Washington once again. On January 18, the leaders met with President Wilson and demanded that the federal government seize the packinghouses. They maintained that this was the only way to keep them operating during the war. The president called for further arbitration: the government called the packers to Washington and forced them to meet with union representatives. Management ignored Fitzpatrick and the other labor leaders and addressed only the chair. Fitzpatrick got up and walked across the room and introduced himself to J. Ogden Armour. This gesture broke the ice, as did the threat of a government takeover. The result of the meeting was that Walsh and Fitzpatrick were to meet with Carl Meyer and J. G. Condon, representing management, to iron out their difficulties. The SYLC instructed them to work out as many of the eighteen union demands as possible and send the remaining to a newly appointed arbitrator. The unions and management negotiated twelve of the demands in face-to-face negotiations; they submitted the remaining six to Judge Samuel Alschuler, the newly appointed arbitrator.

The court of arbitration opened on February 11, 1918. Alschuler effectively recognized the organization headed by Fitzpatrick as the official representative of the packinghouse workers. After hearing testimony from both labor and management, Alschuler closed the proceedings on March 7. Frank Walsh made an eloquent closing argument restating labor's position. In a 7,000 word document Alschuler set forth his findings on the six questions still in dispute.[43]

The arbitrator granted the eight-hour day and basic forty-hour week, calling for three shifts in those plants operating twenty-four hours a day. Workers were to be paid at time and a half, with double time for Sundays and holidays. Alschuler granted a twenty-minute break for lunch with pay for each eight-hour shift. Wages went up, with the largest increases going to the unskilled. Also, Alschuler ruled that men and women should be given equal pay for equal work. Guaranteed time in the plants was to remain the same as had been agreed to in November 1917.[44]

Alschuler made the award on March 30, 1918. The next day, a crowd of about 40,000 held an Easter Sunday meeting in Davis Square Park to hear the announcement. They represented every race and nationality in the yards. Their cheers roared down the street as first Fitzpatrick and then Kikulski announced the settlement. Kikulski asked if they would support the Liberty Loan Drive, and the mass of packinghouse workers shouted their willingness. Perhaps for the first time the Polish workers of Back of the Yards truly felt at home in their new environment. They had gained control over their economic lives through the SYLC and with the help of the federal government. The crowd hailed Alschuler, Fitzpatrick, Foster, Walsh, and Kikulski as great American heroes.[45]

Letters of congratulation streamed into union headquarters. Some began to encourage Foster and Fitzpatrick to move on from the packinghouse industry to the other great unorganized mass production industry on the South Side—steel. It seemed obvious that the same circumstances that had made the organization of Packingtown possible now could be taken advantage of in South Chicago and across the nation.[46]

As in the meatpacking industry, unionism had a long tradition of failure in steel. Large and powerful companies, led by the United States Steel Corporation, dominated the industry. Whereas management was highly organized, workers were not. Labor confronted many of the same problems it faced in the Chicago stockyards: an ethnically divided workforce, large numbers of unskilled workers, the rivalry of craft unions who generally could not act as a united front, a steel union that had been shattered by several struggles with management that resulted in low morale among the rank and file, and a national industry that could work effectively against any organizing attempts. Despite these problems, steelworkers attempted several times to take control of their economic situation.

The earliest effort at organizing Chicago steelworkers resulted in the Friendship Union Lodge founded in 1869. Heaters made up most of its membership. The lodge led efforts to unite other groups of skilled men into the Associated Brotherhood of Iron and Steel Heaters, Rollers, and Roughers in 1872. Two years later the organization had a membership of 700 in twenty-eight locals. It did not allow the lower paid rolling men to join. Already, in this early period, labor made the mistake of segregating the workers into different classes. This resulted in a separate organization founded in Chicago in 1870—the Iron and Steel Roll Hands of the United States. A third organization, the Sons of Vulcan, made up of puddlers, had its strength in the East and traced itself back to 1861. These organizations became entrenched early in the history of the industry. They combined in 1876 for mutual support to form the Amalgamated Association of Iron and Steel Workers. At the peak of its power in 1891, the union had over 24,000 members and was one of the leading unions in the American Federation of Labor.

The organization, centered in the iron mills west of the Alleghenies, met the needs of the industry well. The union negotiated uniform pay scales, bettered working conditions, and kept the independent ironworkers in check. The Amalgamated Association guaranteed the mills a steady supply of puddlers and rollers. The union provided a stabilizing force in the chaotic iron industry. Although bitter fights took place, both sides respected each other.[47]

Organized labor had a harder time spreading into the newly established steel mills. When iron firms entered the manufacture of steel, they generally accepted the Amalgamated Association into their new departments. New steel mills, however, resisted the union. Still, it enjoyed some success there too. The union organized both the Homestead and Jones and Laughlin works in the Pittsburgh area. Steel companies in Ohio and Illinois generally recognized the Iron and Steel Workers. In 1892 roughly one-half the steel industry had a contract with the Amalgamated Association, but east of the Alleghenies steel plants went unorganized.

The advance of technology put the Amalgamated Association in a difficult position, just as it had the meatpacking unions. Skilled workers saw many of their jobs eliminated and their position in the industry eroded; consequently, the power of the union also began to ebb. The Amalgamated Association generally acquiesced and the contract with South Chicago's Illinois Steel required the membership to aid in technological advancement. As jobs disappeared, so did union lodges, but the organization did not complain.

Indeed, the union often gave in to management demands, thus further eroding its reputation among the rank and file and emboldening steelmakers, who desired complete freedom from union interference, especially as competition and economy drives became fiercer. Management came to see the union as a serious obstacle to efficiency. The steelworkers organization enforced many regulations dealing with production; management saw this as an unfair hindrance and an attempt by the union to take control of the mills. This was, of course, the same complaint that the packers had made about the Amalgamated Meat Cutters in 1904.

A wage dispute led to the famous confrontation with Carnegie Steel at Homestead in 1892. Management felt that the union had to go. The fierce and violent strike that erupted spelled the beginning of the end of the Iron Workers as a powerful organization. Other companies joined Carnegie Steel in its move against labor. By 1900, not one large plant in western Pennsylvania recognized the union. The defeats in the East, however, did not have an immediate effect on the Chicago lodges. In 1891 eighteen locals operated in the Chicago district. By 1902 seventeen remained active. The union had a friendlier relationship with management of the mills in the Midwest, but the writing was on the wall.

At the turn of the century various mergers occurred in the industry, resulting in the consolidation of the Carnegie, Federal, and National Steel companies and of several steel-finishing firms into the United States Steel Corporation. This huge trust gained control over the American steel industry. In the hope of stabilizing its position, the corporation did not move at first against the Iron and Steel Workers. It inherited both the union and non-union plants of the merging companies. South Chicago's Illinois Steel was part of the huge trust, and the Amalgamated Association remained entrenched in the South Works.

The union moved to test the strength of U.S. Steel in 1901, the year of its formation. It failed miserably. In South Chicago, the local unions refused to strike against the South Works. The Amalgamated Association expelled the two Illinois Steel lodges and did not readmit them until 1904. Generally, the labor movement had misjudged both its own and the U.S. Steel Corporation's power. Labor leaders believed that the position of the skilled workers remained powerful enough to force the newly formed trust to recognize the union. The Amalgamated Association did not allow the unskilled into its membership, even though the continual mechanization of the mills had enhanced the position of the unskilled at the cost of the skilled. This resulted in disaster. United States Steel pressed its advantage and drove the union out of fifteen plants; the unionized workers held their position in only eight first-class tin mills. Furthermore, U.S. Steel forced the Amalgamated to agree not to spread into other plants. The union never recovered from the 1901 settlement.

The post-1901 Amalgamated Association was a meek organization. Hounded from most mills, it refused to take any stand that might seem hostile to U.S. Steel or the industry in general. Management tried to avoid further conflict and slowly removed the Amalgamated from the mills where it still held its position. One strike occurred in 1904, and the U.S. Steel Corporation defeated the union again and drove it from the corporation's western hoop mills. In other places, the Amalgamated Association's locals disappeared without even a fight. The last of the steel-mill unions ceased operation in 1903, and those remaining in the tube mills went under in 1907 and 1908. United States Steel simply closed down union mills and, after some time, offered to reopen them if the men would drop the union. Still, the U.S. Steel Corporation was not willing to force the issue with the union because it served management's purpose in providing skilled men and giving it an advantage over independent companies. Also, the corporation got a competitive advantage over other steel and tin plate producers by demanding uniform standards in all union mills. The independents almost always had to deal with the Amalgamated Association and therefore abide by union regulations. In turn, the corporation, whose mills for the most part were unorganized, could do as they pleased and gain an advantage over the competition.[48]

The Amalgamated Association continued to lose what little standing it had in the industry. On June 11, 1909, U.S. Steel announced that the twelve union mills of the American Sheet and Tin Plate Company would be run as open plants after June 30. This resulted in a strike that lasted from July 1, 1909, to August 27, 1910. The conflict did not involve the South Chicago plants, from which the union had already been driven, but the defeat of the Amalgamated Association meant the end of organized labor in the industry. From then on, U.S. Steel and the independents followed an antiunion line. The companies used all the usual methods to cripple labor, such as use of labor spies and strike-breakers, blacklisting, controlling the press, curtailing of civil liberties, and certain features of the so-called welfare programs that management used to try to buy off the workers. Eventually management established employee representation plans. The effect of the openly hostile attitude toward labor from 1909 to 1918 was the disappearance of organized labor despite a renewed AFL attempt to enter the mills in 1912.

This abortive drive resulted from unorganized mass strikes in the industry. Despite a call for the inclusion of the unskilled among the ranks of the union, the Amalgamated Association quickly moved away from this position. The lodges that still existed in the small independent mills felt safe and did not want to disrupt their relationship with management. The small union membership was conservative and secure. Once again labor failed to organize the steel industry. Still, the possibility of revival remained. As in the meatpacking industry, events far removed

from South Chicago and other steel centers made a new movement among steelworkers more than just a hope.[49]

The declaration of war in Europe cut off the supply of immigrant labor for the mills just as it had done for the packinghouses; it also increased the demand for American steel. Suddenly a shortage developed and steelworkers found themselves a
valued commodity. However, the industry had a tremendous
reputation for crushing unions and it seemed all powerful on the
eve of the United States' entry into the war.

After the victory in the stockyards, Foster and Fitzpatrick felt
encouraged to launch an attack against the greatest of antiunion
trusts, U.S. Steel. On April 7, 1918, one week after the Davis
Square meeting announced the Alschuler Award to the packinghouse workers, Foster presented a resolution to the Chicago Federation of Labor to start a national campaign to organize the
steelworkers. Twelve unions endorsed the resolution and sent it
to the AFL convention, which met in St. Paul from June 10 to
20, 1918. The resolution, which the AFL adopted by a unani-
mous vote, called for a united effort by all unions and city central
labor bodies involved in the industry. President Samuel Gompers
called another conference in Chicago thirty days later to consider
concerted action. Representatives of all the unions involved attended. As the AFL deliberated, time started to run short for the
campaign.[50]

On August 1, thirty union leaders attended the meeting in
Chicago presided over by Gompers. It led to the formation of the
National Committee for Organizing Iron and Steel Workers. The
unions elected Gompers chairman, but because of his busy schedule, they selected John Fitzpatrick temporary chairman and actual
head of the committee. The committee named Foster secretary-
treasurer, the position he held in the packinghouse campaign.
The same combination that had brought success to the labor
movement in the meatpacking industry now set out to organize steel.

Foster and Fitzpatrick planned to use the same methods that
had been so successful in the stockyards, that is, a united federation of all the unions involved in the industry. This way, the advantages of industrial unionism could be had without raising the

specter of "one big union" before the various internationals who undoubtedly would have opposed it. As in the packing industry, the committee linked unions in an alliance that presented them with the possibility of a victory over the steel companies. It was also recognized that the drive would have to be national in scope because of the way in which the industry was arranged. Finally, the campaign would have to be quick in order to take the industry by storm. Foster wanted the internationals to raise a $250,000 fund. He called for a plan that included mass meetings and the formation of workers' committees.[51]

Although supportive, the international unions were unwilling to make such a grand commitment; they made a vague promise to provide organizers and offered $100 each toward support of the drive. Although Foster had hoped for a great deal more money, he had to make good with quite a bit less. The initial pledge gained $1,500 for support of the committee. By the close of the year, only $6,322.50 had been raised. Beginning with 1919, the twenty-four unions involved agreed to pay a total of $5,000 a month, proportionately assessed on each union according to delegation strength at the AFL convention. Even so, contributions consistently fell below the monthly levy. As to supplying organizers, the unions and the AFL showed little support.

Because of the realities of the situation, the national campaign had to be forsaken. The national committee decided to concentrate on Chicago. This proved a fatal mistake. In order for the Foster and Fitzpatrick plan to succeed, it had to be national in scope and speedily executed. By limiting the drive, the unions allowed the steelmakers to prepare for battle. Also, peace broke out in Europe. The armistice of November 11, 1918, removed many of the conditions that had given organized labor the advantage. By 1920 Foster retrospectively pointed out that too much time had been wasted and that the lack of support by the conservative trade unions condemned the plans to failure from the beginning.

Some positive actions, however, did come out of the August 1918 meeting in Chicago. The steel unions agreed to work together and set a uniform fee of $3 apiece for new members. All the unions but three accepted the proposal. This was substantially lower than the fee for several of the craft organizations. The unions also established a standard application form. They put workers who joined in a common pool to be distributed according to union jurisdiction at a later time. Local unions in steel centers came together in steelworkers' councils modeled after the Stock Yard Labor Council in Chicago. The individual craft unions, however, did not lose their independence. They maintained control over their members and directed the work of their organizers, which led to duplication and a waste of more time.

Despite these problems, the national committee launched its campaign in the Chicago area in September 1918. Organizers held mass meetings, and workers responded positively to the new organizational drive. As in the packing industry, workers flooded the union halls. Steelworkers had never acted before in this manner. It was obvious that something new was happening to the industry.

The change in attitude resulted from the war. Government involvement in labor relations during the conflict was especially significant. The July 31, 1918, War Labor Board decision concerning the Bethlehem Steel Works in South Bethlehem, Pennsylvania, which, among other things, prohibited the company's antiunion policies, presented an important turning point. So did the Alschuler decision in the packing industry. The government now recognized the rights of workers to organize, thus giving labor a confidence it never had before. Also, the tight labor market reinforced the position of the men as they joined the union. In fact, no employer opposition was evident during the Chicago organizational drive. Grievances could now be openly expressed without the fear of firing and blacklisting. Steelworkers also had major complaints; the war had brought a return to the practice of the seven-day week in the continuous-operation departments because of the labor shortage. Also, the twelve-hour day was more common in 1918 than it had been eight years earlier. These conditions, as well as the rate of pay, prompted the steelworkers to flock to the union halls. The war itself had a great influence. Immigrants whose brothers and sons served in the U.S. Army began

Liberty Bond rally, Pressed Steel Company, ca. 1918. The federal government and private businesses encouraged immigrant communities to support the war effort during World War I by purchasing Liberty Bonds. The Polish community is said to have purchased the largest number of Liberty Bonds of any immigrant group. *(Courtesy of the Southeast Chicago Historical Project/Columbia College—Chicago)*

to see America as their permanent home. They purchased Liberty Bonds in large numbers. Since American propagandists portrayed the war as a war for democracy, it gave the union an excuse for demanding industrial democracy. All of this added up to a more militant steel workforce.

The success of the Chicago campaign encouraged the national committee to broaden its attack. On October 6, the committee held the first mass meeting in Cleveland. Soon workers signed up in steel centers all over the country. The unions hoped for the same result they had had in the Midwest, but workers in other areas did not respond as quickly. Management put the basic eight-hour day into effect in the industry on October 1, 1918, and this cut into the union's appeal. The committee also moved its headquarters to Pittsburgh on the same date in order to prepare for an assault at the heart of the industry.

But with the end of the war a reaction began to set in. On November 17, 1918, Bethlehem Steel told the government that it no longer felt obligated to run its plant by the agreement with the War Labor Board. The industry began to move against the labor movement. As the fighting stopped, the national committee had scored an impressive but only partial victory in organizing the workers. With the advent of peace, the unions faced the hostile steelmakers without the support of the government that had proved so important. The advantage on which Foster had banked with a quick and massive campaign had been lost.[52]

While Polish Americans reached out to other groups in the realms of social work and organized labor in an attempt to defend their communities, politics proved to be a different matter. Poles found it difficult to unite with, much less become allies with, other groups.[53] In 1923 the *Chicago Society News*, a Polish monthly newspaper designed to serve the younger members of the Polish American community, complained of Polish American political vulnerability. It pointed to the fact that Polonia was not well organized and therefore was poorly served by the American political system. The *Chicago Society News* stated that the first Chicagoan to die in World War I was a Pole, but still Poles had little recognition and even less power in the city's politics.[54]

The Polish press constantly made this lament. The previous October the *Dziennik Zjednoczenia* called for unity in an article endorsing Edmund J. Jarecki for county judge. The newspaper indicated the importance of the county judgeship by quoting an unnamed Democratic leader: "You need a county judge and city judges to protect you in some of the police courts; and that poor families will get the proper care from the county department." The newspaper admonished its readers to remember Jarecki and the Democratic party on election day. Earlier in April 1922 the *Dziennik Zjednoczenia* proclaimed: "We will be persecuted here as we were in Prussia, because the Poles here have no less a number of obstinate enemies." The newspaper encouraged women to vote for Polish candidates now that they had the franchise. It did, however, warn women not to neglect their families by going to political meetings; rather they should read the newspapers in order to learn about politics.[55]

Other Polish newspapers also commented on Polonia's lack of political solidarity. The *Dziennik Związkowy* in 1916 proclaimed, "It seems that there is no other nation so little skilled in politics as are the Polish people. . . . The main fault of our political impotence is jealousy." The newspaper further pointed to the fact that Poles often divided along class and old world regional lines and therefore lost important chances in the political game while other groups united and won many gains: "Among us Poles, on the other hand, our people inquire from what part of Poland the Polish candidate comes, whether he is a good Catholic or a nationalist, and whether he is rich." In the face of such divisions the *Dziennik Związkowy* called for solidarity behind Polish candidates no matter what their political affiliation. The newspaper called for Polish Americans to register their membership in "one single powerful Polish family."[56] The Catholic-controlled newspaper *Dziennik Chicagoski* lamented factionalism as early as 1891: "We are ignored because we lack solidarity." In continuing frustration over the lack of Polish political progress in Chicago the *Dziennik Chicagoski* affirmed some thirty years later:

Whoever is familiar with our city politics knows only too well how the Irishmen, the most notorious political tricksters in the entire country since the earliest times, manipulate continually and invariably the divergent ambitions of private groups or individuals within the non-Irish nationalities against one another in order to promote thereby their own selfish interest.[57]

After years of frustration the *Dziennik Chicagoski*, which had continuously supported the Democratic party and all Polish candidates regardless of political affiliation, could blame only the Irish for Polonia's lack of solidarity.

Polish Americans had a long history of loyalty to the Democratic party both on the South Side and across the city, but still they often divided into factions within that party or when the Republican or some third party offered a Polish candidate. The Polish newspapers reacted to this by constantly calling for support of Polish candidates despite factional or party affiliation.

In the American city in the nineteenth and early twentieth centuries politics meant jobs. Patronage remained an important political prize. Polish Americans expected to take part in the spoils of victory. After Carter Harrison II's mayoral victory in 1897, the *Zgoda*, the organ of the Polish National Alliance, demanded that because of Polish support for the young Harrison, several Poles who served on the police force and the fire department should receive promotions.[58]

Political appointments were central to the political process. August J. Kowalski, who had been the first Pole elected to the city council in the aldermanic elections of 1888 as a Republican but later became a Democrat, made that point at a Democratic party rally in South Chicago in 1894. In February of that year Kowalski, who lived on the North Side, had been appointed superintendent of the Water Pipe Extension Department. During the South Chicago gathering he told the Polish Democrats, in a speech the *Dziennik Chicagoski* called eloquent, that the only party they could depend on was the Democratic party. He claimed that under the Democrats over four hundred Poles had found employment with the city and two hundred and fifty worked in his department alone. Peter Kiolbassa, Chicago's foremost Polish Democrat, also spoke to the meeting, which was preceded by a parade through the Polish district.[59]

That same year as an economic depression spread across the city and a strike involved many Poles in the nearby Pullman community, radical politics also raised its head in South Chicago. The Polish anarchist J. Rybakowski came to the Steel Mill District and attempted to establish a branch of the Workers Alliance. The *Dziennik Chicagoski* claimed that the "anarchic pestilence is creeping even into peaceful South Chicago." Earlier the newspaper had proclaimed that a person who accepts socialistic ideology cannot be a Polish patriot.[60] The Polish Catholic newspaper reacted strongly to Polish-born socialists and others who tried to influence events in both Poland and the United States. This was important in Chicago, where class interests were often central to neighborhood politics and to the appeal of the Democratic party. The *Dziennik Chicagoski* warned workers in 1895 not to be duped into voting for a third party because this would ensure a Republican and capitalist victory.[61] Some twenty years later the *Polonia*, a South Chicago newspaper controlled by local Catholics, also used this appeal. It proclaimed the Republican party as the party of the capitalists who exploit and oppress the working class. *Polonia* proclaimed the Democratic party as the champion of progress and freedom. The South Chicago newspaper further said that Republicans had always been unfavorable to the Poles, and that a Republican victory would hand the nation over to the trusts while Democrats protected workingmen.[62] In part the Polish press continued to react to the persistence of Polish socialist organizations and to their newspaper, the *Dziennik Ludowy*.

Polish political aspirations in South Chicago, like those of other Polish communities across the city and the country, suffered from the fact that many Poles had not become American citizens. In the Steel Mill District John Koziczynski became active in local Democratic politics in the early 1890s. Koziczynski helped many Polish immigrants to obtain their citizenship papers. He organized citizenship classes in the neighborhood and also mass meetings for the South Chicago Democrats. In 1892 the *Daily Calumet*, the local English language newspaper, gave Koziczynski and the Poles much of the credit for the Democratic victory in the 33rd Ward. Three years later Koziczynski remained active in local politics, speaking at mass meetings in March of that year at Templins Hall at 88th Street and Commercial Avenue in Immaculate Conception Parish and at Retman's Hall on 84th and Buffalo streets in the Bush neighborhood.[63]

Another Polish American, Martin Wiora, also emerged in the 1890s as a major Democratic leader in South Chicago. In 1896 he received his party's nomination for alderman. In part this may have been a reaction to the nomination of Charles Witkowski and Robert Lenart as Independent party candidates for aldermen in the same ward.[64]

South Chicago's Polish community soon had another leader emerge as a force in local and citywide Democratic politics. Julius F. Smietanka was born in Chicago in 1871. Raised on the Lower West Side in St. Adalbert's Parish, Smietanka graduated with honors from Kent Law School in 1894 and was admitted to the bar. Smietanka moved to South Chicago, where he became involved in helping Poles to obtain citizenship papers. A member of Immaculate Conception Parish, he resided at 9024 South Escanaba Street. His firm, Smietanka, Pease, and Pokey, maintained law offices downtown. Smietanka obviously also traveled in non-Polish circles and quickly became involved in the larger world of Democratic politics. In 1905 Smietanka became the first Pole to be nominated for the position of judge of the Illinois Superior Court.[65] Although he did not win the election, Smietanka remained a force in Democratic politics. In the crucial years just prior to World War I, Democrats won most of the important Chicago, Cook County, and federal positions. Carter Harrison II, who won his fifth and last term as mayor in 1911, appointed Smietanka to the Board of Education. In 1917 Woodrow Wilson appointed Smietanka Chicago's internal revenue collector. In these various positions Smietanka helped other Polish Americans gain government positions.[66]

While Julius F. Smietanka became powerful through various appointments on the citywide and federal levels, South Chicago's Poles continued to play a role in local politics. Francis Chamski became the Democratic candidate for representative of South Chicago's Ninth Congressional District in 1914. John J. Sulski also played a part in local politics. "Citizen" Wisniewski was nominated as a candidate for the canal commission in 1908.[67]

In Back of the Yards Polish politics saw a good deal of initial division, especially in the ranks of the local Democratic organization. Various individuals worked to try to organize the Stock Yard Polonia politically. Michael Gryszczynski played an important role in the early politics of the Polish community in the Town of Lake, the township that originally included the Back of the Yards and became part of Chicago during the annexation of 1889. In 1893 he presided over a meeting held at Columbia Hall. Three years later Gryszczynski ran for the position of clerk of the Town of Lake as a Democrat.[68]

Various Polish political clubs appeared over time in the Back of the Yards. In 1894, the same year that violence erupted in the neighborhood during the depression and the Pullman strike, Polish political clubs appeared in the taverns and halls of the Stock Yard District. The Sobieski Political Club of the Twenty-ninth

Ward, named after the famous Polish king who had vanquished the Turks at Vienna in the seventeenth century, held monthly meetings at 4557 South Page Street. Organized in 1891 with Valentine Piasecki as president, the club claimed five hundred members. Leaders proclaimed that the goal of the organization was simply to get better political offices for Poles in the Stock Yard District. Despite the fact that the Sobieski club had existed for three years it seems to have suffered from some internal instability. In January 1894 Piasecki was reelected president along with an entire slate of new officers. By the following March, although Piasecki remained the driving force behind the organization, various new officers now held office.[69]

At the same time that the Sobieski club attempted to represent the Back of the Yards Poles, another organization called the Polish Independent Political Club of the Town of Lake met at Zenon Bykow's hall at 45th and Wood streets, also in the Twenty-ninth Ward. This organization claimed 284 members and had been in existence for two years. John Eitman served as president while Zenon Bykow, the hall proprietor, sat on the executive committee. Forty-eight members attended the August 1894 meeting.[70]

Also in the 1890s the businessman Bronisław F. Kowalewski emerged as a key figure in Stock Yard District Polonia. In 1896 a new political organization, the Polish-Bohemian Democratic Club of the Town of Lake, held its first meeting at Prasecki's hall at 48th and Wood streets in the Thirtieth Ward. About forty people attended the meeting and elected Kowalewski president of the organization with P. D. Winnicki as secretary. Michael Gryszczynski along with various other Polish and Bohemian Democrats addressed the group. This attempt at Pan-Slavism in the Back of the Yards seems to have been short-lived. In 1897 the Polish Citizens' Club of the Thirtieth Ward held its first meeting at Columbia Hall down the street from the meeting place of the old organization. Kowalewski addressed the crowd and made a special plea to Polish American youth. He told them to become the mouthpieces for their parents who had a problem with the English language during the upcoming campaign. Kowalewski expressed hope that all Poles in the area would join despite political affiliation. Kowalewski wished to promote Polish candidates on both major political tickets. In this way the Stock Yard District businessman echoed the plea of the major Polish newspapers, which hoped to promote Polish unity and therefore have both the Republicans and the Democrats knocking at their door. Kowalewski became the financial secretary of the new organization.[71]

Bronisław F. Kowalewski remained an important force in the Stock Yard Polonia over the next thirty years. Kowalewski was elected president of yet another nonpartisan organization, the Polish Citizens Club of the Town of Lake, which held its first meeting in the St. John of God parish hall on April 21, 1912. The official statement of purpose by Kowalewski and the organization spoke to the ongoing problem of factionalism in Polonia and to the fact that many Poles still did not hold American citizenship papers: "We ask all of our countrymen, who desire to become citizens, to join. The Citizens Club not only assists you in obtaining your naturalization papers, but it gives lectures in the English language as well as other aid; such as trying to reduce taxes."[72]

In a September meeting the 29th Ward Non-Partisan Polish Citizen's Club of the Town of Lake, as the organization then called itself, endorsed all Polish candidates in the November 5, 1912, election and called for Polish unity across party lines. The statement of the organization also noted that it would work for "the mutual good of the Polish element of Chicago without malice toward anyone because of any previous hardships we may have suffered in battling the politicians of other nationalities."[73] Kowalewski's group therefore issued a call for extracommunal cooperation in the political sphere while demanding political unity among the Poles. At this time John Golombiewski began to appear as a perennial Republican candidate for Congress from the Fourth District, which included the Back of the Yards. His Republican affiliation presented a constant and perhaps the most serious problem for the onetime alderman in his various races for office in the Stock Yard District.[74] Republican affiliation did not always prove to be such a major problem, as is witnessed by the career of the North Side Polish politician Jan Smulski. Nevertheless, South Side Polish Republicans seem to have done poorly.

While leaders like Kowalewski attempted to organize Polonia on a neighborhood basis, the call for a citywide organization appeared at various times. Here too factionalism often raised its head. In 1918 several Polish Democrats including Julius Smietanka formed the Woodrow Wilson Polish American League as a citywide Democratic organization. Meanwhile the older Polish Democratic League lead by Joseph L. Lisak also called for unity and claimed the support of Democratic boss Roger Sullivan.[75] Factionalism remained a problem.

Although Poles under the leadership of John Kikulski and others made progress in organized labor, politics was not as successful an endeavor for Polonia as a whole. One reality seems important. Chicago's politics presented a difficult sphere to break into with the goal of domination. This was especially true for a new immigrant group like the Poles, which contained a high number of noncitizens within their ranks. Also, politics remained alien to the peasant experience of the majority of Polish Americans. Only in the last third of the nineteenth century, and then primarily in Austrian-occupied Galicia, did peasants begin to emerge as a political factor.

Furthermore the church and labor organizations spoke more directly to immigrant concerns. Polish peasants had a long relationship with the Catholic church; and unity along class lines in Poland, especially with regard to the hated gentry, also provided a long established tradition that included the jacquerie. Involvement in Western-style democratic politics, on the other hand, was a relatively new experience. Moreover, Polish Americans shared a perception that American politics in general and Chicago politics in particular remained corrupt and dominated by the Irish. Politics could be viewed as a way to get work in Chicago. In this way it helped the community, but the peasants' unfamiliarity with it and a lack of interest in citizenship often frustrated the Polish American middle class, who tried to rally their numerous working-class compatriots.

As 1918 came to a close, the Polish working-class communities of South Chicago and Back of the Yards had much to celebrate. The war had ended, and newly resurrected Poland emerged on the political map of Europe. In Chicago both the packinghouse and steel-mill workers enjoyed viable labor organizations. The higher wages and more secure jobs of the war years brought a sense of prosperity to the two industrial communities. Even in the political sphere Polonia had made some progress. The war for democracy abroad seemed to mean greater security and freedom at home. The winter of 1918–19, however, brought not only a killer influenza epidemic but also the erosion of political gains made by organized labor during the war.

The spirit of nativism reemerged and eventually resulted in the Palmer raids and immigration restriction. Chicago witnessed both labor and racial violence in 1919. First, labor lost its position in the steel industry. Later in 1921 and 1922 the meatpackers drove the unions out of the Chicago stockyards. The basis for this damage to the fortunes of South Side Polonia was laid earlier in 1918, when at the height of victory the seeds of defeat were sown.

CHAPTER SIX

Years of Crisis, 1918–1922

As the war came to an end, success and security seemed a fact for the Polish community. For the first time since the end of the eighteenth century a free and independent Poland appeared on the map of Europe. In America, Polish Americans expected to take their place among other citizens because of their patriotic support for the war. Finally, in Chicago the Polish packinghouse and steel-mill workers had helped to forge unions to represent themselves and others. The increased wages and financial security of the war years brought a sense of prosperity to the two communities. Polish workers bought homes and local shopping districts expanded. The corner of 47th Street and Ashland Avenue, in the heart of the Back of the Yards, saw marked improvement. Cement sidewalks replaced the old wooden ones, and the city drained and paved streets. The parishioners of Sacred Heart were well on their way to paying off the parish debt. With the coming of the peace sea lanes opened again and Poles could be reunited with their families. Some might return to Europe, but others would come to Chicago to replace them. Polonia looked to the future with optimism in 1918.

The immediate postwar period, however, proved to be one of trial for the Polish working class in Chicago. Even nature seemed to attack them in the fall of 1918, when a killer influenza epidemic struck the nation and the city. Upon the arrival of peace in the United States the establishment branded labor leaders as dangerous radicals and watched the so-called new immigrants with suspicion as agents of international communism and racial degeneration. Black and white conflict reached dangerous proportions. Polonia found itself under attack on all fronts as it faced the period after the armistice.

In the spring of 1918 few paid any attention to the first traces of an influenza epidemic in the United States because the country's eyes and ears followed the tragic events occurring on the western front. Germany launched a massive offensive in order to win the war before the American military effort could make a difference. The Allies attempted to hold out while the United States hurried to make good its commitment. Meanwhile, over one thousand workers at the Ford plant in Detroit were sent home with influenza in March. The disease was not listed as a reportable contagious infection. In Haskell, Kansas, authorities reported 18 cases, resulting in 3 deaths. Reports swamped United States Public Health Service agents. Influenza hit hard in the San Quentin penitentiary with its cramped quarters. During April and May 500 of the 1,900 prisoners contracted the disease. Three died. Most deaths during the spring outbreak were attributed to pneumonia. The index of the *Journal of the American Medical Association* did not even list the influenza outbreak of early 1918.

The United States did not have a network of health departments that could effectively gather data on the subject. The only accurate numbers came from the army and institutions like San Quentin. Reports attributed many of the deaths to pneumonia, a common cause of death in 1918. Also, many expected that diseases would break out among soldiers and sailors gathered from all parts of the country and confined to military bases. There seemed to be no real reason for alarm. Airborne diseases often took their toll on enlisted men; too many lived in too tight quarters, and men from rural areas had not built up the resistance that soldiers raised in the city had. Those between the ages of twenty-one and twenty-nine years had the highest illness ratio. This was unusual and marked the epidemic that hit the United States on both ends of 1918.

Apparently the doughboys carried the disease to Europe. By May, influenza spread throughout the European theater of war, and Allied nations suffered greatly. The first German troops to contract the disease were those on the extreme western front.

The summer of 1918 saw the United States passing through the warm weather with little evidence of Spanish influenza. At the same time, it ravaged other continents and began to mutate into strains capable of surviving various conditions. Meanwhile, more than 1.5 million Americans traveled back and forth between Europe and the United States in the greatest wartime migration to date. This set the scene for a tremendous outbreak in the United States. Troops were quartered in small areas, and they often passed through major cities on their way to points of embarkation, of which New York was the major port. As the war continued, nature prepared its own offensive against the United States.

Three ports vital to the Allied war effort felt the impact of the virus in August 1918: Freetown, Sierra Leone; Brest, France; and Boston, Massachusetts. Brest was a major port of arrival for the American Expeditionary Force and also served as a training base for the French. The connection between Brest and Boston was obvious. The first reported cases of influenza in August in the United States took place among naval personnel at Commonwealth Pier in Boston. The new strain proved extremely virulent and the disease spread quickly. On August 27 two or three sailors came down with symptoms of the grippe. On August 28 officials reported 8 more cases and 58 turned up the next day. The sickness had returned to North America in a much stronger form.[1]

The influenza epidemic did not reach Chicago until around September 21, when the first death resulting from it was recorded. From that point on it rapidly increased. Once again the outbreak was associated with the military and, as in the case of Boston, with the navy. Thirteen days before the reported death in the city, influenza struck the Great Lakes Naval Training Station, thirty-two miles to the north. Within a week 2,600 were hospitalized in a naval facility designed to take care of 1,800. The navy canceled all liberty on September 19, but by that time the sickness had spread.[2]

The epidemic first touched the northern suburbs of Chicago, which lay close to the naval base. On September 16 the Department of Health warned the public that a possibility of an outbreak of Spanish flu existed. The city posted announcements on streetcars and on the elevated trains throughout Chicago. The health department made influenza a reportable disease, placing it in the same category of seriousness as other killers. One of the principal complications that arrived with influenza was pneumonia, which had been a reportable disease in the city only since 1910. The deaths from both increased dramatically over the following weeks.

The virus moved southward toward Chicago. Reported cases on the North Side of the city (north of 12th Street) exceeded those on the South Side during the first and fifth weeks of the epidemic. Deaths, however, were more numerous on the North Side of Chicago for the first three weeks. The disease especially hit the crowded river wards, where much of the North Side Polish population lived. The West Side of the city felt the full fury of the epidemic in the fourth week and the greatest relative number of deaths occurred there. The Southwest Side, which in the divisions established by the Department of Health included the Stock Yard District, felt the greatest impact. Cutting the city in two along a line running down 12th Street, city officials counted 3,941 deaths north of the line and 4,257 south of it during the period from September 21 to November 18, 1918. Both the Back of the Yards and South Chicago lay in the district south of 12th Street.[3]

Unseasonably cold weather aggravated the problem. The city did not require many landlords to supply heat before October 1 and they refused to. A lack of fuel and the problem of fixing heating equipment in time to deal with the weather also complicated matters for those in working-class districts who provided their own heat with wood- or coal-burning stoves. The Department of Health attempted to deal with the problem and forced landlords to supply adequate heat to those buildings not heated by the tenants. Doctor John Dill Robertson, the city's health commissioner, spoke out against the owners: "If I find evidence against any greedy landlord having turned off the heat and the tenant dies, I shall ask the state's attorney to indict him on a charge of murder."[4] Because of this statement from the commissioner and the quick action taken by the department, most landlords complied. Extensive coverage in both the English and foreign language press facilitated the heating of apartments. A threat to publish the names of landlords who did not provide heat brought further positive action.

The city took other steps to attempt to control the epidemic. As early as September 16 the Department of Health posted placards warning against the danger of passing germs by spitting, coughing, and sneezing. On September 21 a statement in the newspapers warned persons having influenza symptoms to stay home in bed. The chairman of the medical section of the National Council of Defense, Franklin H. Martin, telegraphed the local medical section and asked that an Illinois Influenza Commission be established. One was immediately appointed. Its role was advisory, not administrative. State and local health departments could adopt recommendations made by the commission. The matters considered ranged from the decision to open or close schools to the manner in which funerals were to be conducted.

The commission decided that places of business, churches, and schools should not be closed. On September 28 the commission held a meeting of representatives of agencies interested in children. After a thorough debate they made a decision to keep the schools open. The reasons given were that they could act as an information-gathering place concerning neighborhood health, and that it would also be possible to watch over the children and keep them under better conditions during the day than if they were allowed to roam the streets, alleys, and tenements. Also, an organized medical staff existed to inspect the schools. The commission requested the superintendent to superheat the schools so that classrooms could be flushed with fresh air periodically. Later the school board decided that the schools should keep their windows open at all times. Children were allowed to wear their coats. These measures remained in effect until November 16, by which time conditions had greatly improved.

As the epidemic worsened, the city took measures to prevent large gatherings of people. On October 12 officials decided to close the city's many dance halls. By October 13 the city closed all theaters and five days later canceled all gatherings not essential to the war effort. The city prohibited smoking on streetcars. Officials banned all public funerals and limited attendance to ten mourners.

Archbishop Mundelein issued an order to all Catholic pastors on October 17 suspending evening services and missions and prohibiting long sermons. He limited the length of Masses to forty-five minutes with only five minutes for preaching. The cardinal asked that all churches be thoroughly ventilated between Masses. Pastors posted extra ushers to request those coughing or sneezing to leave. The various Protestant churches took similar action.

The influenza epidemic peaked on October 17, twenty-six days after the initial outbreak in Chicago. The number of deaths attributed to influenza or pneumonia on this day stood at 381 out of a citywide total of 520. The health department counted 2,395 new cases. The death rate during this fifth week of the epidemic stood at 63.0 per 1,000 based on an annual rate; after this the disease declined rapidly. During eight weeks a total of 8,510 persons died of influenza and pneumonia. The increase in the death rate from all causes as compared to the three previous years was 99.2 percent. From September 21 to November 16, doctors reported 37,921 cases of influenza and 13,109 cases of pneumonia in the city of Chicago.

Spot maps published by the Department of Health show the location of the reported deaths caused by the virus. For the week ending October 5, 1918, the disease hit the North Side hardest. The following week showed a dramatic increase on the South Side, but the majority of deaths occurred north of 12th Street. Both the Back of the Yards and South Chicago reported few cases. The week ending October 19, however, witnessed a serious outbreak in the Stock Yard District and a somewhat lighter one near the steel mills. In Back of the Yards the epidemic centered in the area between Ashland Avenue and Robey Street (Damen Avenue) on the east and west and 43rd Street and Garfield Boulevard on the north and south. In South Chicago the disease hit the Bush hardest. The next week saw an intensification of this trend. In Back of the Yards the area affected spread east to Racine Avenue. All three of the Polish parishes in the neighborhood lay in the flu zone. The week ending November 2 saw the tailing off of the disease, but many deaths still occurred in the Back of the Yards. As the virus spent itself in the city the results were the same for the packinghouse and steel areas. The probable reason for the fewer reported deaths in South Chicago was its proximity to the lake and lake winds. The Department of Health stated, however, that it believed that the number of actual cases reported was misleading, that many were not reported or misdiagnosed.

When the eight-week period ended, the ethnic groups that had suffered the most included the Bohemians, Poles, and Lithuanians. These made up three of the largest groups living in the crowded working-class wards in general and the Stock Yard District and South Chicago in particular. The death rate attributed to influenza and pneumonia for foreign-born Bohemians increased 5,450 percent, for Poles 5,362 percent, and for Lithuanians by 4,400 percent. The white population as a whole saw an increase of 2,610 percent, while African American deaths increased at a rate of 1,400 percent.[5]

Local institutions attempted to deal with the epidemic. In the Back of the Yards the University of Chicago Settlement House established an emergency hospital in its gymnasium. The settlement stood in the area of the neighborhood hurt most by the disease. Miss McDowell and her staff responded quickly to the crisis in the crowded district near the packinghouses.[6]

The influenza epidemic continued to decline until November 30, 1918, after which it raged again, reaching a second peak on December 14. Deaths attributed to it also increased until just before Christmas, when a gradual decline set in until the end of the year. This second wave was typical of outbreaks in other American cities.[7]

The epidemic presented the first of the postwar trials of the South Side Poles, who had been hard hit by the disease. The next three years brought economic and social problems to the forefront. Polonia greeted the armistice of November 11 with great joy, but one of its major effects signaled an uncertain future for packinghouse and steelworkers.

From 1890 to 1915 Chicago's black population rose from fewer than 15,000 to over 50,000 people. This increase was to be overshadowed in the next four years by the so-called wartime great migration, which would bring 50,000 southern blacks to the city. The growing African American population was more confined to a certain district than it had been before 1890. Whereas from the beginning most blacks lived south of the downtown business district, there was an increasing tendency to have them live in prescribed areas. The creation of the Black Belt on the South Side and the smaller West Side ghetto, along with other concentrations, resulted.

In 1900 blacks were still relatively well distributed in Chicago, and as late as 1910 they lived in less segregated areas than did Italians. As the number of African Americans grew, however, they did not spread evenly throughout the city but became concentrated in certain neighborhoods. An obvious segregated housing pattern emerged. However, in 1910, blacks did not entirely occupy more than twelve blocks. In many mixed areas the races lived together without hostility. But as the black community spread east of State Street into more middle-class areas, violence increased.

By 1910 the South Side ghetto stretched south from 12th Street along State Street as far as 39th Street. Between 1910 and 1914 the district absorbed over 10,000 new migrants, but the saturation point had been reached. The area had to expand. Most of the southerners settled in the section between State Street and the Rock Island Railroad tracks to the west. This was the poorest and most run-down part of the Black Belt. As the wartime influx of newcomers occurred, housing demands and costs skyrocketed in an already inflated market.[8]

Rents were high in the Black Belt even before the advent of the great migration. A 1912 survey of housing conditions in both the South Side and West Side ghettos revealed that African Americans paid comparatively higher rents than any other ethnic group. Half the residents of the Polish North Side, the Bohemian West Side, and the Back of the Yards paid less than $8.50 a month for a four-room apartment; half the tenants in the part of the Black Belt studied paid at least $12.00 for the same space. Also the homes in the area generally stood in poorer condition than even those in either the Back of the Yards or South Chicago.[9]

Hostile whites surrounded the Black Belt. The working-class

Irish, traditional enemies of Chicago's blacks, lived to the west. To the east native whites and middle-class Jews occupied the desirable lakefront wards. To the south resided Jews and the rising Irish American middle class of Washington Park described by James T. Farrell, especially in his Studs Lonigan trilogy. The continued migration of blacks to Chicago created an explosive situation. Another deadly crisis was the outbreak of racial and ethnic violence that followed the influenza epidemic.[10]

On Sunday, July 27, 1919, Eugene Williams, a seventeen-year-old black, was swimming in Lake Michigan off 27th Street. He and several of his friends had built a raft and floated across the invisible boundary that separated the black and white beaches of the South Side. A lone white man began to throw rocks at the boys; one struck Williams in the head and he drowned. This event happened shortly after an intrusion of the white beach by four blacks that resulted in a rock fight between the races. That July was an especially hot one and the racial confrontation that began on the beach quickly spread across the city. A huge riot resulted that eventually brought the state militia to Chicago and altered race relations for the next fifty years.[11]

Racial tensions had been building in Chicago for some time. They rose throughout the North as the migration of blacks became a national phenomenon. Race riots occurred in Springfield, Illinois, in 1908, then in East St. Louis in 1917. A week before the Chicago riot, Washington, D.C., witnessed racial clashes. In Chicago between July 1, 1917, and the day Williams drowned, twenty-four racially motivated bombings occurred, more than half of them in the six months just prior to the race riot. The bombs struck homes of isolated blacks in once all-white neighborhoods and the offices of realtors who sold or rented to blacks outside the Black Belt. All but four of these bombings took place in middle-class areas to the south or east of the traditional black district in neighborhoods that felt threatened by racial change. Violence also took place along the western boundary of the ghetto. Friction was obvious between Irish-dominated working-class neighborhoods bordering Wentworth Avenue and the black community. Gang attacks on blacks posed a serious problem for some time and frequently occurred the spring before the riot. They reached a climax just five weeks before Williams' death when whites killed two blacks on June 21. Twice before the riot racial violence seemed inevitable, and the chief of police sent several hundred extra patrolmen into the district where trouble seemed likeliest to occur. The heat of July did not improve matters as Chicagoans of all races headed for the beaches.[12]

After Williams drowned, his friends went to the 25th Street beach. They returned with a black policeman to point out the man they believed had thrown the rock that struck the boy. Officer Daniel Callahan, the white policeman on duty, refused to make the arrest and prevented the black officer from doing so. The boys ran back to the "colored" beach and told the crowd what had happened. Blacks began to rush toward the 29th Street beach. A crowd gathered around Callahan and rumors spread quickly through the South Side. One had a white boy drowning, another had Callahan preventing the rescue of a black drowning off the white beach. The crowd grew restless. Officer Callahan then turned and arrested a black on the complaint of a white. As a paddy wagon pulled up to take the prisoner to the station, volleys of rocks and bricks passed between the black and white crowds. James Crawford, a black man, drew a revolver and fired into a group of policemen, hitting one. A black policeman returned fire, fatally wounding Crawford. Other shots rang out and the riot began. The black crowd moved against the whites and beat four, stabbed five, and shot one. The violence spread quickly. White street gangs from west of the Black Belt became involved. Between nine o'clock that night and three o'clock the next morning, whites beat twenty-seven blacks, stabbed seven, and shot four. Race war had broken out.

Daybreak saw little violence. Monday was a workday, and both races headed for their places of employment. The peace did not last, however, as white mobs molested blacks returning home from the stockyards in the afternoon. These attacks happened largely in the area between the yards and the Black Belt. African Americans leaving the packinghouses at 3:00 P.M., 4:00 P.M., and later found themselves confronted by white crowds armed with bats and clubs. The police seemed helpless in dealing with the attacks. Mobs pulled trolleys from their wires and boarded the cars.

They dragged blacks to the streets and beat them. Four blacks and one white assailant died. Whites beat thirty black men severely in the stockyard area clashes.

The death of John Mills was typical of those that occurred that afternoon and evening. A mob of about three to four hundred whites attacked the eastbound 47th Street car near Normal Avenue in Canaryville, the predominantly Irish district to the east of the yards. Twenty-five to fifty men boarded the vehicle and beat the blacks with bats and bricks. The blacks ran for their lives. Mills ran down Normal Avenue. A white hit him on the head with a brick. Before he could run again, another young rioter hit him with a scantling. Four others were beaten, but only Mills died.

Rumors of white attacks on blacks spread throughout the ghetto, resulting in further violence. Blacks stabbed an Italian peddler to death at 3638 South State Street at 4:50 P.M. Eugene Temple, a laundry owner on the same block, died in a like manner about forty minutes later while leaving his establishment. An African American crowd demonstrated outside Provident Hospital, a black institution, because two whites who had been wounded while making an automobile raid down State Street had been taken there. Black mobs stabbed six whites, shot five others, and badly beat nine more. Four whites died.

The most serious confrontation took place at the intersection of 35th Street and Wabash Avenue. At this corner stood Angelus House, a white-occupied apartment building in the middle of the Black Belt. Once again rumors played an important part in the violence. Word spread in the neighborhood that a boy had been shot by a sniper from the fourth floor of the structure. A black mob besieged Angelus House. About one hundred patrolmen, some mounted, responded. They searched for the white who reportedly fired the shot but could not find him. By this time the black community had lost all confidence in the Chicago police. The crowd had grown to about fifteen hundred when a brick hit an officer. The police grouped and fired. Four blacks died and police injured many. After this, both races showed signs of panic.

Small groups began to gather to terrorize members of the opposite race. White gangs in the districts bordering the Black Belt grew bolder. They attacked the homes of African Americans living in "invaded" territory. Automobile raids into the ghetto also frequently occurred. Gangs of white men and boys drove down streets firing indiscriminantly. Blacks returned their shots. By midnight Monday night seventy-one whites and one hundred fifty-two blacks had been injured along with six of unrecorded race. Since the drowning of Eugene Williams the day before, authorities counted two hundred seventy-five casualties.

A transit strike hit the city on Tuesday morning. This stopped violence on public transportation but it presented further problems for Chicagoans, especially blacks. African Americans had to walk to work through hostile, Irish-dominated neighborhoods in order to reach their jobs in the stockyards. The scene for more violence had been set. Idle men gathered at street corners. Race violence spread to the Loop, where white soldiers and sailors led a group in the beating and killing of blacks and the destruction of white-owned property. Race war broke out on the West Side, where an Italian mob killed Joseph Lovings. Meanwhile South Side gangs sprang up everywhere along Wentworth Avenue from 47th to 63rd streets. Mobs burned black homes in mixed areas.

Wednesday saw a lessening of violence. The riot seemed to have peaked. The Irish and black working-class districts still provided storm centers, but the furor cooled down. The governor mobilized the state militia Monday night. It was not until Wednesday evening, however, that it was asked for help. Rain also fell on Wednesday night, driving the crowds indoors. Violence became sporadic and the riot appeared to be under control if not over. At that point, the 6,200 militiamen moved out of the armories and into the district bounded by Wentworth and Indiana avenues on the west and east and 18th Street and Garfield Boulevard (55th Street) on the north and south. They had orders to draw no color line and to shoot as a last resort. The soldiers cracked down especially hard on the white gangs or so-called athletic clubs.

Whites met blacks returning to the stockyards on Thursday morning with more antagonism and violence. A riot occurred in the livestock pens. Except for this, however, the riot area remained quiet. Also, the transit strike came to an end. It seemed that the violence had finally ceased with the incident in the Union Stock Yards.[13]

On Saturday morning the meatpackers, after discussing the problem with the heads of the militia and police, arranged for a return to work under the cover of machine guns. Signs and fliers were posted calling men and women back to their jobs. Black groups also supported the move. The Stock Yard Labor Council, however, warned against a reopening of the plants on Monday, August 4. The unions called for a cooling-off period. J. W. Johnstone, Martin Murphy, and John Kikulski approached the packers and government officials at the secret meeting at the Blackstone Hotel and attempted to get the packers to back down. The leaders of the Stock Yard Labor Council laid the blame for the race riot on the packers for their attempt to divide the workers in the stockyards and accused them of fanning the flames of racial hatred. They told the representatives of the packers that the only way to stop the riot was to bring the black workers back to the plant as union members. The packers refused to do so. The *New Majority*, the official newspaper of the Chicago Federation of Labor, stated that "the profiteering meat packers of Chicago are responsible for the race riots that have disgraced the city." The newspaper also claimed that the meatpackers subsidized black politicians and preachers in order to fight against the union. The mostly black Local 651 of the Meat Cutters Union passed a race riot resolution demanding equality and protection for the black stockyard workers. The resolution also claimed that some whites wanted to drive the blacks from the industry. The packers ignored the plea of the SYLC and moved to reopen the plants. It took further violence to stop management from completing their plans.[14]

At about 3:15 A.M. that same morning, August 2, fires swept through forty-nine houses in the Polish and Lithuanian section of the Back of the Yards. The first fire broke out in the home of Karol Wanata at 4351 South Wood Street. The wind spread the fire quickly. Immigrants claimed that four blacks had set the initial blaze. Fires broke out throughout the area between Wood and Lincoln streets north of 45th Street. The *Dziennik Chicagoski* printed an interview with J. Hezlinziak of 4408 South Honore Street, who said that he had been in his cellar at about 2:30 A.M. when he heard a noise in the alley and saw someone coming toward his house. He went to his apartment and got a revolver. Hezlinziak claimed that about five minutes later he saw a black start a fire. He fired two shots as the culprit fled. An hour later the neighborhood was in flames. Generally, however, witnesses seemed to be confused about who started the fires.[15] Governor Lowden blamed radical anarchist plotters. Others said that the Poles had set the fires in order to attack the Lithuanians.[16] All in all the danger of another racial explosion seemed imminent and the militia poured into the area. The 2nd Infantry Division of the Illinois militia proceeded to occupy the district bounded by Ashland Avenue and Robey Street from 55th Street north to the Chicago River. The packers and Governor Lowden announced shortly thereafter that it had become clear that black workers could not return to work safely on Monday. They now heeded the union's warnings.[17]

The authorities never set specific blame for the conflagration. The grand jury investigation claimed that the white athletic clubs had started the fires in order to incite the East Europeans against the blacks; Irish Americans predominated in these clubs. While investigators argued about who set the blaze, the Polish community quickly decided who the perpetrators were. Reverend Louis Grudzinski, pastor of St. John of God Parish, acted as a spokesman for the three Polish pastors in Back of the Yards. In a statement published in the Polish newspapers Grudzinski called for the Poles to remain peaceful. In an early version of Grudzinski's statement that appeared in the *Dziennik Chicagoski* Grudzinski openly blamed the Irish. The priest claimed that "the Irish want to blame the riot on the Poles." In later versions "other nationalities" replaced the Irish as perpetrators of the attack on the Polish parish of Sacred Heart and the Lithuanian parish of the Holy Cross. The *Dziennik Chicagoski*, however, seemed a little confused. In the column next to Grudzinski's statement the newspaper blamed blacks for the attack![18] The *Dziennik Związkowy*, the newspaper of the Polish National Alliance, warned the Poles to beware of their real enemies. The newspaper seemed to agree with Rev. Louis Grudzinski. The *Dziennik Związkowy* claimed that the burned-out district was being used to cause race war and was not the result of the race riot. The newspaper warned its readers to be peaceful. The Reverend Francis Karabasz, pastor of Sacred Heart Parish, and Rev. Alexander Skrypko of St. George's Lithuanian Parish in Bridgeport came to the aid of the homeless. So did Rev. Stanisław Nawrocki of Our Lady of Perpetual Help Parish also in Bridgeport, who donated $1,150 for the victims of the fire. Morris and Company provided food for the homeless.[19]

The next night witnessed a similar attack on Grudzinski's parish, which bordered the Irish neighborhoods to the east. This time residents spotted the gangs and drove them off. Bronisław F. Kowalewski, a businessman and local resident, stated emphatically that the assailants were not blacks but the "traditional" enemies of the Poles from the area to the east of St. John's. Obviously he too blamed the Irish.[20]

Kowalewski made his remarks at a special meeting held August 4 at the Guardian Angel shelter. He acted as president of a resolutions committee formed to convey the opinion of the Poles from the Back of the Yards to the rest of Polonia and Chicago about the recent rioting. It seems that this resolutions committee was an outgrowth of the local citizens committee organized during World War I to promote the enlistment of Poles in Back of the Yards into the Polish army being raised in France. Generally important local businessmen, fraternal organization leaders, and priests made up these citizens committees.[21] The gathering was well attended and the pastors of the three Polish parishes were present. The dynamic Reverend Louis Grudzinski gave the first speech. Grudzinski seems to have been crucial in cooling the tempers of the stockyard Poles. A charismatic leader, he had served as pastor of St. John of God Parish since 1909. Grudzinski told the crowd to arm itself with patience, to take everything coolly. Grudzinski said, "We must not be moved by agitators and then be condemned for having caused the black pogrom." He maintained that whites in blackface had caused the fires and exploded, "It could not have been the blacks because they have always worked in harmony with the Poles in the packinghouses. They also belong to the union." Grudzinski claimed that the Poles had not taken part in the riot.

"Citizen" Garpiel followed the pastor. He told of the attack on the neighborhood around St. John's. Garpiel said that he too had heard blacks threaten whites, but never Poles. After this W. Wresinski, a director of the Polish National Alliance (PNA), spoke. He said that as of late blacks had been working in the stockyards and that they fraternized so well with whites that there had been little room for misunderstanding. Wresinski also emphasized black membership in the union, which was obviously a sore point for white workers. He said that it should be understood that blacks had been exploited by capitalists and at times had been used to break strikes. Once again the PNA director stated that there had been no racial battles in Polish neighborhoods and no need for troops.

The resolutions committee made the following statement:

We citizens of Polish descent meeting at the Guardian Angel Shelter and representing 6,000 Poles put forth the following resolution:
We recognize the sad fact that the terrible race war was brought to our neighborhood by conspirators who hoped to involve the Poles and blame the riots on them.
We also recognize that the Polish homes burnt down were destroyed by those who hoped to agitate us against the blacks in revenge.
We ask our brothers to remain peaceful and to have cool blood. We desire that the conspirators be brought before the law of the city and the state.
    —Fr. L. Grudzinski, W. Wresinski, B. Kowalewski, Dr. P. Lownik, B. Galecki, Ig. Sciagalski, Ed. Bradel—The Resolutions Committee.[22]

Wresinski's remarks concerning capitalist exploitation echoed those made in the *Dziennik Związkowy* after the second day of rioting. An article in the back of the newspaper discussed the riot and then offered a short history of the black experience in America. It ended with the terse question, "Is it not right they should hate the whites?"[23]

The manner in which the *Dziennik Związkowy* handled the race riot is of interest. On July 28, the day after the killing of Eugene Williams and others, the newspaper's headline dealt with military events in Eastern Europe:

WAR WITH UKRAINE ENDS!
She Yields to Poland
Polish Army Enters Ukraine to Push Bolsheviks Out

There was no mention of the racial fighting taking place on the South Side. The first news of the riot occurred the next day in the above-mentioned article concerning black history. Also in the column entitled "Z Town of Lake," which dealt with local events in the Back of the Yards, the newspaper reported interracial fighting along Ashland Avenue from 35th Street south to 63rd Street. The article described the streetcar attacks.[24]

On July 30 the newspaper ran a front-page cartoon showing Uncle Sam looking toward Poland and protesting Jewish pogroms. Blacks and whites fought behind the figure. The caption read "On the Occasion of the Black Pogrom in America." The Polish newspaper responded to America's criticism of the new Polish state's inability to control antisemitic violence. It was obvious to the Poles, if not to the Americans, that the United States was being hypocritical.

On the same day the *Dziennik Związkowy* noted that the stockyards had been shut down by the fighting and the transit strike. It also quoted a foreman as saying that blacks had stayed home in order to fight whites. Other stories concerning the riot were listed throughout the newspaper. Generally, the reporting was neutral if not slightly pro-black. It related a story of one African American soldier who had fought in the Canadian army. He had felt that the crowds would respect his uniform, but he was wrong. The newspaper quoted him as saying, "I don't know why they attacked someone like me. I did what I could to help their homelands, for that I get this beautiful reception." In a report on the Angelus House riot the *Dziennik Związkowy* claimed that blacks could not show their faces on the street.[25]

But by August 2 the newspaper was starting to identify African American interests with those of the packers. Responding to the packer attempt to open the plants on Monday, the newspaper claimed that management had used the blacks as a weapon against the union and the working class. The article related rumors of a plan to bring more blacks up from the South in case of a strike by the union. "The blacks are to be brought in by the elevated train and protected," the newspaper stated. The *Dziennik Związkowy* continued:

The meat barons want to use the race riot under the cover of the police and military to smash the union and to return to the ways they ruled the packinghouses five years ago. . . . All the blacks who live on the South Side have friends in the persons of Swift, Armour, Wilson, Morris, and the others. As soon as they hear there is hunger in the black quarters they send an abundance of food. We wonder if they would be so concerned if they knew hunger stalked their white workers, in particular their union workers? We know they would not be so concerned.

The article noted that the Wabash Avenue YMCA and Jesse Binga's bank were passing out packers' checks to black workers unable to leave the Black Belt.

The same issue also contained other antipacker statements. In an article entitled "Dzial Robotniczy" (Worker's column) the newspaper attacked the English language papers as being tools of the meatpackers. Discussing the high cost of meat, the newspaper asserted that the meat trust, and not consumers or farmers, caused the inflated prices.[26]

On August 4 the newspaper discussed the calamity in the Stock Yard District. It called the fire one of the worst in history, leaving many homeless and several dead including children. Once again the daily stated that it was not blacks but some other outside element that perpetrated the crime in order to arouse the Poles. It compared the fires to those in black areas started by whites with gasoline-filled bottles.[27]

The *Dziennik Związkowy* obviously reacted to the race riot on several levels. Originally it had hardly reacted at all. The newspaper was printed on the North Side in the area near the intersection of Division Street with Ashland and Milwaukee avenues— far from the riot district. Serving to a large extent the community known as Polish Downtown, it did not immediately react to what looked like an Irish-black confrontation on the South Side. In fact the newspaper seemed to be fair to the African American position. After the fires in the Back of the Yards the newspaper attempted to gather information and to keep the community calm. It used no inflammatory language, unlike the English language papers, and the Polish daily constantly shifted blame away from the blacks. The readers would have little difficulty guessing that the real enemies referred to were the Irish, who lived both among them and to the east and south in Bridgeport, Canaryville, Fuller Park, and Englewood. The daily's one article that seemed antiblack really spoke to questions of class interests, hitting on the theme of capitalist exploitation of black workers. This was basically the same stand that the speakers at the Guardian Angel meeting took on August 4.

The interesting connection made by the *Dziennik Związkowy* between blacks and Jews was important. The newspaper represented not only the Polish working class, which made up the great majority of Polish Americans, but a growing entrepreneurial group. The gazette contained several antisemitic remarks. The Jewish population in the Polish districts often settled along the major business streets and operated small stores. The rising Polish-American business community found itself in competition with them. Advertising for the Liberty Clothing Company, which opened stores in both the Polish Downtown and Back of the Yards, referred to the firm as Polish. The advertisement further reminded the readers to recall the saying *"Swój do Swójego"* or "Patronize Your Own." This was a reminder not to buy in non-Polish, that is, Jewish, shops. A few lines later there was an announcement of a meeting of the Commercial Club of the Town of Lake to be held in the Polish theater on 46th Street and Ashland Avenue. The newspaper emphatically stated, "There are no Jews in the organization." In an article about South Chicago, six days later, a story told of a Jew taking advantage of a Pole. The article included the same saying, *Swój do Swójego.*[28]

The struggle between Polish Christians and Jews must be viewed in the European context. Pogroms were taking place in Poland. The American press rightfully condemned these. The *Dziennik Związkowy* pointed out that the so-called civilized West also had its pogroms, most evident now in the riots. What Kowalewski reacted to at the Guardian Angel meeting included the accusation that Christian Poles in Europe slaughtered Jews. He said that the Poles in Back of the Yards should remain calm. The riots were started by enemies who wanted to be able to say, "Look, the Poles are even holding black pogroms here."[29]

The Catholic-controlled *Dziennik Chicagoski* covered the race riot extensively and gave it headlines from the day it broke out. The newspaper tried to present the facts but was obviously confused by the various reports coming from the Back of the Yards. This newspaper, published by the Resurrectionist Fathers, was not as pro-union in its reportage as the *Dziennik Związkowy*. It nevertheless also cautioned its readers to be calm and not to riot. The *Dziennik Chicagoski* also blamed the riot on the Republican mayor of Chicago, William Hale Thompson. In an editorial titled "Whose Fault?" it blamed Thompson for not asking earlier for the militia and for favoring blacks over whites. The *Dziennik Chicagoski* was obviously referring to the fact that Thompson had tried to bring blacks into his Republican organization. The Resurrectionist newspaper maintained a pro-Democratic party stance in American politics.[30] The editorial cartoons of the *Dziennik Chicagoski* criticized American society for its racial problems. A July 31 cartoon depicted Chicago as a weeping woman standing before an open history book with two black pages marked "strikes" and "race riots." The caption read "Two dark pages in the city's history." A cartoon appearing on August 2 pictured a black armed with a razor fighting with a gun-wielding white while onlookers of various nationalities watched from a grandstand. The Ukrainian onlooker simply laughed. A cannibal made the sarcastic remark of "How civilized!" A Bolshevik stated, "And this is Democratic America!" A Turk laughed and said, "So Free!" Finally a Mexican sarcastically remarked how much cleverer the Americans were than he was. The editorial cartoon was captioned "The Racial Pogrom." The newspaper also expressed the opinion that the fires in Back of the Yards were part of a conspiracy to involve the Poles. The *Dziennik Chicagoski* claimed that the Polish section of the Back of the Yards was peaceful and that the militia was not necessary in those areas.[31]

The *Naród Polski*, the official organ of the Polish Roman Catholic Union, took the most violent stand on the race riots. It compared the East European pogroms to the race riots and took a much more antisemitic and antiblack stand. The daily said that both groups deserved the treatment. The Catholic newspaper also claimed that Germans and Bolsheviks controlled both Jews and blacks. After this, the *Naród Polski* called upon Poles to be calm. "Let there not be any of us staging pogroms."[32] Obviously there was a schizophrenic reaction to the black and Jewish problem. The South Side Polonia seems to have taken the calmer approach of the *Dziennik Związkowy*, which saw the race riot as an outgrowth of capitalist exploitation and of the class struggle. This remained, of course, the official view of the community as expressed by the pastors and others who spoke at Guardian Angel, as well as that of the packinghouse unions.

Mary McDowell of the University of Chicago Settlement House maintained that the Polish community did not take part in the racial violence. She blamed it on athletic clubs that consisted of second- and third-generation Americans. The chief offenders were the Ragen Colts, who were among those who attacked blacks leaving the yards on the Monday after the drowning of Williams. McDowell also claimed that skin color did not concern the foreign born as it did Americans. Whereas Poles and Lithuanians did not get along and violence had been committed against the first Italian family to settle in Back of the Yards, not much antagonism existed between Poles and African Americans. In fact, when the first black family moved into the neighborhood on Gross Avenue, not far from the settlement house, the Poles greeted them. Polish residents invited the family to weddings, christenings, and other social affairs. The man of this household was a cattle butcher and a union member who came to the district after the 1904 strike. During the riot a Slovak apparently saved a black from being trampled by horses on the corner of 47th Street and Ashland Avenue. Even after the 1919 race riot the black family on Gross Avenue remained in the district.[33]

The assertion that the Polish community did not take part in the riot was, however, not entirely true. Still, the evidence of Polish participation is not overwhelming. This may have been a result of geography. The Polish districts did not lie next to the Black Belt but were separated from it by predominantly Irish-American neighborhoods. Streetcar attacks did take place in Polish neighborhoods, but these areas were ethnically integrated. Among those Chicagoans listed as either victims or perpetrators of assaults no distinctly Polish names appear. There are, however, four that are Slavic and they may have been Poles. Two of these were victims attacked in the Black Belt, and two were involved in the livestock pen riot on the Thursday after the fighting had peaked. The fires set in the Polish-Lithuanian quarter on August 2 give credence to the view that the immigrants did not take part in the fighting, since the incident evidently was an attempt to provoke the residents into joining the race riot. Also, although the *Dziennik Związkowy* should not be taken as the only voice of Polonia, the newspaper's attitudes did reflect a much weaker antiblack view than might have been expected. Perhaps the Poles had not yet been assimilated into the tradition of American racism in 1919. Certainly the future would be different, but in this period class, not race, seems to have been a greater concern for the immigrant communities. When African Americans acted as strikebreakers, Poles reacted very violently, but there had not been intense interaction between the two groups. Because blacks were less involved with organized labor after the riot, they presented more of an economic threat to organized white workers. The race riot initiated a new era in black-Polish dealings and set the course for race relations in the city for the next fifty years. For the immediate aftermath it accelerated the competition between African Americans and white ethnics on the South Side while setting up a permanently segregated housing pattern.[34]

After the initial call for organization of the steel industry in 1918, the unions began to make progress, especially in the Chicago District, where the campaign had begun. While the embers of the race riot cooled, the South Side braced for yet another crisis as the steel companies and the unions headed for a collision. When the World War came to an end the labor movement seemed to be united and militant. The victories of the war years established the unions as a strong force in the life of both the country and Chicago. The government's support and the lack of a surplus labor force during the fighting had placed organized labor in a very good strategic position. The Chicago Federation of Labor (CFL), led by John Fitzpatrick, moved to establish the militant labor movement as a political force. In 1919 the Farmer-Labor party, which was founded to a large extent by the CFL, put forward a full ticket for the city elections that included Fitzpatrick for mayor and John Kikulski for city clerk. Organized labor seemed to be on the verge of establishing itself permanently as a force in the city and in the large mass production industries. Steel would prove to be the test. As the spring of 1919 saw the defeat of the Labor party, so it also marked the beginnings of the conflict that determined organized labor's role in Chicago for the next twenty years.[35]

The federal government's intervention in the steel industry proved to be crucial for the unions. The War Labor Conference Board recognized the workers' right to organize. Behind these recommendations stood the veiled threat of nationalization, which prompted the steel companies and other manufacturers to go along with the government's demands. But as the war ended, steel manufacturers began to mobilize. The industry moved quickly before the mass organization campaign could spread throughout the nation. On October 1, 1918, the National Committee for Organizing Iron and Steel Workers moved its headquarters to Pittsburgh and opened the national campaign after its success in the Chicago District.[36]

When Bethlehem Steel announced in November 1918 that it no longer felt obliged to tailor its labor relations to the decision of the War Labor Board, the counteroffensive began. Steel was determined not to allow its workforce to be organized by Foster and Fitzpatrick or anyone else. Judge Elbert H. Gary, who headed U.S. Steel, called for fairness toward workers so that they would not flock to the union. "It will cost some money," he warned, "but I do not think that very important in comparison."[37]

Management attempted another way to counteract the labor movement, its employee representation plans (ERPs). This device gained popularity during the war. Because federal regulations required that management deal with employees through shop committees, the ERPs offered the steel bosses a chance to circumvent the intent of the regulations. The plans provided a refuge from interference from Washington. A third way to deal with workers' organizations was simply to mobilize local authorities to break up meetings and outlaw gatherings. The civil rights of many were taken away in the name of law and order. For the most part, attacks on liberty did not appear in the Chicago District.[38]

Nevertheless the owners could not stop the national committee's efforts. Workers flocked to the union halls with their complaints. The new organization quickly became a force in the industry, but the steel magnates refused to deal with it. The question of whether the companies would recognize the unions became one of power. The firms led by U.S. Steel stood determined not to. The union had to make the next move. In the end the strike, which hit the entire nation, was a contest over recognition of the new labor organization.[39]

One of steel's first propaganda moves against the national committee was to brand its leadership as Reds and to claim that only the foreign born had joined the union. This device, management hoped, would divide the workers along ethnic lines and also help brand the leadership as Bolshevik. With the outbreak of the Russian Revolution, the fear of radicalism seized the public mind. The steel companies targeted William Z. Foster, whose background included membership in the IWW. John Fitzpatrick, in an attempt to clear his colleague's name, asked Judge Alschuler to give his opinion of Foster. Alschuler replied on March 28, 1919, that Foster seemed to be "particularly intelligent, honorable, moderate, tactful, and fair." The judge further pointed out that although Foster might have entertained radical ideas in his youth, nothing occurred in their relationship that implied that he still held these views. The Stock Yard Labor Council, which Foster and Fitzpatrick had helped to establish, sent their support. J. W. Johnstone wrote Foster that the packinghouse workers stood united behind him, and that this propaganda contained "poison gas" sent up by war profiteers who feared the advance of labor.[40]

The Interchurch World Movement's investigation of the steel strike decried the red-baiting of the steel companies. In particular the report condemned the attack on Foster, especially the re-printing of Foster's *Red Book*, an old syndicalist tract, as if Foster had reissued it. The steel companies distributed the book to news-papers, government officials, and local pastors with the intent of discrediting the union movement. They asserted that Bolsheviks pervaded the organization. This claim became a major issue as time went on and as a steel strike seemed imminent.

Union literature both before and during the strike was rather conservative. In fact Foster kept the issue of a labor party out of all union material until Fitzpatrick ordered it included. Gener-ally the unions confined all leaflets to traditional union oratory and did not reflect any radical influence. Investigators found one bundle of Communist handouts, but union officials had confis-cated them and thrown the distributor out of the union hall. A piece entitled "Forward to Bleed and Die" was translated into Polish to read "Forward to Wade Through Blood!" The Polish organizer refused to distribute it, saying, "My people are all good Catholics. They won't stand for advice like that." The union her-alded the organizing drive not as a radical movement but as one more step in the struggle for democracy.

Local leaders, however, seemed less concerned with maintain-ing a conservative posture. Generally they maintained the official AFL position, but the rank and file also influenced them. As a result they used radical rhetoric. In fact, the workers seemed to be more eager for action than the national leadership. The steel-workers pushed for a confrontation with management. The very facts that had made the organizational campaign a success now threatened to bring it into possibly suicidal struggle. Workers wanted to press their demands; the national leadership hoped to hold them back until organizational activities could be completed. Demands for action flooded the national committee headquar-ters in Pittsburgh. Leaders finally decided to call a conference on May 25, 1919, at Pittsburgh's Labor Temple. They hoped that this conference would help to constrain the rank and file's mili-tancy so that the important task of union building could go on before a confrontation.

The Pittsburgh conference resulted in increased militancy.

Representatives from the nation's mills moved the organization further along the road to battle with management. The meeting ended in a call for the twenty-four unions associated with the national committee to request meetings with the steel companies in order to discuss wages, hours, conditions, and the recognition of collective bargaining.

Samuel Gompers wrote to Judge Gary on June 30, 1919, asking for a parley. The AFL leader pointed out that over 100,000 men from the steel mills belonged to the ranks of organized labor and that the future of the new organization seemed bright. Gary ignored the letter. On July 8 Gompers reported this to the national committee. The result was an almost immediate explosion. Local unions threatened strikes all over the steel districts. On July 20 the national committee was forced to decide whether to call for a strike vote. The motion passed by a margin of twelve to two.[41]

Each international union voted separately and the balloting took a month. There was no hurry because the national committee was certain that the vote would lead to a strike. In fact, the events after July 20 helped the unions to gather additional strength. Foster reported on July 28 that "the campaign is going like a house afire now." He told Fitzpatrick that the Amalgamated Association was going along with the strike vote and that there would be cooperation all along the line.[42] When the voting ended on August 20, approximately 98 percent of the ballots called for a strike. The delegate from the South Chicago Trades and Labor Assembly claimed that the members of his organization voted at a rate of 150 to 1 in favor of the confrontation with the companies if the latter refused to talk with the national committee.[43]

The July 20 meeting resulted in the propositions that the national committee hoped to discuss with the big steel corporations. *Bulletin No. 2* of the national committee listed them as follows:

1. Right of collective bargaining.
2. Reinstatement of all men discharged for union activities with pay for lost time.
3. The eight-hour day.
4. One day's rest in seven.

5. Abolition of twenty-four hour shifts.

6. Increase in wages sufficient to guarantee an American standard of living.

7. Standard scale of wages for all crafts and classifications of workers.

8. Double rates of pay for all overtime work and for work on Sundays and holidays.

9. Check-off system of collecting union dues and assessments.

10. Principles of seniority to apply to maintaining, reducing and increasing working forces.

11. Abolition of company unions.

12. Abolition of physical examination of applicants for employment.[44]

The bulletin, issued in Pittsburgh ten days after the resolution passed, appeared in six languages. The principal concern of the organizers headed the list. If management recognized the unions, the rest might fall into place. After the issue of legitimacy, the issue of time and wages was the most important. While the steel companies probably forced the confrontation over the first demand, the workers fought primarily for issues affecting their daily lives.

The strike began on September 22, 1919, and shook the nation and the entire industry. Immigrant communities across the nation supported the struggle. Observers claimed that, of all the workers, they remained most loyal to the unions. The American born, on the other hand, proved more reluctant to join the movement. David J. Saposs observed that the immigrant was more likely to act in a group, and this made him a better union member. Perhaps this was because the immigrants filled the ranks of the unskilled and their position in the industry was rather precarious. Edward J. Evans, the secretary-treasurer of the Chicago District Organization Committee, saw the foreigners as less fearful. He also pointed out that they had a better attendance record at meetings and took part in the proceedings. The organizers had to be very careful, however, about national sensibilities. Evans said that it was better to have the less numerous nationalities addressed first at a meeting because those who have heard the talk in their own language tended to leave the meeting. The committee employed Russian, Italian, Lithuanian, Croatian, and Polish organizers in South Chicago and at the other mill gates.[45]

Three days after the unions called the strike they claimed that 340,000 men had walked out. Reportedly 90,000 had struck in the Chicago District, which included Gary and other Indiana centers. Plants closed down all over the area despite a press attack on the unions that started even before the strike had begun. The local newspapers reported as early as September 19 that the steel companies had a half-billion-dollar war chest to smash the labor organization. Continually during the strike Chicago and other area newspapers exaggerated the number of workers returning to the plants in an attempt to break morale.[46]

In South Chicago the local Polish newspaper *Polonia*, published by Rev. Francis M. Wojtalewicz, spoke out against the strike before the union called it. On September 18, in an article entitled "We Do Not Want A Strike!" the paper claimed that most South Chicago workers, both Polish and American, did not want a conflict. "The winter is coming," the newspaper observed. "What will happen to the strikers and their families? This question is not asked by just one father, but by all." In the same issue, however, the newspaper described a strike in neighboring Hammond at the Standard Steel Car Company. It reported that as the organizers tried to convince the workers to maintain their solidarity, the local police fired into a gathering. The first to be wounded was a Pole, Wawryn Dudka. Five Poles fell before the bullets of the company and city police, who fired over one hundred rounds. The article described the funerals and ended with a call to protest: "Americans and Poles stand up as citizens to protest these things done to our countrymen!" The *Polonia* obviously worried that such violence would occur in South Chicago if the steel strike became a reality. Yet, despite its call for a stop to the slide toward confrontation, it exhibited indignation over the killing of the Polish workers across the state border.[47]

On September 25 the *Polonia* reported that 18,000 workers had struck in South Chicago. The neighborhood remained calm despite the presence of five hundred patrolmen and forty mounted police. The first steel mill to close was the Federal Furnace Works on 108th Street. All the steel establishments in Chicago followed except the Wisconsin Steel plant in South Deering, where about 60 percent of the men remained on the job. After a talk with representatives of the employees, however, management agreed to close the plant temporarily. The strike went well and the plants seemed to be paralyzed. The men finished the tasks at hand before leaving their jobs and departed as if at the end of another workday. Captain Nootbar of the Chicago police ordered extra men into the district. Three other captains, twenty-two lieutenants, and forty sergeants assisted him during the buildup. Tension filled the air as groups of workers stood around the various mill gates. Several clashes occurred in South Chicago, including one at 92nd Street and the B&O Railroad tracks. Unfounded rumors that strikers killed three policemen spread through the area. The Polish newspaper advised caution and calm.[48]

The *Dziennik Chicagoski* published an editorial cartoon on September 24 captioned "The Son of Vulcan Listens to Seducers." It portrayed a steelworker with a demon marked "radicals" sitting on his shoulder and whispering in his ear. The same newspaper reported on the next day that roughly one thousand striking steelworkers watched the local train stations and searched each train as it arrived for strikebreakers. The newspaper also noted rumors that management planned to bring in southern blacks to work the mills. On September 28 the *Dziennik Chicagoski* reported that a crowd of strikers' wives chased an automobile carrying five strikebreakers out of the South Works and pelted the scabs with bricks. Police detective T. J. McGrath suffered a broken hand in the confrontation.[49]

Meanwhile steel management called for a return to work. One of the staff members of Illinois Steel's South Works said that the company would send a car around for those willing to come back to work. Company officials claimed that about four hundred men came to work in that manner on September 24. The union called this a lie. Leo Rogan, the union secretary in South Chicago, charged that the steel company burned wood and anything else it could in order for smoke to come out of the stacks so as to convince the strikers that the plants continued to operate.[50]

The records of Illinois Steel's South Works point to the initial effectiveness of the strike. According to the "South Works Personnel Activities Record, 1917–1920," only 20.8 percent of the employees working at the time of the strike call reported to work on October 15, 1919. The records of the Illinois Steel Company actually broke down the returning strikers by nationality group. American-born whites led the strikebreakers with over 1,200 crossing the picket lines, which made up just under 50 percent of the number working on September 22. Fifty-seven percent of the black workers employed by the South Works before the strike continued to work on October 15. Their number (241), however, was small. The observations of labor organizers and others that the foreign born actively supported the strike are borne out by the company's records. On October 15, 93 percent of the German Poles still observed the strike call. Nearly all the Austrian and Russian Poles remained away from the plant. Generally speaking, all the foreign-born, both Eastern and Western European, communities observed the strike.[51]

The majority of the population of South Chicago supported the strike. Even most Americans backed the union. The length of the workday remained the biggest complaint of the strikers. As one South Chicago worker put it, "A man works, comes home, eats and goes to bed, gets up, eats and goes to work." Another simply said that he worked "just like a mule."[52]

Not all the men struck. Some felt the strike was wrong. One Polish machinist who had worked at the South Works for fifteen years called the strikers crazy. He stayed home for six weeks but returned to work when his foreman agreed to convey him back and forth from the plant. Many of the men returned after about six weeks. One worker referred to his co-workers as "sheep," claiming that they did not stick together. Another mentioned that all the men except those on salary went out but that management brought strikebreakers in after six weeks. He claimed that the men who held the better jobs returned to work first.[53]

As the strike dragged on, rumors of a surrender from both sides filtered through South Chicago. In the second week, the South Park Commission refused to allow a union rally in Bessemer Park near the Polish parish of the Immaculate Conception. Organizers held the rally instead at the corner of 92nd and Anthony streets. The neighborhood remained fairly quiet, but occasional explosions of violence broke out. On Monday, September 29, a gun battle broke out in early morning near the South Works. Tension filled the air as the steel companies began to use every means possible to break the spirit of the strikers. Management claimed that many had already returned to work and that more planned to do so shortly. Meanwhile, a red glow over the mills at night gave the local populace the impression that the plants continued to operate. Although the union claimed that it was only a trick, it had a negative effect on morale.[54]

Angry mobs often greeted returning workers and members of management. On October 5 strikers congregated near the 83rd Street Illinois Central railroad station to continue their vigil for strikebreakers. They also stopped cars to look especially for blacks. James Mulaney, a white from the Stock Yard District, was driving a car near the South Works when a crowd attacked him at the intersection of 86th and Saginaw streets. A brick hit him in the face. He was rushed to the South Works' hospital. Meanwhile management taunted the unions with a declaration that the mills operated at a better rate than at any time since the strike began. Mill gates saw further skirmishes as some of the union men tried to prevent strikebreakers from entering the plants. Crowds pelted blacks with bricks as they approached the mills. The *New Majority* claimed that the ranks of organized labor remained unbroken in South Chicago. On October 4 that newspaper declared that 95 percent of the men in the South Chicago mills remained on strike. The *New Majority* further declared: "We are in the midst of a revolution. . . . It is a revolution to overthrow the autocracy of the Steel Trust." Meanwhile union members patroled the streets trying to keep the peace. These men wore white ribbons clearly marked "picket." The park commissioners remained obstinate and refused to allow the unions to hold rallies in Bessemer Park. As a result, the Gassman brothers, local merchants, donated a hall for union meetings.[55]

Meanwhile the tragedy of violence and military occupation shook nearby Gary, Indiana. Authorities seemed more conciliatory in Chicago. On October 7 unions held an orderly parade led by an escort of 150 soldiers in uniform and a cavalcade of mounted police under the direction of Captain Nootbar. The parade carried many protest signs, including one that attacked the press and read: "Press of the Trusts—You Will Not Lie To Us!!!" Four days later the *New Majority* printed an appeal for the workers to stick by the unions in three languages, including Polish. It was the first time that the labor newspaper had made a direct ethnic appeal to Chicago's workers. John Fitzpatrick addressed a crowd of roughly eight thousand workers on Friday, October 17. Two days later Fitzpatrick claimed victory for organized labor.

Accounts of nativist reactions to the strike appeared in the Polish press. *Polonia* also reported that foreign-born workers planned to flee the country. The newspaper pointed out that American chauvinists blamed the immigrants for the strike and called for their deportation. In East Chicago and Indiana Harbor over 1,000 workers reportedly withdrew their savings from local banks and prepared to leave for Europe. Even naturalized citizens seemed to be ready to leave the United States. *Polonia* claimed, however, that most of those leaving were not Poles but Balkans.[56]

With the violence in Gary came repression. Local officials banned both the *Strike Bulletin* and the *New Majority*, the official organ of the Chicago Federation of Labor, in Indiana Harbor. Chicago also banned the *New Majority*. In Gary the local land company, which U.S. Steel controlled, threatened to evict strikers from their homes. The newspapers continued their nativist attacks on the union and the workers. The *Chicago Tribune* blamed "Balkan Blood" for the strike violence. There was no reference to the fact that management used ethnic and racial prejudice to divide the workers. The companies used blacks with a great deal of success as strikebreakers. In fact their importation into Gary led to the riots of early October. United States Steel brought roughly 30,000 to 40,000 blacks into the mills during the strike. Management told other ethnic groups that their rivals now had their jobs while they continued to strike; friction between Italians and Serbs resulted.

By the middle of November all the mills in the Chicago District, except those in Waukegan and Joliet, operated at from 50 to 85 percent of their normal capacity. Of the 90,000 men who struck in the district on September 29, only 18,000 remained out by December 10, 1919. The unions finally called off the strike on January 8, 1920. It had been broken weeks before.[57]

The Polish community in South Chicago had remained loyal to the labor movement. In many ways the strike of 1919 had been a communal one. But the labor organization was not sufficiently developed to win a long struggle with the companies led by U.S. Steel. The period after World War I witnessed a period of extreme public reaction. The nationalism of the war had been stirred up again but was now directed against the steelworkers. The companies, meanwhile, moved quickly to exploit this situation in their attack against the supposedly "Red" leadership of the unions and later against the rank and file, especially in Gary and in the Pittsburgh District. United States Steel, which had encouraged Americanization classes during the war, apparently fostered the belief among workers that it was a branch of the government and that anyone interfering with steel production acted against the federal government.[58]

The year 1919 marked the beginning of the end of the success of the wartime labor movement. Steel provided a crucial test for the system of organization that developed out of the Stock Yard Labor Council. This organization remained intact as 1919 ended, but the packing industry soon followed steel down the road to conflict. The Polish community in the Back of the Yards looked at the events in South Chicago with well-founded apprehension.

As the fighting stopped in Europe, packinghouse workers faced their own crisis in the Chicago stockyards. The year 1919 was to be a critical one for the labor organization in the meat-packing industry, just as it had been in steel. Although the problem did not come to a head for two years, the seeds of the confrontation had already been planted in the months after the armistice. The packers, who had to operate under close governmental scrutiny, moved carefully but directly against the organization that Foster and Fitzpatrick launched in 1917. The Stock Yard Labor Council, which had proved so successful in uniting the various factions among the workers, male and female, black and white, now faced internal divisions and a united group of packers determined to throw off the control of the federal government and to destroy the power of the unions. The Amalgamated Meat Cutters and Butcher Workmen, leaders of the lost 1904 strike, involved themselves from the outset in the creation of the Stock Yard Labor Council in Chicago. After about a year, however, they began to agitate against the council. The industrial union tendencies of the Chicago organization ran against the grain of the Butcher Workmen. Finally, in early 1919 they moved against the organizers who had won the Meat Cutters and other affiliated unions so many members. The secretary-treasurer of the union, Chicagoan Dennis Lane, quickly became a bitter foe of Jack Johnstone, who took Foster's place after the latter had gone to Pittsburgh to organize the steel industry, and of Martin Murphy, John Kikulski, and John Riley. Lane singled out Kikulski and Riley as two troublemakers who were trying to destroy the Meat Cutters' Union. Kikulski, of course, was instrumental in organizing the foreign born in general and the Poles in particular. Riley was an important black organizer.[59]

Lane claimed that the three leaders—Johnstone, Kikulski, and Martin Murphy—of the SYLC had openly tried to discredit the AFL union. The disagreement actually went back to 1918 and eventually led to violence and charges on both sides. Lane claimed that armed thugs attacked him after a meeting of the Stock Yard Labor Council on July 21, 1919.[60] Foster, on the other hand, stated that Lane, along with Simon O'Donnell of the building trades union, had attempted to take control of the council by force. Big Tim Murphy, an ally of Lane, openly threatened to kill Foster. Although the Butcher Workmen's attempted takeover of the SYLC was stopped, the fight became more bitter.[61] Dennis Lane and the Amalgamated moved through traditional AFL channels to try to discredit the Stock Yard Labor Council. Even as organized labor in Chicago faced the severe test of the steel strike, the organization that had sparked much of labor's progress in the two mass production industries of steel and meatpacking began to witness a civil war. The Stock Yard Labor Council struggled through the fall of 1919 to the summer of 1920 to maintain itself, but it died under the impact of intrigue, scandal, and even murder. Leaders of the SYLC moved quickly to try to stop the damage caused by the 1919 race riot, but it resulted not only in a racially and ethnically fragmented working class, but also in the nightmare of dual unionism during the difficult readjustment period following World War I. In the midst of the riots and the strikes that followed, the Amalgamated Meat Cutters announced the formation of an organization separate from the SYLC. The Butcher Workmen demanded that their locals pledge allegiance to this new organization called Chicago District Council No. 9. By the fall a third labor council, the Mechanical Trades Council, appeared. Most of the allied skilled trades that had belonged to the SYLC joined this third organization.[62]

The race riot ended with black workers being escorted into the stockyards by the militia on August 7, 1919. About 5,000 white workers under the leadership of the SYLC walked out on strike in protest of the stationing of the militia in the yards. By August 9, the *Dziennik Chicagoski* reported that about 36,000 packinghouse workers had answered the strike call. This strike led to an open break between the Amalgamated Meat Cutters and the SYLC. Dennis Lane refused to support the strike outwardly because of its questionable legality under the Alschuler agreement, but in reality because of his continuing argument with Johnstone, Kikulski, and Martin Murphy, the SYLC leaders. On August 17 Local 87 of the Butcher Workmen moved its headquarters from Columbia Hall (Słowacki Hall), where the SYLC and Local 554, the big Polish local run by Kikulski, had their offices.[63] Alex Nielubowski served as president of Local 87. The secretary-treasurer of the Amalgamated Meat Cutters, Dennis Lane, also belonged to this local. The thirty-four-year-old Nielubowski had long been associated with the Butcher Workmen and the AFL. Born in Chicago, he spoke Polish fluently. He began working at Swift's cattle kill at the age of thirteen in 1898 and took part in the 1904 packinghouse strike. Nielubowski became an AFL organizer in 1912 and served in various packing centers before returning to Chicago to head the skilled cattle butchers local. Nielubowski now saw himself in the middle of the factional dispute between the charismatic Kikulski and the Butcher Workmen.[64]

Johnstone, Kikulski, and Murphy represented the more radical leadership associated with William Z. Foster. They had worked

Columbia Hall (Julius Słowacki Hall), 1930. This hall in the Back of the Yards served as headquarters for the predominantly Polish locals of the Amalgamated Meat Cutters and Butcher Workmen during the 1921–22 packinghouse strike. Columbia Hall also provided a home for various Polish American organizations. Pictured here is the first national congress of the Polish Highlanders Alliance of North America. *(Courtesy of the Polish Highlanders Alliance of North America)*

hard to create an organization in the stockyards that could overcome racial, ethnic, and craft divisions among workers. Kikulski in particular had preached racial harmony to his vast following of Polish and East European immigrants. The early summer of 1919 saw various attempts to promote working-class solidarity across racial lines. This hope died as one of the victims of the riot. Johnstone later claimed that his foe Dennis Lane had simply disappeared during the riot and that Frank McElroy of the Butcher Workmen had said, "We have got the niggers out of the stockyards, now let's keep them out."[65]

Indeed the SYLC leadership seemed to hold fast against a renewed attempt by the Butcher Workmen to take over the council. The Amalgamated Meat Cutters and Butcher Workmen's official union newspaper, the *Butcher Workman,* claimed that Johnstone,

Kikulski, and Murphy had set themselves up as self-appointed "emancipators." The newspaper also condemned the race riot strike. Lane and the Butcher Workmen's leadership felt that Johnstone and Kikulski were too aggressive in their attitude toward the packers. Finally the union called the SYLC leadership obstructionists and claimed that they had a mad desire to control the labor movement.[66]

In November 1919 the *Butcher Workman* published the International's version of the conflict. It claimed that the Amalgamated Meat Cutters had established Chicago District Council No. 9 because of the "questionable activities of the Chicago Stock Yard Labor Council." The newspaper attacked the three leaders of the SYLC. The *Butcher Workman* pointed to J. W. Johnstone's IWW past and his friendship with Foster. The newspaper explained that Murphy had only joined the union in the spring of 1917 when he worked as a hog butcher at Agar's and accused him of being antiunion. Finally it ridiculed Kikulski as a "large man with a HA-HA laugh that arouses one's suspicions as to its sincerity and honesty." It then made the accusation that Kikulski had stolen funds from Local 554. Kikulski was a prime target of the Butcher Workmen at this point because he enjoyed the almost unquestioned loyalty of the Polish and East European immigrants. The Amalgamated tried to break the workers' attachment to Kikulski, perhaps hoping to replace him with Nielubowski.[67]

John Kikulski had a long-established reputation in the Polish community. He was an active and important member of the Polish National Alliance and the Polish Falcons, a patriotic paramilitary group that supported the movement for Polish independence. When a schism occurred in that organization in 1912 Kikulski helped to heal the break. He also worked as an AFL organizer for the Wood Cutters Union.[68] Kikulski ran on the Labor party ticket for city clerk in April 1919. In that election Kikulski's rhetoric called for the working class to take power in America: "We mean to put our own constitution on these laws." He had worked closely with some of the clergy, especially Rev. Louis Grudzinski at St. John of God Parish in the Back of the Yards. Kikulski also attempted to organize veterans returning from the war. In January 1920, while he was embroiled in the labor civil war in the stockyards, Kikulski organized the Soldiers, Sailors and Marines Club. This organization and Kikulski were accused by Captain Wrobel (also a Polish American) of the Third Illinois Reserve Militia of threatening his life and the lives of other members of the militia. The militia company apparently lost a good part of its membership after Kikulski claimed it was a tool of the meatpackers. In December 1919 the choir of St. John of God Parish entertained the veterans' organization, a sign that Rev. Louis Grudzinski supported the radical veterans' group. John Kikulski therefore enjoyed a broad base in the Polish community and, at least until the fall of 1919, in the ranks of organized labor.[69]

The argument between the Amalgamated Meat Cutters and the Stock Yard Labor Council continued through the fall and winter of 1919–20. In October the Butcher Workmen asked the Chicago Federation of Labor that it unseat Butcher Workmen Local Union Nos. 116, 212, 219, 554, 649, 650, 658, and 609 with their approximately 30,000 members. The Amalgamated had earlier expelled these unions for not joining Chicago District Council No. 9. The motion carried unanimously, but it was referred to the CFL's executive board. John Fitzpatrick was in Pittsburgh at the time dealing with the steel strike, so the problem was put on hold. The *New Majority* explained that the controversy was of momentous consequence for organized labor and that the CFL hoped to act as a mediator between the two organizations. In November the CFL announced that a meeting between the warring parties would be held to try to bring peace to the labor movement.[70]

In January Johnstone approached the Chicago Federation of Labor and offered the SYLC's resignation from that body in order to prevent a rupture between the CFL and the AFL. Johnstone praised the Chicago federation, and Kikulski told of attempts by "certain" interests to inject race hatred into the situation in the stockyards. He told the CFL that he had been approached by the packers to sell out the labor movement. The CFL gave the SYLC a vote of confidence and offered aid in the future. At the February 1, 1920, meeting of the Chicago federation, delegate Hans Pfeiffer of Butcher Workmen's Local 484 complained that the SYLC had attempted to disrupt his union by taking away several hundred of its members and forming a Polish local not connected with the Amalgamated Meat Cutters. Fitzpatrick responded by blaming the Amalgamated for the trouble in the yards and said that it was being used by the packers to destroy the SYLC.[71]

The following month a compromise was apparently found in the conflict. On February 15 Martin Murphy told the CFL that an agreement had been reached with the Amalgamated Meat Cutters. A new council would be formed and reaffiliated with the Chicago Federation of Labor. However, packinghouse workers voted to reinstate the entire SYLC organization. Dennis Lane and the Amalgamated refused to accept the election results and would not charter the newly formed council. Lane encouraged District Council No. 9 to continue its existence. Before this problem could be resolved, Johnstone brought charges against John Kikulski to the CFL at its April 14 meeting. He had first made these charges at a March 15 meeting of the new SYLC. The charges that the *Butcher Workman* had brought up in October of the misuse of funds by Kikulski once again surfaced.[72]

Johnstone claimed that $7,000 in union funds intended as strike aid to a local in Detroit was missing. The day after the March meeting the Amalgamated Meat Cutters District No. 9 met and elected Kikulski the new president. Kikulski left the SYLC and joined forces with Dennis Lane and the Amalgamated Meat Cutters. Over the next few weeks charges and counter-charges flew as the labor civil war in the stockyards entered a new phase. Kikulski in turn accused Johnstone of stealing funds. The local's books disappeared and the Amalgamated came to Kikulski's defense. Delegate Pfeiffer of the Amalgamated's Local No. 484 asked the CFL to pass a resolution finding Kikulski innocent. On May 12, 1920, the CFL received a letter from Locals 212, 484, 554, 649, 650, 658, and District No. 9 in support of Kikulski and protesting the CFL's investigation of the entire affair. Kikulski's immigrant workers rallied behind him. The CFL, however, denied Pfeiffer's resolution. It instead exonerated Johnstone, who brought the books of his union to be examined by the CFL.[73]

On the night of May 17 Kikulski drove to his Northwest Side home after a union meeting at Columbia Hall in Back of the Yards. Two men jumped out of a taxi and clubbed and shot him.

Kikulski died at Norwegian Deaconess Hospital four days later. Police questioned several people, including Johnstone. The *Dziennik Chicagoski* claimed that suspicion automatically fell on Johnstone and Martin Murphy. Kikulski's wife told the newspaper that he had worried about his life because of his troubles with other union leaders and that he carried a revolver because he feared an attack. Dennis Lane admonished the police for believing the suspects, who claimed they knew nothing of the attack. The *Dziennik Chicagoski* also criticized the police. The newspaper claimed that "this Pole was like salt in the eye of the Irish. Only after his death are the police looking for his killers only because they must."[74]

On May 25 Kikulski received a hero's funeral from the church of St. Hyacinth in the Avondale neighborhood on Chicago's Northwest Side. A crowd gathered outside Kikulski's home at 2650 North Central Park Avenue before dawn. Fathers Grudzinski, Tyrcha, and Bubacz from St. John of God escorted his body to the church. Over 10,000 mourners filled the church beyond capacity and spilled out onto the street. The crowd included black unionists. An honor guard of Polish Falcons marched behind Kikulski's coffin as a band played Chopin's funeral march. Delegations came from a score of unions and marched to the church as a body. The funeral procession to St. Adalbert's Cemetery in Niles included over 200 cars. The *Dziennik Chicagoski* claimed that over 150 of these came from the Back of the Yards area. Kikulski's friend Rev. Louis Grudzinski officiated at the cemetery. The stockyard priest praised the slain leader and admonished workers everywhere and Poles in particular to keep alive that which Kikulski had started. Stanley Rokosz, who helped organize steelworkers in Pittsburgh during the 1919 strike and who would eventually succeed Kikulski as president of District Council No. 9, spoke next.[75]

Like Kikulski, Rokosz was well known in Polonia and had been an active member of the Polish National Alliance. Also like Kikulski, Rokosz was obviously murdered because of his union activities in the stockyards. Rokosz died less than a year after Kikulski when he was attacked in a similar fashion at 35th Street and Ashland Avenue near the yards. He died twelve days later on April

20, 1921, at Cook County Hospital. At that time he was no longer president of District Council No. 9, having resigned as of January 1. The Polish Local 554 offered $1,000 as a reward for evidence of his killers, but as in the case of Kikulski the police never charged anyone with the murder.[76]

The civil war in the stockyards ended shortly after the death of Kikulski. The Stock Yard Labor Council faded away in the summer of 1920. Johnstone and Murphy's organization never recovered after Kikulski's move back into the Amalgamated Meat Cutters. Whether Kikulski was guilty of having stolen from Local 554 as Johnstone and his supporters claimed became academic as the immigrant workers remained loyal to the Pole. Even after Kikulski's death the Polish packinghouse workers remained in District Council No. 9. Much of the fighting among the various factions seems to have been ethnic in nature. The older ethnic groups often did not get along with the newer groups like the Poles and later the Mexicans. Add the problem of race, and the fragmentation of the stockyard workers must have seemed inevitable, especially after July 1919. Ethnic feelings and even international politics compounded the problems facing organized labor in Chicago.[77]

The Polish community had become rather wary of the Chicago Federation of Labor and the radical wing of the labor movement in Chicago. Much of this had to do with international politics. The CFL supported the workers' government in the Soviet Union when the communist state found itself in a war with the newly resurrected Polish state. The *New Majority* carried news of the Soviet Union's battle against its enemies and often referred to Polish imperialism. After an article in the CFL's journal accusing Poland of imperialism in August 1920, the *Naród Polski* editorialized that workers were being misled by their leaders. The newspaper pointed out that many workers had protested the recent CFL resolution condemning Poland for its war against the USSR. The newspaper, known for its antisemitic stand, claimed that "some American or English Jew, standing at the head of a labor union, desires to control the destiny of Poland." As in the case of the race riot the *Naród Polski* quickly proposed that an international German and Jewish conspiracy existed against Poland.[78]

The Chicago Federation of Labor itself seemed on the defensive after the murder of Kikulski. The *New Majority* remained silent about the attack on Kikulski and his death. On the day after his death the newspaper still carried the minutes of the CFL meeting accusing him of wrongdoing. The same was true in the case of Rokosz. The *New Majority* never mentioned the issue. The whole episode seemed to disappear from the pages of the CFL newspaper. In March 1921 the *New Majority* carried an article describing the 1917 organizing campaign in the yards and made no mention of the Stock Yard Labor Council, Kikulski, Johnstone, or Murphy. The March 1921 version sounded much like the version published by the Amalgamated Meat Cutters in their newspaper during the height of the controversy over the rival councils.[79]

The drive to organize all stockyard workers was effectively destroyed first by the race riot and then by the civil war between the SYLC and the Butcher Workmen. Many new workers, especially southern blacks, arrived in the packinghouses. These new men and women had no loyalty to the labor movement, and the badly divided unions had little hope of attracting them to the ranks of organized labor. This would prove to be crucial to the coming conflict as the meatpackers prepared a postwar attack on all labor unions in their plants.[80]

Even though the packers had profited greatly in the period before and during the war, the period immediately following the fighting proved difficult. The packers used their hardship as an excuse to move against the labor organization. In 1919 labor still seemed strong. As in previous struggles management chose to bide its time before forcing a confrontation. A campaign to prove how poorly the packers fared financially preceded the attack on labor.

Armour and Company claimed in its 1920 annual report that because meat exports had virtually stopped, the industry faced a growing problem. In fact, the latter part of 1919 brought a decline in meat prices and a drastic drop in exports. In 1921 the company reported that the previous year had to be considered the severest economic test in the history of the industry. According to management, 1920 was a year of tremendous readjustment and loss. While prices continued to fall, operating costs continued to rise. Armour called the following year the most disastrous in the life of the company and of the industry in general. It began with large carryovers of by-products and other commodities that had been inventoried and sold at a great loss.[81]

Riding the crest of the postwar reaction, the major packers decided to move against the union. On February 26, 1921, the Big Four notified the government that they would no longer abide by the wartime agreements. The Chicago Federation of Labor's *New Majority* claimed that the packers were joining the railroads in trying to destroy organized labor. The Amalgamated Meat Cutters called an emergency meeting to try to deal with the new problem. In turn the CFL passed a resolution at its March 6 meeting demanding that the meat companies return to arbitration. In mid-March the *New Majority* claimed that the companies wanted to force a strike and cause another race riot. The newspaper stated that the American Unity Labor Union and Colored Welfare Club, which claimed to represent 6,000 black packinghouse workers and which had voted to accept a 20 percent reduction in wages for skilled workers and a 10 percent cut for the unskilled, was simply a company union. The newspaper pointed to the fact that the organization had no connection with either the AFL or the Butcher Workmen. A vote taken at the end of March showed that Butcher Workmen members overwhelmingly favored a strike. Hans Pfeiffer of the Amalgamated Meat Cutters reported to the CFL that the meatpackers openly replaced white union workers with blacks, thus creating another tense racial situation on the South Side. As April approached, confrontation seemed unavoidable, but management avoided it by agreeing to return to arbitration for six months. Nevertheless a short livestock handlers strike did break out in May, when about 1,500 employees struck the Union Stock Yard and Transit Company.[82]

On July 7, 1921, the Chicago packers asked Judge Alschuler to allow a wage cut of 5 cents per hour. Management claimed that wages made up 45 percent of their production costs and that they had lost millions of dollars despite the wage cuts agreed to the previous March. The unions, of course, reacted negatively to the wage cut, and the 1921 AFL convention in Denver backed the packinghouse workers in their protest. The convention charged that the packers wanted to take advantage of the postwar slack by reasserting the open shop policy and establishing company unions.

The arguments went on for several more months until November 1, when the Amalgamated Meat Cutters voted to strike, setting the walkout for November 15. The union claimed a membership of 100,000 nationwide, with 40,000 union workers in Chicago alone. The Big Four responded on November 9 with a proposal to reduce wages further. The fifth largest packer, Chicago's Nelson Morris Company, was expected to follow their lead. Management also claimed that the threatened Butcher Workmen's strike would have no impact on their operations.[83]

Louis F. Swift spoke for the packers. He claimed that Swift and Company workers earned $7.50 more a week than steelworkers and $6.70 more than cotton workers. The *New York Times* quoted Swift as appealing to his workers: "It must be apparent to you, to your foremen and to your workmen that this step in wage cuts must be taken."[84] Meetings of the so-called plant congresses followed the announcements. These were employee representation plans much like those established in the steel industry. Swift and Company first developed them to take the place of unions and federal arbitration and to serve as a forum for employee grievances. By this time, all the large packers had adopted the system.

On November 18, 1921, the news spread that the Swift plant congress had voted to cut wages, leaving the adjustment to the company. At the same time, Armour and Company announced that representatives of 26,000 employees voted for and fixed a reduction effective November 28. Wilson and Company was expected to announce a pay cut the next day. The new agreement affected plants all over the West. Reports stressed that the workers had voluntarily agreed to the wage scale. The reaction of the Amalgamated Meat Cutters was quick and predictable. The union secretary, Mr. Burns, said, "We gave the right to call a strike in October. If a working agreement satisfactory to the organization as a whole cannot be reached, a strike will be the result."[85]

On December 5, at six in the morning, the strike began. The first day was fairly peaceful, and the union claimed that 12,000 men and women had honored the call to walk off their jobs. The police appeared everywhere, but the strikers remained calm and the union had not yet established a picket line. The neighborhood around the yards seemed so quiet that one Chicago police lieutenant predicted that the strike would end in forty-eight hours.[86]

The next day, however, brought the first violence as workers attempted to cross the picket lines. Outbreaks occurred all over the Stock Yard District. A crowd beat a woman strikebreaker and her father on the corner of 46th and Bishop streets. The largest eruption took place at the intersection of 43rd Street and Ashland Avenue near one of the main entrances to the yards. A crowd attacked a streetcar and beat a strikebreaker unfortunate enough to be caught on it. The police waded into the crowd using their clubs to disperse the strikers and their sympathizers.[87]

December 7 saw more violence. The *Dziennik Związkowy* referred to it as "Bloody Wednesday." One person died and the police shot several score as the Stock Yard District went back to war. The radical Polish socialist newspaper, *Dziennik Ludowy*, claimed that the packers had planted "agents provocateurs" recruited from their private police forces to start the riots. The newspaper warned the workers to maintain solidarity and not to be provoked into violence. The riots started at about 4:00 P.M., when the packers let out their loyal workers for the day. A crowd of about one thousand strikers greeted them as they came out of the 43rd Street and Ashland Avenue gate. The crowd surged forward calling the workers scabs and threatening them. A major confrontation with police began as a striker unhooked the trolley of a streetcar filled with strikebreakers. The crowd chanted at the police and called them "black cossacks." The police department had put one thousand extra men into the Stock Yard District to reinforce the usual contingent of five hundred.[88]

The crowds that took part in the fighting on Bloody Wednesday consisted of both strikers and their spouses and children. Many of them, of course, also worked or had worked in the packinghouses, but the participation of women not employed in the industry was also evident. The *Dziennik Związkowy* accused the police not only of being tools of the "Swine Barons" but also of charging into crowds of defenseless women and children. An editorial cartoon in the *Dziennik Związkowy* portrayed the packers as nobles locked up in their palaces with packinghouse workers attacking the fortress. One reason for the radicalism of the newspaper was its correspondent, Stanley Nowak, then a young brother of packinghouse union members. Later Nowak became an auto industry labor organizer in Detroit during the 1930s.[89]

As Chicago read the stories of the Wednesday rioting, the fighting began again on Thursday. Riots broke out again. Snipers fired up and down the streets of Back of the Yards. Nearly one hundred and fifty injuries resulted during the violence of December 8. Mounted police repeatedly charged into mobs of strikers and their adherents, who congregated on street corners despite the efforts of half the city's police force.[90]

The characterization of the Back of the Yards women as defenseless by the Polish newspapers seems hardly true. When the violence of December 8 erupted, the police, angered by the previous day's fighting, began to attack everyone within their reach. On Marshfield Street they searched door-to-door for guns and ammunition. The local women met the police with unique weapons. The area's Slavic women emptied the stores of supplies of red pepper and paprika. When mounted police attacked a crowd, the women threw the substances into the eyes of the horses. Once the horses panicked and dislodged their riders, the police found their eyes filled with pepper and paprika. The police retaliated with motorcycle patrols, only to find Ashland Avenue littered with broken glass and tacks spread by the women and children of the neighborhood.[91] The *Dziennik Związkowy* recorded the wounding of twenty-three Poles that day, including nine women. All the women had been beaten by police clubs or trampled by the mounted police. Similar events occurred the following day as women again joined active rioters. Police beat and arrested them. One Chicago police captain blamed women for all the violence. "The whole trouble in this strike lies with the women. They are behind the men, pushing them on." Mary Janek, a Back of the Yards resident, provided much of the leadership for the women who participated in the strike demonstrations.[92]

On December 9 the *Dziennik Chicagoski* wrote: "The fight between labor and capitalism had finally started. The strikers are battling for their rights, but the police are interfering."[93] The socialist *Dziennik Ludowy* claimed that the struggle in Back of the Yards was apolitical. The newspaper editorialized: "The strike in the stockyards does not have a political nor a revolutionary character. It is simply an economic problem. . . . There are no communists involved. When the provocations are stopped, when the police treat strikers as citizens and not like huns then there will be peace."[94]

Not everyone in Polonia agreed with either the *Dziennik Chicagoski* or the *Dziennik Ludowy*; the conservative Polish newspaper, *Dziennik Zjednoczenia*, published by the Polish Roman Catholic Union, also warned the Poles against violence. On December 9 the newspaper claimed that Poles were "too emotional" to take part in strikes. The *Dziennik Zjednoczenia* advised: "If someone desires to strike let him do so, but if anyone desires to work he should not be compelled to strike by beating, threatening, or any other violence; for such action would be terrorism, a limitation of personal liberty, which is despotism not democracy."[95]

The striking Polish packinghouse workers obviously did not heed the call of the *Dziennik Zjednoczenia* for peace as the rioting continued. On the same day as the conservative appeal of the newspaper, Judge Dennis Sullivan handed down an injunction against the strikers. In commenting on the workers' behavior he said, "All rights are relative: the line comes when actions are a benefit to themselves and an injury to others."[96] The union called for a parley with management on the same day. Dennis Lane said, "We will win if the men stick. Things are looking better than they ever did." But in reality they were not looking good, as it was reported that management had already imported 8,000 strikebreakers. Many of them were black. The tragedy of the 1919 race riot now paid its dividends to the stockyard workers.[97]

The Polish community stayed loyal to the union until the very end. This was true except for a few strikebreakers who broke with both the union and the community. Violence exploded throughout December as more and more men filtered back to work. Strike meetings were held in the hall of S.S. Peter and Paul Catholic Church, a Polish parish just to the northwest of the stockyards. The union also held daily meetings at Słowacki Hall (Columbia Hall) across the street from St. Joseph's Polish Church. Polish organizers were present daily. The tailor's union lent Leo Krzycki to the Meat Cutters to help the Polish organizers. Alex Nielubowski served District Council No. 9 as president and provided leadership in Back of the Yards. The *New Majority* reported that the Amalgamated Meat Cutters held daily outdoor rallies attended by over 10,000 people. The Amalgamated Meat Cutters' *Butcher Workman* reported that a mass meeting held at 47th Street and Western Avenue drew a crowd of over 25,000. These meetings and rallies continued well into January.[98] In the middle of that month a mass meeting at Słowacki Hall resulted in violence as the police fired into a crowd of unionists. A police officer critically wounded Anthony Marczak, a striking twenty-eight-year-old packinghouse worker, in the back.[99] Throughout January the Polish newspapers reported that the police continued to arrest strikers. The Poles of the Back of the Yards, however, saw a friend in the local judge on duty at the stockyard police station, who dismissed most of the cases. Polish organizations decided to honor Judge Trude as a friend of labor with a special dinner at Zajdzinski's restaurant just after the first of the year. On January 30, 1922, the *Dziennik Chicagoski* reported that the union still held strike meetings at Słowacki, Mickiewicz, and Pulaski halls in Back of the Yards. Despite these signs of unity, the constant clashes between scabs and strikers throughout December and January proved that the union was losing.[100]

Just after Christmas a black strikebreaker fired a gun into a crowd of union men. This took place in the Pilsen neighborhood north of the Stock Yard District. The person wounded was referred to as a strike sympathizer rather than a striker. In the Back of the Yards some Poles began to break ranks and go back to work. A crowd chased strikebreaker Walter Damowicz through the streets of the neighborhood to his home on Honore Street, where he turned and fired at the crowd, hitting Sophie Wyka, a bystander. Other strikebreakers saw their homes pelted with bricks during the strike. The crowds did not seem to work in a random fashion but knew who their targets were and where they lived. Still, as the strike dragged on into the coldest part of the winter the economic realities of life in Chicago began to wear away at the strikers' resolve.[101]

Part of the problem was the result of the civil war that had raged in 1919 and 1920 among the unions themselves. On December 18 Alex Nielubowski addressed the Chicago Federation of Labor and asked that the citywide labor body help the stockyard strikers by convincing the engineers, teamsters, and firemen to honor the picket lines. The CFL complied with the request, but the skilled trades unions refused to agree. Financial aid from outside unions also remained meager. The problem of working-class fragmentation once again proved to be a fatal problem for the packinghouse workers.[102]

Although aid from outside the Stock Yard District and from other unions involved in the packing industry seemed scarce, the unity of the Polish community remained strong. Indeed the various clashes between strikers, strikebreakers, and police can be seen as an attempt by the Polish community to enforce not only labor solidarity but also communal solidarity in the face of increasingly overwhelming odds. This communal unity developed on several levels, of which street fighting was only the most obvious.

The Polish community in Chicago by 1920 had developed, as John Bukowczyk has pointed out, a diverse social world occupied not only by industrial workers but also by the ethnic lower middle class, which thrived during the years of mass immigration and beyond. A small professional and business class provided leadership along with the clergy, who remained powerful throughout Polish American society.[103] Before World War I these various groups had struggled with one another for power within Polonia and for ideological reasons had often fought with one another and even become embroiled in European politics. The various ethnic leaders dealt with the problem of assimilation and of retaining a sense of Polishness, or *Polskość*. Victor Greene, in a recent study of several major ethnic groups including the Poles, has pointed to the role that these leaders played as interpreters of America for their constituency.[104] The Polish National Alliance and the Polish Roman Catholic Union often fought with each other over a multitude of issues. Polish newspapers reflected these ideological and class conflicts within Polonia. However, after World War I and the revival of the Polish state, American Polonia found itself under a nativist attack and also under intense economic pressure. This pressure threatened the very existence of the community and all its members, including workers, priests, professionals, and small business owners. To an extent the community saw the 1921–22 packinghouse strike as part of this attack. Although the various groups could disagree they had to come together to save the community.

The Meat Cutters strike resulted in a large degree of unity in Polonia. Even the conservative *Dziennik Zjednoczenia*, which had praised the Palmer raids and had condemned the American Federation of Labor, saw fit to call for aid to the strikers and their families. After the strike ended, the newspaper defended the workers for striking against terrible conditions and pay cuts. Nevertheless the *Dziennik Zjednoczenia* did maintain that Polish workers had been duped into striking once again. In July 1922, five months after the failure of the strike, it referred to Polish workers as the "goat of sacrifice" for non-Polish labor leaders.[105]

The reality of the difficult times after World War I stimulated a good deal of ethnic middle-class support for the unions. Just before Christmas 1921 the Polish Businessmen's Association of the Town of Lake (Back of the Yards) heard proposals for ways of helping striker families. Two weeks later the *Dziennik Chicagoski* wrote that thanks should be given to "the priests, church societies, and Polish businessmen within the locale of the Town of Lake for trying to fulfill the needs of the unfortunate strikers." The Polish newspapers indeed listed various organizations and individuals who donated money or food to the strikers. The White Eagle Dairy Company donated fifty quarts of milk daily. The 47th Street Businessmen's Association donated fifty baskets of food. On January 11, 1922, the *Dziennik Chicagoski* reported that the Businessmen's Association of the Town of Lake had collected $450.25 in cash and $567.00 in food for the strikers. The Poles of Hegewisch on the far Southeast Side of the city sent $25.00. Lists of individuals who came to the strikers' aid included J. J. Pesicka, the president of Depositors State Bank in Back of the Yards, and Bronisław F. Kowalewski, the banker, real estate developer, and president of the local citizens committee who had provided leadership during the race riot. Father Louis Grudzinski of St. John of God Parish donated $100.00 to the strike fund. Various other Roman Catholic priests were listed among those who gave money for the strike fund. The *Dziennik Zjednoczenia* itself donated $100.00 shortly after the strike ended to help the families of packinghouse workers who could not get their jobs back.[106]

The support of the clergy should not be considered simply a Polish American phenomenon. Priests like Grudzinski and the two other Polish Back of the Yards pastors did come from working-class backgrounds. They therefore understood many of the problems their parishioners faced. Grudzinski in particular seems to have been very supportive of the labor movement. The Catholic church in Chicago, however, also supported the stockyard unions. The archdiocesan newspaper, the *New World*, editorialized against the packers and supported the strike. Just before the strike broke out the *New World* praised the work of the unions as essentially Christian because they acted as an uplifting force in society. On December 16 the Catholic newspaper published an article written by the National Catholic Welfare Council of Social Action concerning the stockyard strike, stating: "There is a grave danger that the packinghouse workers will lose the strike and go back to worse than the evil conditions prevailing before the war." The meatpacking companies responded by writing letters to the *New World* that claimed that the December 16 article included many misstatements. The *New World* answered by printing a point-by-point refutation of the packers' claims written by Father R. A. McGowan, the assistant director of the Social Action Department of the Catholic Welfare Council. The Polish pastors thus had the sympathy of a good part of the Catholic religious establishment in their support of the strike.[107]

As Bukowczyk has observed in his study of the Bayonne, New Jersey, Polonia, members of the lower middle class were closely related to the workers in their neighborhoods. Many of them had originally worked in the packinghouses or mills. The priests, storekeepers, and professionals also depended on their neighbors for their livelihoods. It is not surprising that they would support the workers' cause. In fact the workers demanded that the lower middle class live up to the ideals of community that they had brought with them from Poland. The Polish communal response to industrial conditions in America reinforced class unity during an American industrial struggle. The communal response made the extracommunal response possible.[108]

Despite the unity of the Polish community during the winter of 1921–22, the Amalgamated Meat Cutters and Butcher Workmen lost the strike. As early as January 9, 1922, an Armour and Company spokesman could claim: "There is no matter of dispute between management and employees."[109] The union called the strike off on February 1. Two weeks later the *Dziennik Chicagoski* reported that many strikers remained out of work. The management of the packinghouses had blacklisted them. Immigrant workers quickly learned the realities of the class struggle in America. The bitterness of the strike lasted for nearly fifteen years before another organizational attempt could be undertaken.[110]

The question remains: Why did the Polish community support both the steel and the meatpacking strikes? The success of the labor movement in organizing Polish neighborhoods on the South Side during World War I, although to a great part resulting from the special conditions of the era, could not have happened without a new found stability in the immigrant community.

By the end of 1919, the Poles had passed the first crucial test of settling in Chicago. The initial hurdles had been taken by the immigrants; they had mastered the very basic process of settlement, of adjusting and surviving with a degree of dignity in the new industrial setting in which they found themselves. This process was by no means automatic, but once the settlement had taken on the appearance of stability with the establishment of viable neighborhoods, Poles could reach out to others to attempt to transform American urban society.

Conclusion

The defeat of organized labor in steel and meatpacking after World War I marked the end of an era for the Polish working-class communities of Chicago's South Side. The intense period of settling-in and of organizing viable communal institutions had passed. A dramatic period of reaching out beyond ethnic walls to other working-class groups had also come to an end, but an end marked by defeat. The huge labor organizations formed during the war disappeared almost overnight. The working class returned to what some called normalcy. It returned to fragmentation and relative powerlessness. Organized labor and effective multiethnic neighborhood organizations reappeared in both South Chicago and the Back of the Yards but not until the late 1930s. During the Great Depression extracommunal organizations appeared once again, and once again they were built on the resilient communal structure established during the immigrant generation's settling-in period. The communal structure remained crucial. It spoke to the possibility of unity as well as to the disunity that often racked the American working class.[1]

The communal nature of Chicago's Polish community proved important for the working-class organizations of the World War I period. The definitions of the terms *neighborhood* and *community* are crucial for understanding both the Polish and the working-class experience in Chicago and the United States. As Caroline Golab has stated, "Neighborhood and community were never synonymous."[2] Many different groups shared the same kind of geographic space as existed in Back of the Yards or South Chicago, but they often did not interact with one another. *Neighbor-*

hood is a geographic term. *Community* implies a social relationship, a sharing of common goals, cultural or otherwise. Neighborhoods were spatially integrated but socially segregated. As Louis Wirth pointed out in his classic study *The Ghetto*, immigrant groups who lived side-by-side with one another still had separate "inner" lives.[3] This often led to working-class fragmentation, but the strong communal nature of these inner lives also provided working-class organizers with an opportunity to bring these groups together at various times in the history of the working class. The nature of American industrial society forced this issue periodically on the various ethnic, religious, and racial groups that found themselves living in it. Group interests became class interests in the caldron of American industrial society.

Both the Back of the Yards and South Chicago are representative of nineteenth-century industrial neighborhoods in metropolitan settings. The large industries that dominated them created their special ambience. They also determined the types of neighborhoods and communities that developed. These were working-class neighborhoods with large ethnic working-class communities. The mass production industries, steel and meatpacking, had many common attributes. Large workforces, low pay, long hours, dangerous working conditions, and a large semi- and unskilled labor pool resulted in much the same kind of neighborhoods and communities that developed in the two South Side Chicago locations.

Technology played a vital role in the creation of these two neighborhoods. The technology that made mass production industries possible shaped the work experience of their inhabitants. Great advancements in transportation technologies brought Polish and other immigrants to them. The neighborhood system that developed in Chicago after the Civil War, and of which these two districts were a part, was based on hard economic realities, geography, and the cultural baggage that the inhabitants brought with them.

These industrial neighborhoods were based on a firm economic/symbolic base rooted in the steel and meatpacking industries. The communities that developed in these areas brought with them a good deal of tradition, which resulted in the complex of communal institutions that developed rather quickly after the initial ethnic pioneers arrived in the Back of the Yards and South Chicago. In turn, block life became very important, as the city block was the center of the most intense social interaction available in the city. Finally the families that made their homes in the Steel and Stock Yard districts sought protection in these neighborhoods and in their institutions from the uncertainties of life in industrial America. In the end it proved impossible for any single group to deal with the problems of the new industrial order. Reaching out to other groups for common defense helped to overcome fragmentation. The success of this extracommunal approach was based on the communal nature of these people. The various ethnic workers and residents of these areas had one thing in common. The industries that stood at the center of their neighborhoods affected everyone. Despite the fact that these districts were part of the streetcar metropolis, they acted as walking cities in their own right. The residents faced the same concerns as their neighbors despite ethnic or religious differences. Common problems helped to overcome the divisiveness of ethnicity and religion for the American working class.

Race became the one factor that split the newly united working class during the World War I era. For Polish Chicagoans this was less an immediate problem because they had not yet been fully assimilated into the racial prejudices of American culture. Yet they were deeply affected when the race riot broke out in 1919 and left behind a shattered labor movement. The period between 1917 and 1922 was one of mounting class and racial hatreds. Because of the unending manipulation of the working class by management, the hostility between the races led to what some saw as the ultimate fragmentation of the working class. This too did not prove true. The 1930s saw a good deal of interracial cooperation at the workplace, but still race and racism worked to weaken the labor movement. Common goals often fell prey to competition between various working-class groups.

The immigrant generation left much for succeeding generations of Polish Americans. It also left much upon which to build working-class unity in Chicago. The parochialism of the ethnic neighborhood often led to conflict between groups. Gerald Suttles called the neighborhood a place to be defended.[4] It also, however, provided a firm institutional base that could be mobilized for working-class unity. If one looks at the hundreds of little villages that made up working-class Chicago, one can see both the strength and the weakness of the American working class. The villages of steel mills and packinghouses provided a firm base for the development of countervailing power for workers in Chicago. The experiences of the period from 1880 to 1922 prove the viability of both the communal and extracommunal responses to industrialism made by Polish and other working-class Americans.

In the end it must be recognized that the Polish peasants who made their way to Chicago to work in the steel mills and packinghouses of the South Side were not straw men or women. Rather they were people of flesh and blood who tried to make sense of the new industrial order that presented both opportunities and problems to them. The economic, technological, and social revolutions of the nineteenth century produced certain realities. Polish peasants tried to make sense of these new conditions and to profit from them. They attempted to take control of their own lives. The realities of class in America forced them to be assimilated into the American working class. The Polish tradition of communalism allowed them to be active participants in it. The past helped create the future.

Notes

Introduction

1. *Poles in America: Their Contribution to a Century of Progress* (Chicago: Polish Day Association, 1933), p. 215; *The Sun* (Chicago), May 3, 5, 7, 1884; [Rev. Alfred Abramowicz], *Diamond Jubilee, 1882–1857: Immaculate Conception, B.V.M.* (Chicago, 1957), p. 21.

2. William I. Thomas and Florian Znaniecki, *The Polish Peasant in Europe and America*, edited and abridged by Eli Zaretsky (Urbana and Chicago: University of Illinois Press, 1984). This is the most recent edition of *The Polish Peasant* to appear. I use the original five-volume work in the body of the book but will make reference to the 1984 edition in the introduction.

3. The publication of Madison Grant's *The Passing of the Great Race* in 1916 is the most obvious of the racist tracts that attacked Eastern and Southern European immigration to the United States. The Dillingham Commission also pointed to the problem of assimilation of these "new" immigrants: Maldwyn Allen Jones, *American Immigration* (Chicago: University of Chicago Press, 1970), pp. 177–81, 268–77.

4. James T. Carey, *Sociology and Public Affairs: The Chicago School* (Beverly Hills and London: Sage Publications, 1975), p. 101.

5. Thomas and Znaniecki, *Polish Peasant* (1984 abridged ed., pp. 205–7, 226–33, 289.

6. Eli Zaretsky, "Editor's Introduction," in ibid., pp. 4–5, 32–35.

7. Polish Americans were especially upset with Clifford Shaw's *The Jack-Roller: A Delinquent Boy's Own Story* (Chicago: University of Chicago Press, 1930), which dealt with the life history of a Polish American boy. Burgess' work concerning South Chicago delinquents also enraged Polonia. See Steven Schlossman and Michael Sedlak, *The Chicago Area Project Revisited* (Santa Monica: Rand Corporation, 1983), pp. 15–19.

8. Zaretsky, "Editor's Introduction," p. 21.

9. Ibid., pp. 35–47.

10. For a discussion in English of the transformations of peasant life in nineteenth-century Poland see Stefan Kieniewicz, *The Emancipation of the Polish Peasantry* (Chicago: University of Chicago Press, 1969); Ewa Morawska's work on East Europeans who settled in Johnstown, Pennsylvania, also demonstrates the impact of this new freedom on peasants from the "other" Europe. See *For Bread with Butter* (Cambridge: Cambridge University Press, 1985).

11. Immanuel Wallerstein and others have discussed the creation of a capitalist world-economic system. See esp. Immanuel Wallerstein, *The Modern World System I: Capitalist Agriculture and the Origins of the European World-Economy in the Sixteenth Century* (New York: Academic Press, 1974), and *The*

Modern World System II: Mercantilism and the Consolidation of the European World-Economy, 1600–1750 (New York: Academic Press, 1980). Oscar Handlin first presented the metaphor of the uprooted peasant/immigrant in his *The Uprooted* (New York: Grosset & Dunlap, 1951). A recent study by John Bodnar has replaced uprooted with transplanted. See his *The Transplanted* (Bloomington: Indiana University Press, 1981).

12. For a discussion of the impact of Catholicism and nationalism on American Polonia see Victor Greene, *For God and Country: The Rise of Polish and Lithuanian Ethnic Consciousness in America, 1860–1910* (Madison: State Historical Society of Wisconsin, 1975), and Joseph John Parot, *Polish Catholics in Chicago, 1850–1920* (DeKalb: Northern Illinois University Press, 1981). For a treatment of the negative impact of Polish communalism see Edward Kantowicz, *Polish Politics in Chicago, 1888–1940* (Chicago: University of Chicago Press, 1975). John Bukowczyk's general study of American Polonia, *And My Children Did Not Know Me: A History of the Polish Americans* (Bloomington: Indiana University Press, 1987), discusses many aspects of the Polish community-building process.

13. Morawska, *For Bread with Butter*, p. 24.

14. James R. Barrett, *Work and Community in the Jungle: Chicago's Packinghouse Workers, 1880–1922* (Urbana: University of Illinois Press, 1987).

15. For a discussion of the importance of immigrant culture and its impact on the American working class see Herbert G. Gutman, *Work, Culture, and Society* (New York: Vintage Books, 1977), p. 14. David Montgomery also makes much the same argument in "To Study the People: The American Working Class," *Labor History* 21 (Fall 1980): 507. Richard Julius Oestreicher's important study, *Solidarity and Fragmentation: Working People and Class Consciousness in Detroit, 1875–1900* (Urbana: University of Illinois Press, 1986), discusses both fragmentation and solidarity as integral parts of the urban working-class experience.

16. Steven J. Ross discusses the growth of working-class culture and the Knights of Labor in *Workers on the Edge: Work, Leisure, and Politics in Industrializing Cincinnati, 1788–1890* (New York: Columbia University Press, 1985).

17. The literature on Chicago's neighborhoods is voluminous. The work of sociologists and urban anthropologists complements that of urban historians. For a sociological overview see Albert Hunter, *Symbolic Communities: The Persistence and Change of Chicago's Local Communities* (Chicago: University of Chicago Press, 1974). The most recent community fact book also gives short histories and census statistics for Chicago's various communities. See Chicago Fact Book Consortium, eds., *Local Community Fact Book, Chicago Metropolitan Area, Based on the 1970 and 1980 Censuses* (Chicago: Chicago Review Press, 1984). For a historical overview of many of the city's neighborhoods see Dominic A. Pacyga and Ellen Skerrett, *Chicago: City of Neighborhoods* (Chicago: Loyola University Press, 1986).

18. For the views of early sociologists see Gerald D. Suttles, *The Social Construction of Communities* (Chicago: University of Chicago Press, 1972), p. 9, and Ulf Hannerz, *Exploring the City: Inquiries Toward an Urban Anthropology* (New York: Columbia University Press, 1980), pp. 65–72. Louis Wirth made the classic sociological statement on urban life in his "Urbanism as a Way of Life," *American Journal of Sociology* 44 (July 1938): 1–24. For a contemporary view of immigrant neighborhoods in a literary form see Upton Sinclair, *The Jungle* (1905; reprint ed., New York: Viking Press, 1947).

19. Caroline Golab, *Immigrant Destinations* (Philadelphia: Temple University Press, 1977), p. 129.

20. Louis Wirth, *The Ghetto* (Chicago: University of Chicago Press, 1928), pp. 282–83.

21. Daniel T. Rodgers, "Tradition, Modernity, and the American Industrial Worker: Reflections and Critique," in Theodore K. Rabb and Robert I. Rotberg, eds., *Industrialization and Urbanization: Studies in Interdisciplinary History* (Princeton: Princeton University Press, 1981), p. 241.

22. Alice Kessler-Harris, *Out to Work: A History of Wage-Earning Women in the United States* (New York: Oxford University Press, 1982); Herbert Hill, "Myth-Making as Labor History: Herbert Gutman and the United Mine Workers of America," *International Journal of Politics, Culture and Society* 2 (Winter 1988): 132–200; James R. Grossman, *Land of Hope: Chicago, Black Southerners, and the Great Migration* (Chicago: University of Chicago Press, 1989).

23. Ira Katznelson argues that these are the four appropriate ways to discuss working-class culture in "Working-Class Formation: Constructing Cases and Comparisons," in Ira Katznelson and Aristide R. Zolberg, eds., *Working-Class Formation* (Princeton: Princeton University Press, 1986), p. 9.

24. Roy Rosenzweig, *Eight Hours For What We Will: Workers and Leisure in an Industrial City, 1870–1920* (Cambridge: Cambridge University Press, 1983), pp. 52–53. Rosenzweig discusses the similarity of backgrounds of saloonkeepers and their customers in Worcester, Massachusetts.

25. David Montgomery has argued that working-class ideals stressed mutuality. Earlier Selig Perlman argued for the collective mentality of the labor movement. Although these arguments were generally made concerning skilled workers, the Polish worker in America also seems to fit this pattern. See Montgomery, "To Study the People," p. 499.

26. Ladislas Reymont, *Peasants*, 4 vols.: *Autumn, Winter, Spring, Summer* (New York: Alfred A. Knopf, 1924).

27. David Montgomery, "Gutman's Nineteenth-Century America," *Labor History* 19 (Summer 1978): 423.

28. Jonathan Prude, "The Family in Context," *Labor History* 17 (Summer 1976): 424. For the important role of ethnic leaders in the acculturation of immigrants into American society see Victor Greene, *American Immigrant Leaders, 1800–1910: Marginality and Identity* (Baltimore: Johns Hopkins University Press, 1987).

29. For a discussion of the mistaken notion of closed ethnic communities see Stephen Thernstrom and Peter R. Knight, "Men in Motion: Some Data and Speculations about Urban Population Mobility in Nineteenth Century America," in Rabb and Rothberg, *Industrialization and Urbanization*, p. 195.

Chapter 1

1. Brinley Thomas, *Migration and Urban Development* (London: Metheun, 1972), pp. 60–62.

2. Immanuel Wallerstein, *The Modern World System I* (New York: Academic Press, 1974); see chap. 2 for Wallerstein's views on this system.

3. Thomas, *Migration and Urban Development*, p. 4.

4. Alexander Gieysztor et al., *History of Poland* (Warsaw: PWN [Polish Scientific Publishers], 1968), pp. 584–86.

5. Helena Znaniecka Lopata, "Polish Immigration to the United States of America: Problems of Estimation and Parameters," *Polish Review* 21 (1976): 105.

6. Joseph A. Wytrwal, *America's Polish Heritage: A Social History of the Poles in America* (Detroit: Endurance Press, 1961), p. 79; Theresita Polzin, *The Polish Americans: Whence and Whither* (Pulaski, Wisc.: Franciscan Publishers, 1973), p. 59.

7. Gieysztor, *History of Poland*, pp. 370–94, 423–51, 632–33.

8. Robert F. Leslie, *Polish Politics and the Revolution of November 1830* (London: Athlone Press, 1956), pp. 279–80.

9. Robert F. Leslie, *Reform and Insurrection in Russian Poland, 1856–1865* (London: Athlone Press, 1963), pp. 113, 216–17.

10. Gieysztor, p. 525.

11. Stefan Kieniewicz, *The Emancipation of the Polish Peasantry* (Chicago: University of Chicago Press, 1968), pp. 172–82.

12. Zbigniew Stankiewicz, "The Economic Emigration From the Kingdom of Poland Portrayed on the European Background," in Celina Bobinska and Andrzej Pilch, eds., *Employment-Seeking Emigrations of the Poles World-Wide XIX and XX C* (Cracow: Jagellonian University Press, 1975), p. 30.

13. Ibid., pp. 32–33.

14. Kieniewicz, *Emancipation of the Polish Peasantry*, pp. 172–82.

15. Adam Galos and Kazimierz Wajda, "Migrations in the Polish Western Territories Annexed by Prussia (1815–1914)," in Bobinska and Pilch, *Employment-Seeking Emigrations*, p. 58.

16. Andrzej Pilch, "Migrations of the Galician Populace After the Turn of the Nineteenth and Twentieth Centuries," in ibid., pp. 82–83.

17. Piotr S. Wandycz, *The Lands of Partitioned Poland, 1795–1918* (Seattle and London: University of Washington Press, 1974), pp. 276.

18. Gieysztor, pp. 548–56.

19. Paul Fox, *The Poles in America* (New York: Arno Press and New York Times, reprint of 1922 ed., 1970), p. 58; Wytrwal, *America's Polish Heritage*, pp. 130, 139.

20. William J. Cronon, "To Be The Central City: Chicago, 1848–1857," *Chicago History* (Fall 1981): 130.

21. Bessie Louise Pierce, *A History of Chicago*, 3 vols. (Chicago: University of Chicago Press, 1937–57), 1:176–77.

22. For an overview of Chicago's immigrant/ethnic history see Melvin G. Holli and Peter d'A. Jones, eds., *Ethnic Chicago* (Grand Rapids: William B. Erdmans, 1984).

23. Phyllis Bate, "The Development of the Iron and Steel Industry of the Chicago Area" (Ph.D. diss., University of Chicago, 1949), p. 9; William Parkhurst, *History of the Yards, 1865–1953* (Chicago: Union Stock Yard & Transit Company, 1953), p. 11.

24. Parkhurst, *History of the Yards*, p. 12; Rudolph Alexander Clemens, *The American Livestock and Meat Industry* (New York: Ronald Press, 1923), p. 6; *Chicago Daily Tribune*, December 22, 1940; Vivian Palmer, comp., "Documents: History of Bridgeport Community" (mimeo.), document no. 1, informant S. H. Kelly, interviewed August 1924.

25. Swift and Company was founded in 1855 and moved to Chicago in 1875. Libby, McNeill and Libby was founded in 1868: the Libby plant opened

in 1888 adjacent to the Chicago stockyards, where the firm operated until 1961. Armour and Company started killing hogs in 1870, cattle in 1878, and sheep in 1880. By 1890, all the major packers had plants near the Union Stock Yards, with the exception of Wilson and Company, which was not formed until 1916 after the reorganization of the Schwarzchild and Sulzberger Packing Company (S & S Packing Co.). See Bessie Louise Pierce, *A History of Chicago*, 3 vols. (Chicago: University of Chicago Press, 1957), 3: 108–44; Howard C. Hill, "The Development of Chicago as a Center of the Meat Packing Industry," *Mississippi Valley Historical Review* 3 (December 1923): 253–73; U.S. Court of Appeals, *Chicago Stockyards Company vs. Commissioner of Internal Revenue* (October term, 1941), p. 89; Louis F. Swift, in collaboration with Arthur Van Vlissingen, Jr., *The Yankee of the Yards* (Chicago and New York: A. W. Shaw, 1927), pp. 6–7; Alvin Howard Sanders, *At the Sign of the Stock Yard Inn* (Chicago: Breeders Gazette Press, 1915), p. 302; Lewis Corey, *Meat and Man: A Study of Monopoly, Unionism and Food Policy* (New York: Viking, 1950), pp. 38–40; Bertram B. Fowler, *Men, Meat and Miracles* (New York: Julian Messner, 1952), pp. 93–97; and "Libby's Chicago Handling," *National Provisioner* (August 12, 1961):16. For the most complete study of the development of the packing industry in Chicago see Louise C. Wade, *Chicago's Pride: The Stockyards, Packingtown, and Environs in the Nineteenth Century* (Chicago and Urbana: University of Illinois Press, 1987).

26. Commission on Chicago Historical Landmarks, *Report on The Union Stock Yard Gate* (Chicago, 1971), p. 4; *Act of Incorporation and By-Laws of the Union Stock Yard and Transit Co.* (Chicago: Goodall Printers, 1895); *Chicago Daily Tribune*, January 1, 2, 1866; Parkhurst, *History of the Yards*, p. 12.

27. "First Stock at New Union Yard" (typed MS), Stock Yard Collection, University of Illinois at Chicago; *Chicago Daily Tribune*, December 26, 1865; Charles R. Koch, "A Country Fair Every Day," *Farm Quarterly* (Spring 1965): 80–83, 157–58.

28. Union Stock Yard & Transit Co., *81st Annual Livestock Report, 1946* (Chicago: U.S.Y. & T. Co., 1946), pp. 8–9; *Drovers Journal Yearbook of Figures, 1939* (Chicago: Drovers Journal Press, 1939), p. 195; Chicago Commission on Historical Landmarks, p. 5.

29. Paul Aldrich, ed., *The Packer's Encyclopedia* (Chicago: National Provisioner Press, 1932), p. 195.

30. U.S.Y. & T. Co., *81st Annual Report*, p. 41. See also Secretary of Agriculture, Bureau of Animal Husbandry, *The Department of Agriculture vs. The Union Stock Yard and Transit Co. of Chicago*, docket no. 472 (February 14, 1938), pp. 5–6.

31. Quoted in David Brody, *The Butcher Workmen* (Cambridge: Harvard University Press, 1964), p. 5.

32. See. U.S.Y. & T. Co., *81st Annual Report*; also *Drovers Journal Yearbook*, 1939.

33. Although the G. H. Hammond Company was the first to ship fresh beef in a refrigerated railroad car in 1868, it was Chicago's Swift and Company that revolutionized the process in the 1870s and helped to assure the city's domination of the industry by its success. See Fowler, *Men, Meat and Miracles*, p. 53, and Swift, *Yankee of the Yards*, pp. 185–92.

34. Jozef Chałasinski, "Parafia i szkola parafialna wsród emigracji pol-

skiej w Ameryce. Studium dzielnicy polskiej w Południowym Chicago" (Parish and Parish Schools during the Polish Emigration: A Study of the Polish District in South Chicago), *Przegląd Sociologiczny* 3 (Warsaw, 1935):634. See William H. Rowan, "History of South Chicago" (typed MS), Stephen Stanley Bubacz Collection, University of Illinois at Chicago, Urban Archives, folder 161, p. 9 (hereafter cited as Bubacz Collection), and Gladys Priddy, "South Chicago," in Alfred Abramowicz, *Diamond Jubilee, Immaculate Conception B.V.M. Parish, 1882–1957* (Chicago, 1957), p. 23.

35. Bate, "Development of Iron and Steel Industry," pp. 10–11; Victor Windett, "The South Works of the Illinois Steel Company," *Journal of the Western Society of Engineers* 3 (Chicago, 1898):789–93, 808.

36. The Iroquois Iron Company was built in the 1880s on the south bank of the Calumet River; in the 1890s it moved to a new site just opposite the South Works. Three large mills located in the area around 106th Street: the Wisconsin Steel Division of the International Harvester Company, the Federal Furnace Company, and the Interstate Iron and Steel Company. The Youngstown Sheet and Tube Company also located a plant in the South Chicago area. See Bate, p. 13, and John B. Appleton, "The Iron and Steel Industry of the Calumet District—A Study in Economic Geography" (Ph.D. diss., University of Chicago, 1925), pp. iii–iv. See also Rowan, "History of South Chicago."

37. For a discussion of the creation of the United States Steel Corporation and its effect on workers and their unions see David Brody, *Steelworkers in America: The Nonunion Era* (New York: Harper & Row, 1969), pp. 50–79. See also C. Joseph Pusateri, *A History of American Business* (Arlington Heights, Ill.: Harlan Davidson, 1984), p. 223.

38. Phillip Taylor, *The Distant Magnet: European Emigration to the U.S.A.* (New York: Harper & Row, 1971), pp. 121–23.

39. U.S. Congress, Senate, *Steerage Conditions, Importation and Harboring of Women for Immoral Purposes, Immigrant Homes and Aid Societies, Immigrant Banks*, S. Doc. 753, 61st Congress, 3rd session, 1911, pp. 29–31.

40. Witold Kula, *Listy Emigrantów Z Brazylii i Stanow Ziednoczonych* (Emigrant Letters from Brazil and the United States) (Warsaw: Ludowa Spoldzielnia Wydawnicza, 1973), p. 245, letter 93.

41. Ibid., p. 124, letter 5.

42. Ibid., p. 154, letter 26.

43. U.S. Congress, Senate, *Steerage Conditions*, p. 31.

44. Kula, p. 129, letter 8.

45. Ibid., p. 120, letter 2.

46. Ibid., p. 136, letter 15.

47. Ibid., p. 127, letter 5.

48. Ibid., p. 119, letter 1.

49. Marja Gliwicowna, "Drogi Emigracji" (The Immigrant Road), *Przegląd Socjologiczny* 4 (Warsaw-Poznan, 1936):507.

50. Kula, p. 155, letter 26.

51. Ibid., p. 299, letter 137.

52. Ibid., p. 306, letter 143.

53. U.S. Congress, Senate, *Steerage Conditions*, pp. 32–35; Taylor, *Distant Magnet*, pp. 15–21.

54. Ibid., p. 256, letter 102.

55. Ibid., p. 391, letter 220.
56. Ibid., p. 403, letter 231.
57. Ibid., p. 306, letter 143.
58. Edith Abbott, *Immigration, Select Documents and Case Records* (Chicago: University of Chicago Press, 1924), p. 245.
59. Ibid., pp. 246–48.
60. Ibid., pp. 246–47.
61. Ibid., pp. 344–48, 468–71.
62. Ibid., pp. 470–71.
63. Interview with Mr. Petterson, passenger agent on Chicago and Milwaukee Railroad, 1928, in Immigrants' Protective League Papers, University of Illinois at Chicago, Urban Archives, folder 9; Mary T. Waggamon, "Immigrant Aid: Legislative Safeguards and Activities of the Bureau of Immigration," *Monthly Labor Review* 16 (February 1923):33.
64. Abbott, *Immigration*, p. 471.
65. Gliwicowna, "Drogi Emigracji," p. 505.
66. Ibid., p. 505.
67. Ibid., p. 514.
68. Lask Family interviews, April–June 1932, in Ernest W. Burgess Papers, Regenstein Library, University of Chicago, box 133, folder 7. Hereafter cited as Burgess Papers.
69. Interview with Mrs. Kaczmarek, February 25, 1932, in Burgess Papers, box 133, folder 7.
70. Clemens, *American Livestock and Meat Industry*, p. 263.
71. Frank J. Sheridan, "Italian, Slavic and Hungarian Unskilled Immigrant Laborers in the United States," *Bulletin of the Bureau of Labor* 72 (September 1907):479–80.
72. Gliwicowna, pp. 509–11.
73. Harvey M. Choldin, "First Year in the Metropolis: A Study of Migration and Adjustment" (Ph.D. diss., University of Chicago, 1965), pp. 2–3.
74. Sheridan, p. 474; Chałasinski, "Parafia i szkola parafialna," p. 637.
75. Sophonisba Breckinridge and Edith Abbott, "Housing Conditions in Chicago, III: Back of the Yards," *American Journal of Sociology* 16 (January 1911):436; "The Foreign Born" (typed MS), in Mary E. McDowell Papers, Chicago Historical Society, box 2, folder 12.
76. Gliwicowna, p. 502; Choldin, "First Year," pp. 50–55.
77. Interview with Frank Flynn, vice president of Union Stock Yard & Transit Co., January 1971, in Leslie Orear, ed., *Chicago Stockyards History Interview Series* (Chicago: Illinois Labor History Society, 1971), p. 1; U.S. Congress, Senate, *Final Report and Testimony Submitted to Congress by the Commission on Industrial Relations*, S. Document 415, 64th Congress, 2nd session, 1916, vol. 4, p. 3463.
78. Choldin, p. 75; Chałasinski, pp. 637, 641; Gliwicowna, p. 509.
79. Włodzimierz Wnuk, *Klub Małopolski W. Ameryce* (Malopolski Club in America) (Warsaw: Instytut Wyudawniczy, 1974).
80. Regional groups like the Polish mountaineers often established their own fraternal organizations. The mountaineers established the Polish Highlanders Alliance of America in the late 1920s.
81. Edward R. Kantowicz, *Polish American Politics in Chicago, 1888–1940* (Chicago: University of Chicago Press, 1975), pp. 14–22.

Chapter 2

1. David Brody, *The Butcher Workman* (Cambridge: Harvard University Press, 1964), p. 7; Edna Louise Clark Wentworth, "The History of the Controversy Between Labor and Capital in the Slaughtering and Meat Packing Industries of Chicago" (M.M. thesis, University of Chicago, 1922), p. 25; John R. Commons, "Labor Conditions in Meat Packing and the Recent Strike," *Quarterly Journal of Economics* 19 (November 1904):6; Carroll D. Wright, "Influence of Trade Unions on Immigrants," *Bulletin of the Bureau of Labor* 56 (January 1905):2; Howard Barton Meyers, "The Policing of Labor Disputes in Chicago: A Case Study" (Ph.D. diss., University of Chicago, 1929), pp. 162, 177–83.

2. Balthasar H. Meyer to Mary E. McDowell, April 11, 1912, McDowell Papers, box 3, folder 15A; U.S. Congress, Senate, *Final Report and Testimony Submitted to Congress by the Commission on Industrial Relations*, S. Doc. 415, 64th Cong., 2nd sess., 1916, vol. 4, pp. 3464, 3504–14; sworn affidavit of Mike Matkowski before Florence Carr, notary public, October 26, 1908, in McDowell Papers, box 3, folder 15A; Leslie Orear, *Chicago Stockyards History Interview Series* (Chicago: Illinois Labor History Society, 1971), interview with Frank Flynn, January 1971, p. 1.

3. Rudolph Alexander Clemens, *The American Livestock and Meat Industry* (New York: Ronald Press, 1923), pp. 545–46, 550—51.

4. *Chicago Daily Tribune*, March 6, 1880; U.S. Congress, House, *Conditions in Chicago Stock Yards*, H.R. Doc. 873, 59th Cong., 1st sess., 1906, p. 263.

5. "Wages and Hours of Labor in the Slaughtering and Meat-Packing Industry," *Bulletin of U.S. Labor Statistics* 252 (August 1917):1076; F. W. Wilder, *The Modern Packing House* (Chicago: Nickerson & Collins, 1905), pp. 72, 252–54; W. Joseph Grand, *Illustrated History of the Union Stockyards* (Chicago: author, 1901), p. 54.

6. Wilder, *Modern Packing House*, p. 72.

7. U.S. Congress, House, *Hearings Before the Committee on Agriculture on the So-called Beveridge Amendment*, 59th Cong., 1st sess., 1906, p. 264.

8. Clemens, *Livestock and Meat Industry*, pp. 683–84; John Foster Fraser, *America at Work* (London: Cassell, 1903), p. 156; *Chicago Daily Tribune*, March 6, 1880; Wilder, *Modern Packing House*, p. 75.

9. Upton Sinclair, *The Jungle* (1905; reprint ed., New York: Viking Press, 1947), p. 115.

10. Wilder, *Modern Packing House*, pp. 76–77, 118–19; "Wages and Hours in Meat-Packing, 1917," pp. 1077–78; Commons, "Labor Conditions," pp. 4–9.

11. Wright, "Influence of Trades Unions," p. 2; "Wages and Hours in Meat-Packing, 1917," pp. 61, 1080–81; Commons, "Labor Conditions," p. 10; Wilder, *Modern Packing House*, pp. 241, 270–72.

12. "The Meat Industry of America," *Scientific American*, January 23, 30, 1909; reprint ed., Swift & Co., 1909, p. 11.

13. John R. Commons, "Women in Unions, Meat Packing Industry," *American Federationist* 13 (May 1906):382; Sophonisba P. Breckinridge and Edith Abbott, "Women in Industry: The Chicago Stockyards," *Journal of Political Economy* 19 (October 1911):641; Commons, "Labor Conditions," p. 20; Mary Elizabeth Pidgeon, "The Employment of Women in Slaughtering and Meat Packing," *Bulletin of the Women's Bureau* 88 (Washington, 1932),

pp. 4, 18–19, 23–24; Mary E. McDowell, "Mothers and Night Work," *Survey* 39 (December 22, 1917): 335.

14. Mary E. McDowell, "Labor The Great Strike" (n.d.), typed MS in McDowell Papers, box 3, folder 15, p. 8; Rose J. McHugh to Mary E. McDowell, Chicago, January 14, 1910, in ibid., box 3, folder 15A; Homer D. Call to Mary E. McDowell, Chicago, October 16, 1902, in ibid.; Pidgeon, "Women in Slaughtering and Meat Packing," p. 21; Breckinridge and Abbott, "Women in Industry: The Chicago Stockyards," pp. 648–49.

15. *Third Annual Report of the Factory Inspectors of Illinois for the Year Ending December 15, 1895* (Springfield: Ed. F. Hartman, State Printer, 1896), pp. 10–11; *Fourth Annual Report of the Factory Inspectors of Illinois for the Year Ending December 15, 1896* (Springfield: Phillips Bros., State Printers, 1897), p. 14; *Eighth Annual Report of the Factory Inspectors of Illinois for the Year Ending December 15, 1900* (Springfield: Phillips Bros., State Printers, 1901), pp. 7, 10–11.

16. Florence Kelley, "The Illinois Child Labor Law," *American Journal of Sociology* 3 (January 1898): 492–95; *Eighth Annual Report of the Factory Inspectors*, pp. 26–27; Commons, "Labor Conditions," p. 24.

17. *Eighth Annual Report of the Factory Inspectors*, pp. 5, 21–22, 26.

18. Florence Kelley, "The Working Boy," *American Journal of Sociology* 2 (November 1896): 363.

19. Jan Smolka, *From Serfdom to Self Government: Memoirs of a Polish Village Mayor, 1842–1927*, trans. William John Rose (London: Minerva Publishers, 1941), p. 123; *Eighth Annual Report of the Factory Inspectors*, p. 8.

20. Ernest L. Talbert, *Opportunities in School and Industry for Children of the Stockyards District* (Chicago: University of Chicago Press, 1912), pp. 14–15, 53.

21. For an example of the views of reformers on this subject see *Eighth Annual Report of the Factory Inspectors*, pp. 10–11, and Florence Kelley, "The Working Child," paper presented at Twenty-third National Conference of Charities and Correction, Grand Rapids, Michigan, June 8, 1896, p. 3.

22. Talbert, *Opportunities for Children of the Stockyards*, pp. 14–15, 45; Louise Montgomery, *The American Girl in the Stockyards District* (Chicago: University of Chicago Press, 1912), p. 7.

23. Talbert, *Opportunities for Children of the Stockyards*, pp. 20–34, 47; Montgomery, *American Girl in the Stockyards*, pp. 31, 51–54.

24. *Thirteenth Biennial Report of the Bureau of Labor Statistics of the State of Illinois, 1904* (Springfield: Phillips Bros., State Printers, 1907), pp. 6, 45.

25. Commons, "Labor Conditions," pp. 24–25; *Industrial Relations Report and Testimony*, p. 3465.

26. Talbert, *Opportunities for Children of the Stockyards*, pp. 10, 19, 41.

27. The first law that called for the recording of all industrial accidents of a fatal and nonfatal nature (loss of thirty or more days) was effective on July 1, 1907, after being passed by the Forty-fifth General Assembly of Illinois on May 24, 1907. Prior to this act only employees hurt in transportation and coal mining accidents were recorded and reported on by the state. In 1910 the law changed to call for the report of accidents that caused a loss of fifteen or more days. In May 1912, when the Workmen's Compensation Act became effective, injuries that caused a loss of seven or more days were filed. By 1913 accidents were being reported to various bureaus acting under several laws and were being reported in the industrial accidents reports pub-

lished by the state. Seven-day accidents were reported until June 30, 1913, when the Compensation Act was repealed, and thirty-day injuries were reported to the Bureau of Labor Statistics under the original 1907 law whereas fifteen-day injuries were reported to the chief state factory inspector under the Safety and Comfort of Employees Law of January 1, 1910. See *First Report, Bureau of Labor Statistics Industrial Accidents in Illinois for the Six Months Ending December 31, 1907* (Springfield: Phillips Brothers, State Printers, 1908), p. 7; *Fourth Report, Bureau of Labor Statistics Industrial Accidents in Illinois for the Year Ending December 31, 1909* (Springfield: Illinois State Journal, State Printers, 1911), p. 7; *Seventh Report, Bureau of Labor Statistics Industrial Accidents in Illinois for the Year Ending December 31, 1913* (Springfield: Illinois State Journal, State Printers, 1914), pp. 9–10.

28. *First Report on Industrial Accidents in Illinois*, pp. 14–15.

29. *1907–1910 Annual Reports of the Illinois Bureau of Labor Statistics*.

30. *Third Report, Bureau of Labor Statistics Industrial Accidents in Illinois for the Year Ending December 31, 1909* (Springfield: Illinois State Journal, State Printers, 1910), pp. 30–31; *Fourth Report on Industrial Accidents in Illinois* (1910), pp. 90–91; *First Report on Industrial Accidents* (1907), pp. 76–77; *Second Report, Bureau of Labor Statistics Industrial Accidents in Illinois for the Year Ending December 31, 1908* (Springfield, 1909), pp. 256–57.

31. Floyd Erwin Bernard, "A Study of Industrial Diseases in the Stockyards" (M.A. diss., University of Chicago, 1910), pp. 11–16.

32. Mary E. McDowell, "Beginnings" (typed MS dated 1914), p. 1, in McDowell Papers, box 1, folder 3; Robert Hunter, *Tenement Conditions in Chicago* (Chicago: City Homes Association, 1901), p. 12. Sinclair, *The Jungle*; Breckinridge and Abbott, "Housing Conditions, Back of the Yards"; *Chicago Daily Tribune*, March 6, 1918.

33. "The Back-of-the-Yards Area" (typed undated MS), p. 2, in Settlement House Papers, box 1, folder 2. See also Louise Wade, *Chicago's Pride: The Stockyards, Packingtown, and Environs in the Nineteenth Century* (Urbana: University of Illinois Press, 1986), pp. 157–59.

34. Chicago Plan Commission, *Chicago Land Use Survey, Housing in Chicago Communities—Community Area Number 61, Preliminary Release* (Chicago, 1940), pp. 9–11.

35. Perry R. Duis, *Chicago: Creating New Traditions* (Chicago: Chicago Historical Society, 1976), p. 14.

36. Lloyd Lewis and Henry Justin Smith, *Chicago, The History of Its Reputation (New York: Harcourt, Brace, 1929), p. 275; Tenth Annual Illustrated Catalogue of S. E. Gross' Famous City Subdivisions and Suburban Towns* (Chicago: H. J. Armstrong, 1891), pp. 60–63; Henry Hall, ed., *America's Successful Men of Affairs: An Encyclopedia of Contemporaneous Biography*, 5 vols. (New York: New York Tribune, 1896), 3 : 354; *The Biographical Dictionary and Portrait Gallery of Representative Men of Chicago, Minnesota Cities, and the World's Columbia Exposition* (Chicago: American Biographical Publishing, 1892), p. 81.

37. "New City," *Chicago Sun*, May 3, 1884.

38. Chicago Plan Commission, *Preliminary Release*, Community Area 61, p. 11.

39. Breckinridge and Abbott, "Housing Conditions, Back of the Yards," pp. 437–50.

40. Andrew M. Greeley, *The Communal Catholic* (New York: Seabury Press, 1976), p. 121.

41. Breckinridge and Abbott, "Housing Conditions, Back of the Yards," pp. 434–35; Mary E. McDowell, "Standard of Living" (typed MS), p. 4, in McDowell Papers, box 2, folder 13; "Ordinances Governing and Pertaining to the Department of Health of the City of Chicago Passed April 18, 1881" (revised and authorized to be published as in force on the second day of April, A.D. 1890), ordinance 2233 (1634) (Chicago: P. F. Pettibone, 1891); Eleanor Kroll, "The History of the University of Chicago Settlement House" (typed MS), p. 10, in McDowell Papers, box 1, folder 3A; "Bubbly Creek—Good Bye!" *Central Manufacturing District Magazine* 6 (June 1922):31. See also Joseph Hamzik, "Portion of Pershing Road Was Once a Union Stock Yards Canal Slip," *Chicago, Back of the Yards Journal*, October 4, 1972.

42. Alice May Miller, "Rents and Housing Conditions in the Stockyards District of Chicago, 1923" (M.A. thesis, University of Chicago, 1923), pp. 11–12; Mary E. McDowell, "Civic Experience" (1914), typed MS, p. 3, in McDowell Papers, box 3, folder 14; idem, "City Waste," in Caroline M. Hill, ed., *Mary McDowell and Municipal Housekeeping: A Symposium* (Chicago: Miller Publishing, n.d.), p. 2.

43. McDowell, "Civic Experience," pp. 1–2; Charles J. Bushnell, *The Social Problem at the Chicago Stock Yards* (Chicago: University of Chicago Press, 1902), p. 42.

44. McDowell, "Civic Experience," p. 3.

45. Harry M. Beardsly, "47th and Ashland District Prosperous," *Chicago Daily News*, May 6, 1922.

46. Russell Sage Foundation, "University of Chicago Settlement," from *Handbook of Settlements* (1911), pp. 1–2, in McDowell Papers, box 1; Breckinridge and Abbott, "Housing Conditions, Back of the Yards," p. 434; Mary E. McDowell, "The Significance to the City of its Local Community Life," *Proceedings of the National Conference of Social Work, 44th Session* (Chicago, 1917), 459; Miller, "Rents and Housing, 1923," pp. 6–8.

47. Bushnell, *Social Problem at the Chicago Stock Yards*, p. 38.

48. See City of Chicago Department of Health Reports for 1894–1900.

49. Caroline Hedger, "Health—Summer of 1908" (typed MS), in McDowell Papers, box 2, folder 13; *Report of the Department of Health of the City of Chicago for the Years 1907, 1908, 1909, 1910* (Chicago, 1911), p. 174.

50. *Industrial Relations Report and Testimony*, pp. 3514, 3521, 3464; "Wages and Hours in Meat-Packing, 1917," p. 61; Commons, "Labor Conditions," p. 13; Harold H. Swift, "Guaranteed Time in the Stockyards," *Survey Graphic* (November 1931):122; Mary E. McDowell, "The Great Strike" (1904) (MS) in McDowell Papers, box 3, folder 15, p. 3.

51. Clemens, "Livestock and Meat Industry," pp. 697–98; Harry Rosenburg, "On Packing Industry and the Stockyards" (n.d.), p. 10 (typed MS), in McDowell Papers, box 3, folder 15; Commons, "Labor Conditions," p. 16.

52. Bert Crawford Gross, "Factors Affecting the Origin of Livestock Receipts at Chicago, 1923–27" (M.A. thesis, University of Chicago, 1929), p. 14; *1953 Yearbook of Figures of the Livestock Trade* (Chicago: Chicago Daily Drovers' Journal, 1953), p. 14.

53. Gross, "Origins of Livestock Receipts," pp. 27–34; J. C. Kennedy et al., *Wages and Family Budgets in the Chicago Stockyards District* (Chicago: University of Chicago Press, 1914), p. 14; Breckinridge and Abbott, "Women in Industry: The Chicago Stockyards," p. 647.

54. Kennedy et al., *Wages and Budgets in Stockyards*, pp. 9–14, 19–23; *Industrial Relations Report and Testimony*, pp. 3466–67.

55. Kennedy et al., *Wages and Budgets in Stockyards*, pp. 22–23, 65–75, 80; *Industrial Relations Report and Testimony*, pp. 3466–67.

Chapter 3

1. U.S. Congress, Senate, *Report on Conditions of Employment in the Iron and Steel Industry in the United States*, S. Doc. 110, 62nd Cong., 1st sess., 1913, vol. 3, pp. 43–44, 90, 140, 147–48.

2. Phyllis Bate, "The Development of the Iron and Steel Industry of the Chicago Area, 1900–1920" (Ph.D. diss., University of Chicago, 1949), pp. 31–33.

3. John Bargate Appleton, "The Iron and Steel Industry of the Calumet District—A Study in Economic Geography" (Ph.D. diss., University of Chicago, 1925), pp. 63–71.

4. *Conditions of Employment*, 3:44–47, 87; Bate, "Development of Iron and Steel Industry," pp. 39, 47; Appleton, "Iron and Steel Industry in Calumet," p. 111.

5. *Conditions of Employment*, 3:56–57, 74–76.

6. Bate, "Development of Iron and Steel Industry," p. 149; *Conditions of Employment*, 3:258, 294, 299.

7. Bate, "Development of Iron and Steel Industry," p. 149; "Epidemic of Furunculosis in a Steel Plant Due to Infection Through Grease," *Monthly Labor Review* 9 (September 1919): 296–97; *Conditions of Employment*, 3:214.

8. *Dziennik Chicagoski*, January 6, March 2, 1900; *Conditions of Employment*, 4:11.

9. William Hard, "Making Steel and Killing Men," *Everybody's Magazine* 17 (November 1907): 579–87.

10. Bate, "Development of Iron and Steel Industry," pp. 151–53.

11. David Brody, *Steelworkers in America: The Nonunion Era* (New York: Harper & Row, 1969), pp. 91–92; Bate, "Development of Iron and Steel Industry," pp. 151–53.

12. U.S. Department of Labor, Bureau of Labor Statistics, *The Safety Movement in the Iron and Steel Industry, 1907–1917*, Lucien W. Chaney and Hugh S. Hanna, Report no. 234 (Washington, D.C.: Government Printing Office, 1918), pp. 68–71.

13. Bate, "Development of Iron and Steel Industry," pp. 152–53; Chaney and Hanna, *Safety Movement in the Steel Industry, 1907–17*, pp. 89, 102–03; Hard, "Making Steel and Killing Men," p. 591.

14. Bate, "Development of Iron and Steel Industry," pp. 147, 153; David S. Beyer, "Safety Provisions in the United States Steel Corporation," *Survey* 24 (May 7, 1910): 205–08, 213.

15. Chaney and Hanna, *Safety Movement in the Steel Industry, 1907–17*, pp. 14–17.

16. Brody, "Steelworkers in America," p. 167.

17. Bate, "Development of Iron and Steel Industry," pp. 158, 161; Brody, *Steelworkers in America*, p. 168; "Good Fellow Club as 'Santa Claus,'" *South Works Review* 2 (January 1914): 7–8; *South Works Review* 2 (July 1914): 11.

18. All taken from *South Works Review* 2 (May 1914): 6–7; 2 (February

1914): 10; 2 (August 1914): 13; 4 (August 1916), insert between 6 and 7; 5 (May 1917): 4; 6 (March 1918): 11; 2 (May 1914): 1.

19. Bate, "Development of Iron and Steel Industry," p. 168.

20. John Gillette, *Culture Agencies of a Typical Manufacturing Group: South Chicago* (Chicago: University of Chicago Press, 1901), p. 9; Sophonisba Breckinridge and Edith Abbott, "Chicago Housing Conditions, V: South Chicago at the Gates of the Steel Mills," *American Journal of Sociology* 17 (September 1911): 145.

21. Gillette, *Cultural Agencies: South Chicago*, pp. 12, 22–25.

22. Edith Abbott, *The Tenements of Chicago, 1908–1935* (Chicago: University of Chicago Press, 1936), p. 145; Breckinridge and Abbott, "Housing Conditions, South Chicago," p. 151.

23. Information taken from Breckinridge and Abbott, "Housing Conditions, South Chicago," pp. 146–52, 156–58, 160–74.

24. Department of Health, City of Chicago, *Report of the Department of Health of the City of Chicago for the Years 1907, 1908, 1909, 1910* (Chicago, 1911), pp. 115, 119, 174–76.

25. *Conditions of Employment*, 3: 205.

26. Ibid., 1: xiv; Bate, "Development of Iron and Steel Industry," p. 134.

27. *Conditions of Employment*, 3: 160–70; Bate, "Development of Iron and Steel Industry," pp. 136–37.

28. Brody, *Steelworkers in America*, pp. 35–37.

29. John A. Fitch, "Steel Corporation Labor Report," *Survey* 28 (4 May 1912): 253.

30. Bate, "Development of Iron and Steel Industry," p. 138.

31. *Conditions of Employment*, 3: 205, 214, 232–33; 1: 233–36; Bate, "Development of Iron and Steel Industry," pp. 141–43.

Chapter 4

1. William I. Thomas and Florian Znaniecki, *The Polish Peasant in Europe and America*, 5 vols. (Chicago: University of Chicago Press, 1919), 1: 275, 277.

2. Anthony J. Kuzniewski, S.M., "The Catholic Church in the Life of Polish-Americans," in Frank Mocha, ed., *Poles in American Bicentennial Essays* (Stevens Point, Wisc.: Worzalla, 1978).

3. Ladislas Reymont, *The Peasants*, 4 vols., trans. Michael A. Dziewicki (New York: Alfred A. Knopf, 1925), 1: 175, 178.

4. Thomas and Znaniecki, *Polish Peasant*, 1: 277.

5. Helen Stankiewicz Zand, "Polish Folkways in America," *Polish American Studies* 6 (January–June 1949): 33–36.

6. Helen Stankiewicz Zand, "Polish American Holiday Customs," *Polish American Studies* 15 (July–December 1958): 85, 28, 90; Kazimierz Dobrowolski, "Peasant Traditional Culture," in Teodor Shanin, ed., *Peasants and Peasant Societies* (Harmondsworth, Middlesex, England: Penguin, 1971), p. 285.

7. Thomas and Znaniecki, *Polish Peasant*, 1: 220–21, 226, 228–29.

8. Zand, "Polish American Holiday Customs," p. 84; Reymont, *Peasants*, 2: 20.

9. Ferdynand Kuras, *Przez Ciemnie Zywota* (Through a Dark Life) (Czestochowa: Ksiegarni A. Gmachowskiego, 1925), p. 28.

10. Thomas and Znaniecki, *Polish Peasant*, 1:233–34; Dobrowolski, "Peasant Traditional Culture," p. 288.

11. Dobrowolski, p. 289.

12. Kuras, *Przez Ciemnie Zywota*, p. 23; Reymont, *Peasants*, 1:87–88, 133, 2:212–13; Dobrowolski, "Peasant Traditional Culture," p. 285; Thomas and Znaniecki, *Polish Peasant*, 1:233.

13. Dobrowolski, "Peasant Traditional Culture," pp. 292–93.

14. Ibid., pp. 296–97.

15. Thomas and Znaniecki, *Polish Peasant*, 1:231.

16. Reymont, *Peasants*, 2:268–84.

17. Thomas and Znaniecki, *Polish Peasant*, 1:166–67, 184–86.

18. Jan Slomka, *From Serfdom to Self-Government, Memoirs of a Polish Village Mayor, 1842–1927*, trans. William John Rose (London: Minerva, 1941), pp. 78, 92–93, 15; Thomas and Znaniecki, *Polish Peasant*, 1:30, 138–39, 226; Reymont, *Peasants*, 2:19–20; Piotr S. Wandycz, *The Lands of Partitioned Poland, 1796–1918* (Seattle: University of Washington Press, 1974), pp. 281, 293; Max L. Margolis and Alexander Marx, *A History of the Jewish People* (New York: Jewish Publication Society of America, 1927; reprint ed., Forge Village, Mass.: Atheneum, 1975), p. 718.

19. Helen Stankiewicz Zand, "Polish American Weddings and Christenings," *Polish American Studies* 16 (January-June 1959):24–27. For an excellent description of a Polish wedding see Reymont, *Peasants*, 1:211–37.

20. Thomas and Znaniecki, *Polish Peasant*, 1:87–90, 92–96; Reymont, *Peasants*, 2:118, n. 1.

21. Thomas and Znaniecki, *Polish Peasant*, 1:90, 109–10; Reymont, *Peasants*, 1:155–59.

22. Thomas and Znaniecki, *Polish Peasant*, 1:117–20.

23. Ibid., p. 98; Dobrowolski, "Peasant Traditional Culture," pp. 297–98.

24. Alexander Gieysztor, Stefan Kieniewicz, et al., *History of Poland* (Warsaw: PWN [Polish Scientific Publishers], 1968), p. 535.

25. Peter F. Sugar and Ivo S. Lederer, *Nationalism in Eastern Europe* (Seattle: University of Washington Press, 1971), pp. 34, 337–38.

26. Dobrowolski, "Peasant Traditional Culture," p. 296; Wandycz, *Partitioned Poland*, pp. 220, 222–23; Roman Dyboski, "The Peasant in Modern Poland," *Slavonic Review* 2 (1923):106–07; Lisa Bernault, "Polish Peasant Autobiographies," (Ph.D. diss., Columbia University, 1950), p. 109.

27. Gieysztor, *History of Poland*, pp. 559, 578; Bernault, "Peasant Autobiographies," pp. 228–30.

28. Wandycz, *Partitioned Poland*, p. 226.

29. Gieysztor, *History of Poland*, pp. 559, 577–78.

30. Ibid., p. 578; Dyzma Galaj, *Chłopski Ruch Polityczny w Polsce* (Peasant Political Movements in Poland) (Warsaw: Państowe Wydawnictwo "Wiedza Powszechna," 1969), p. 5.

31. Wandycz, *Partitioned Poland*, p. 278.

32. Galaj, *Chłopski Ruch Polityczny*, p. 9.

33. Benjamin P. Murdzek, *Emigration in Polish Social-Political Thought, 1870–1914* (Boulder, Colo.: East European Quarterly, 1977), pp. 151–55.

34. Thomas and Znaniecki, *Polish Peasant*, 1:192–98; Murdzek, *Emigration in Polish Thought*, pp. 161–62.

35. Gieysztor, *History of Poland*, pp. 602–04.

36. Galaj, *Chłopski Ruch Polityczny*, p. 12.

37. Edward R. Kantowicz, *Polish-American Politics in Chicago* (Chicago: University of Chicago Press, 1975), p. 19.

38. Many scholars have commented on the importance of the parish for Polish Americans. For a look at the role of the parish as an Americanizing force see Daniel S. Buczek, "The Polish-American Parish as an Americanizing Factor," in Charles A. Ward, Philip Shashko, and Donald E. Pienkos, eds., *Studies in Ethnicity: The East European Experience in America* (Boulder, Colo.: East European Monographs, 1980), pp. 153–65.

39. Lewis Mumford, *The City in History* (New York: Harcourt, Brace & World, 1961), p. 310.

40. Kantowicz, *Polish-American Politics*, pp. 19–22.

41. Joseph J. Parot, *Polish Catholics in Chicago, 1850–1920* (DeKalb: Northern Illinois University Press, 1981), pp. 75–78.

42. Victor Greene, *For God and Country* (Madison: State Historical Society of Wisconsin, 1975), pp. 66–84; Lawrence D. Orton, *Polish Detroit and Kolasinski Affair* (Detroit: Wayne State University Press, 1981).

43. *Diamond Jubilee, Immaculate Conception*, pp. 26–30, 83.

44. Reverend Msgr. Harry C. Koenig, ed., *A History of the Parishes of the Archdiocese of Chicago*, 2 vols. (Chicago: Archdiocese of Chicago, 1980), 1: 515–18; Reverend George Lane, *Chicago Churches and Synagogues* (Chicago: Loyola University Press, 1981), p. 233.

45. *St. John of God Jubilee Book, 1907–1957* (Chicago, 1957), pp. 12–13, 34–36; Koenig, *History of the Parishes*, 1:496.

46. Reverend Louis Grudzinski file, Archdiocesan Personnel Records, Archives of the Archdiocese of Chicago. For Grudzinski's role as a leader of Polish priests see Edward R. Kantowicz, *Corporation Sole: Cardinal Mundelein and Chicago Catholicism* (South Bend, Indiana: University of Notre Dame Press, 1983), pp. 77–79; *St. John of God Golden Jubilee Book*, p. 47; and Koenig, *History of the Parishes*, 1:498.

47. Reverend Francis J. Karabasz file, Archdiocesan Personnel Records, Archives of the Archdiocese of Chicago.

48. Various requests for payment included in the Sacred Heart of Jesus Parish (Honore Street) Correspondence File; *Sacred Heart of Jesus Golden Jubilee Book, 1910–1960* (Chicago, 1960), pp. 14–16; Koenig, *History of the Parishes*, 2:872.

49. Josef Chałasinski, "Parafja i Szkola Parafijalna Wsród Emigracji Polskiej w Ameryce. Studium dzielnicy polskiej w Połundniowym Chicago" (The Parish and Parish School during the Polish Emigration to America: A Study of the Polish District in South Chicago), *Przegląd Socjologiczny* 3 (Warsaw 1935):640–41.

50. Zand, "Polish Folkways," pp. 33–37.

51. "Notatki, 1898–1941," (Notes, 1898–1941, of Rev. F. M. Wojtalewicz, pastor of Immaculate Conception B.V.M. Church), February 20, 1898, typed copy in Immaculate Conception B.V.M. Collection at the University of Illinois at Chicago Circle, Urban Archives, folder 1. Hereafter cited as "Notatki."

52. Slomka, *Memoirs*, p. 142.

53. "Notatki," April 17, 1904, March 26, 1899; Zand, "Polish American Holiday Customs," pp. 87–88.

54. Zand, "Polish American Holiday Customs," pp. 85, 90.

55. Helen Stankiewicz Zand, "Polish American Folkways," *Polish American Studies* 17 (July–December 1960): 103.

56. "Notatki," September 3, 1899.

57. Slomka, *Memoirs*, pp. 10, 114; Zand, "Weddings and Christenings," p. 25.

58. Zand, "Weddings and Christenings," p. 25.

59. Thomas and Znaniecki, *Polish Peasant*, 1 : 122.

60. Zand, "Polish Folkways," p. 37.

61. Ernest Poole, "A Mixing Bowl of Nations," *Everybody's Magazine* (October 1910): 554–55.

62. Zand, "Weddings and Christenings," p. 27.

63. Chałasinski, "Parafje Polski w Ameryce," p. 644.

64. "Notatki," April 29, 1900; September 28, 1902; February 25, 1900.

65. Thomas and Znaniecki, *Polish Peasant*, 1 : 266.

66. *Diamond Jubilee, Immaculate Conception*, pp. 137–47.

67. Ibid., p. 147.

68. *Poles of Chicago*, pp. 84–86.

69. Ibid.; *Dziennik Związkowy* (Chicago), January 4, 1918; January 11, 1918.

70. *Dziennik Chicagoski*, February 19, 1900.

71. Ibid., January 26, 1900; "Notatki," November 5, 1899.

72. *Dziennik Chicagoski*, February 22, 1900.

73. *Diamond Jubilee, Immaculate Conception*, p. 29.

74. "Notatki," Dom V, February 8, 1903.

75. *Diamond Jubilee, Immaculate Conception*, p. 29.

76. *Dziennik Związkowy* (Chicago), January 8, 1918.

77. *Diamond Jubilee, Immaculate Conception*, pp. 149, 153.

78. Kuzniewski, "Catholic Church in the Life of Polish Americans," p. 403.

79. Henryk Sienkiewicz, *After Bread*, trans. Vatslaf A. Hlasko and Thomas Bullick (New York: R. F. Fenno, 1897), p. 101.

80. Ellen Marie Kuznicki, CSSF, "The Polish American Parochial Schools," in Frank Mocha, ed., *Poles in America, Bicentennial Essays* (Stevens Point, Wisc.: Worzalla, 1978), p. 436.

81. *Diamond Jubilee, Immaculate Conception*, pp. 75–76.

82. *Polonia* (South Chicago), January 3, 1929.

83. *Dziennik Chicagoski*, February 1, 1900.

84. James W. Sanders, *The Education of an Urban Minority, Catholics in Chicago, 1833–1965* (New York: Oxford Press, 1977), pp. 45–47, 83.

85. Ibid., pp. 60–61, 85.

86. Ibid., p. 115; Jozef Miaso, *Dzieje Oświaty Polonijen w Stanach Zjednoczonych* (History of Polish American Education in the United States) (Warsaw: Panstowe Wydanictwo Naukowe, 1970), p. 292.

87. Anthony Kuzniewski, "Boot Straps and Book Learning: Reflections on the Education of Polish Americans," *Polish American Studies* 22 (Spring 1975): 27.

88. Guznicki, "Polish American Parochial Schools," p. 445; Thaddeus C. Radzialowski, "Reflections on the History of the Felicians in America," *Polish American Studies* 22 (Spring 1975): 24.

89. *Dziennik Chicagoski*, February 1, 1900.

90. U.S. Department of Labor, Bureau of Labor Statistics, *The Safety*

Movement in the Iron and Steel Industry, 1907–1917, Lucien W. Chaney and Hugh S. Hanna, Report no. 234 (Washington, D.C.: Government Printing Office, 1918), p. 41.

91. David Hogan, "Education and the Making of the Chicago Working Class, 1880–1930," *History of Education Quarterly* 18 (Fall 1978):231–32; "When the Immigrant Goes to School," *Intepreter* 5 (December 1926):9.

92. Hogan, "Education and the Working Class," pp. 233–34, 236–37.

93. Helenz Znaniecka Lopata, *Polish Americans—Status Competition in an Ethnic Community* (Englewood Cliffs, N.J.: Prentice Hall, 1976), p. 92.

94. Chałasinski, "Parafje Polski w Ameryce," p. 638.

95. Helen Stankiewicz Zand, "Polish American Leisureways," *Polish American Studies* 18 (January–June 1961):35.

96. Quoted in Norman Sylvester Hayner, "The Effect of Prohibition in Packingtown" (Master's thesis, University of Chicago, 1921), pp. 12–13.

97. Sophonisba P. Breckinridge and Edith Abbott, "Housing Conditions in Chicago, III: Back of the Yards," *American Journal of Sociology* 16 (January 1911):464.

98. Hayner, "Prohibition in Packingtown," p. 12.

99. *Dziennik Związkowy* (Chicago), January 11, 1918.

100. Thomas and Znaniecki, *Polish Peasant*, 5:209.

101. Hayner, "Prohibition in Packingtown," p. 10.

102. *Dziennik Związkowy* (Chicago), January 2, 1918.

103. E. C. Moore, "The Social Value of the Saloon," *American Journal of Sociology* 3 (July 1897):4–5. For a complete discussion of the saloon as a public institution and its role as a community institution, see Perry R. Duis, *The Saloon: Public Drinking in Boston and Chicago, 1880–1920* (Urbana: University of Illinois Press, 1983).

104. Frederick M. Thrasher, *The Gang* (Chicago: University of Chicago Press, 1927), pp. 28–32, 194.

105. Ibid., p. 82; Clifford R. Shaw, *The Jack-Roller* (Chicago: University of Chicago Press, 1968), p. 7.

106. Thrasher, *Gang*, pp. 148–58. For an account of an incident in South Chicago, see *Dziennik Chicagoski*, January 12, 1900.

107. See Shaw, *Jack-Roller*, pp. 97–98.

108. *Dziennik Związkowy* (Chicago), January 2, 1918.

109. Thrasher, *Gang*, p. 174; Dobrowolski, "Peasant Traditional Culture," p. 294.

110. Clifford R. Shaw and Henry D. McKay, *Juvenile Delinquency and Urban Areas* (Chicago: University of Chicago Press, 1972), pp. 60–65.

111. Shaw, *Jack-Roller*, p. 35.

112. Thomas and Znaniecki, *Polish Peasant*, 2:184–85.

113. Ibid., 2:185.

114. Caroline M. Hill, ed., *Mary McDowell and Municipal Housekeeping: A Symposium* (Chicago: Millar, n.d.), pp. 16–17; "The Foreign Born (Immigrants in the Packing Industry), p. 6, typed MS in McDowell Papers, folder 12, box 6.

115. Lopata, *Polish Americans*, p. 100.

116. Thomas and Znaniecki, *Polish Peasant*, 2:185.

117. Victor Greene, *For God and Country* (Madison: State Historical Society of Wisconsin, 1975), pp. 58–59.

118. Ibid., p. 150.

119. Adam Andrzejewski, ed., *Pamiętniki Emigrantów Stany Zjednoczone* (Memoirs of Immigrants to the United States), 2 vols. (Warsaw: Instytut Gospodarstwa Społecznego—Ksiazka i Wiedza, 1977), 2:226–27. For the rise of Lithuanian nationalism, see Wandycz, *Partitioned Poland*, pp. 241–47.

120. Hill, *McDowell*, p. 27.

121. Ibid.

122. Ibid., p. 28.

123. Ernst W. Burgess and Charles Newcomb, *Census Data of the City of Chicago, 1920* (Chicago: University of Chicago Press, 1931), census tract 354.

124. Edward R. Kantowicz, *Polish-American Politics in Chicago* (Chicago: University of Chicago Press, 1975), pp. 118–19.

125. Stefan Włoszczewski, *History of Polish American Culture* (Trenton, N.J.: White Eagle, 1946), pp. 47, 67–68.

126. Zand, "Polish American Folkways," p. 100; idem, "Weddings and Christenings," p. 32.

Chapter 5

1. Daniel T. Rodgers, *The Work Ethic in Industrial America, 1850–1920* (Chicago: University of Chicago Press, 1978), pp. 28–29.

2. Allen F. Davis, *Spearheads of Reform* (New York: Oxford University Press, 1967), pp. 3–14, 103–4.

3. Thomas Wakefield Goodspeed, *A History of the University of Chicago* (Chicago: University of Chicago Press, 1916; reprint ed., Chicago: University of Chicago Press, 1972), pp. 445, 447; Lea D. Taylor, "The Social Settlement and Civic Responsibility—The Life Work of Mary McDowell and Graham Taylor," *Social Service Review* 28 (March 1954):32; John Drury, *Rare and Well Done* (Chicago: Quadrangle Books, 1966), p. 153.

4. Mary E. McDowell, "Beginnings," 1914 (typewritten), pp. 7, 71, in Mary Eliza McDowell Papers, Chicago Historical Society, box 1, folder 1. Hereafter cited as McDowell Papers.

5. Howard Eugene Wilson, "Mary E. McDowell and Her Work as Head Resident of the University of Chicago Settlement House, 1894–1905" (M.A. Thesis, University of Chicago, 1927), pp. 14, 17–19; Mary E. McDowell, "How the Living Faith of One Social Worker Grew," *Graphic Survey* 60 (April 1928):42–43; idem, "A Quarter of a Century in the Stockyards District," in Clyde C. Walton, ed., *An Illinois Reader* (DeKalb: Northern Illinois University Press, 1970), p. 327.

6. Howard E. Wilson, *Mary McDowell: Neighbor* (Chicago: University of Chicago Press, 1928), p. 32; McDowell, "Beginnings," p. 10; Mirriam G. Rappe, "Mary E. McDowell" (typewritten), p. 11, in McDowell Papers, box 1, folder 1.

7. Wilson, "Mary McDowell," pp. 32, 35–36; Russell Sage Foundation, "University of Chicago Settlement," *Handbook of Settlements* (1911), p. 5, in McDowell Papers, box 1, folder 1.

8. Mary E. McDowell, "The Foreign Born (Immigrants in the Packing Industry)" (typewritten), p. 1, in McDowell Papers, box 2, folder 12.

9. "University Settlement Women's Club Minutes," January 3, 1896; February 28, 1901; September 28, 1897, in University of Chicago Settlement House Papers, Chicago Historical Society, box 4. Hereafter cited as Settlement House Papers.

10. *The University of Chicago Settlement Handbook*, p. 1, in Settlement House Papers, box 1, folder 1; "University Settlement Women's Club Minutes," February 28, 1901.

11. Wilson, "Mary McDowell," pp. 143-51.

12. Mary McDowell, "Meeting Educational and Aesthetic Hunger" (typewritten), p. 23, in McDowell Papers, box 1, folder 3.

13. Sage Foundation, "University of Chicago Settlement," p. 4; Mary McDowell, "The Activities of the University of Chicago Settlement" (1908) (typewritten), p. 3.

14. Wilson, "Mary McDowell," pp. 61-63; Mary McDowell, "Summer on the Sidewalks" (typewritten), p. 27, in McDowell Papers, box 1, folder 3.

15. Wilson, "Mary McDowell," pp. 54-58.

16. Mary McDowell, "Our Proxies in Industry," in Caroline M. Hill, *Mary McDowell and Municipal Housekeeping: A Symposium* (Chicago: Millar, 1937), pp. 58-59; U.S. Congress, Senate, Industrial Relations, S. Doc. 415, 64th Cong., 1st sess., 1916, vol. 4.

17. D. E. Proctor, "The University of Chicago Settlement: A Study of the History of its Internal Organization" (typewritten), pp. 36-37, 45-47, in Ernest W. Burgess Papers, University of Chicago, box 138, folder 10. Hereafter cited as Burgess Papers.

18. *St. John of God Jubilee Book, 1907-1957* (Chicago, 1957), p. 37; McDowell, "Our Proxies in Industry," p. 47; interview with Rt. Rev. Monsignor Edward Plewinski, June 16, 1973; "The Back-of-the-Yards-Area" (typewritten), pp. 24-25, in Settlement House Papers, box 1, folder 2.

19. "University Settlement Women's Club Minutes, 1900-1904"; Mary Anderson to George T. Snider, August 24, 1924; John Fitzpatrick to George T. Snider, August 26, 1924, McDowell Papers, box 1, folder 1.

20. Henry Pelling, *American Labor* (Chicago: University of Chicago Press, 1968), pp. 63-66, 71; Howard B. Meyers, "The Policing of Labor Disputes in Chicago: A Case Study" (Ph.D. diss., University of Chicago, 1929), pp. 162-72; McDowell, "Quarter of a Century," pp. 336-37.

21. David Brody, *The Butcher Workmen* (Cambridge: Harvard University Press, 1964), pp. 14-15, 22-25, 35-41.

22. Emily Barrows, "Trade Union Organization Among Women in Chicago" (M.A. thesis, University of Chicago, 1927), pp. 7, 63, 29, 32, 114-15.

23. "University Settlement Women's Club Minutes," January 15, 1903; Barrows, "Trade Unions Among Women," pp. 116-17; Harry Rosenberg, "On Packing Industry and Stockyards" (typewritten), p. 2, in McDowell Papers, box 3, folder 15.

24. Alma Herbst, "The Negro in the Slaughtering and Meat Packing Industry in Chicago" (Ph.D. diss., University of Chicago, 1930), pp. 31-33.

25. Rosenberg, "On Packing Industry and Stockyards," p. 5; "The Community's Interest in the Stock Yards Strike," *The Commons* 9 (September 1904):402-03.

26. *Dziennik Chicagoski*, July 15, 1904.

27. Ibid., July 19, 20, 1904.

28. Mary E. McDowell, "At the Heart of the Packingtown Strike," *The Commons* 9 (September 1904):397-98; *Chicago Daily Tribune* July 13, 1904; Herbst, "Negro in the Meat Packing Industry," p. 53; *Chicago Daily Tribune*, July 21, 1904; "The Community's Interest," p. 404; John Fitzpatrick, "De-

fense of the Strike Policy," *The Commons* 9 (November 1904):550; Rosenberg, "On Packing Industry and Stockyards," p. 7.

29. "The Community's Interest," p. 404.

30. *Chicago Daily Tribune*, July 22, 1904; *Daily Republican* (Joliet), July 27, 1904, in Illinois Annals of Labor History, Chicago Historical Society, folder 1904. The collection is a series of notes taken on labor and industrial-related topics by the WPA from newspapers across Illinois. Hereafter cited as Illinois Annals. See also *Joliet Daily News*, July 27, 1904, Illinois Annals, folder 1904; *Evanston Index*, July 30, 1904, Illinois Annals, folder 1904.

31. *Dziennik Chicagoski*, July 29, 1904.

32. *Chicago Daily Tribune*, August 2, 1904.

33. *Dziennik Chicagoski*, August 4, 8, 1904.

34. James R. Barrett, *Work and Community in the Jungle: Chicago's Packinghouse Workers, 1894–1922* (Urbana and Chicago: University of Illinois Press, 1987), pp. 174–75.

35. Luke Grant, "Labor's Mistakes Where It Was Hard Not to Err," *The Commons* 9 (November 1904):544–45; "Responsibility for Prolonging the Packing Trade Strike," *The Commons* 9 (September 1904):392; "Who Blundered Away the Packing Trade Pact," *The Commons* 9 (August 1904):341; Fitzpatrick, "Defense of the Strike Policy," p. 551; Lewis Corey, *Meat and Man* (New York: Viking, 1950), p. 63.

36. Herbst, "Negro in the Meat Packing Industry," p. 53.

37. Norman J. G. Pounds, *Poland Between East and West* (New York: D. Van Nostrand, 1964), p. 60; Alexsander Gieysztor, Stefan Kieniewicz, et al., *History of Poland* (Warsaw: PWN [Polish Scientific Publishers], 1968), p. 609; Edward R. Kantowicz, *Polish-American Politics in Chicago* (Chicago: University of Chicago Press, 1975), pp. 110–12.

38. William Z. Foster, *American Trade Unionism* (New York: International Publishers, 1970), pp. 21–23; Herbst, "Negro in the Meat Packing Industry," pp. 66–72.

39. Barrows, "Trade Unions Among Women," pp. 118–19; Olive M. Sullivan, "The Women's Part in the Stockyards Organization Work," *Life and Labor* 8 (May 1918):102, 104.

40. Handwritten note giving Kikulski's address as 2848 N. Kildare. It also mentions that he should see Foster at Stock Yards Headquarters: John Fitzpatrick Papers, Chicago Historical Society (hereafter referred to as Fitzpatrick Papers), box 8, folder 41; Herbst, "Negro in the Meat Packing Industry," pp. 65–66; telegram, Frank Morrison to John Fitzpatrick, September 23, 1917, Fitzpatrick Papers, box 6, folder 41.

41. Foster, *American Trade Unionism*, pp. 24–25.

42. John Fitzpatrick to Samuel Gompers, March 26, 1918, Fitzpatrick Papers, box 6, folder 46.

43. William Z. Foster, "How Life Has Been Brought Into the Stockyards," *Life and Labor* 7 (April 1918):66–68, 71; Frank Walsh, *Over the Top at the Yards* (Chicago: Chicago Labor News, 1918). This booklet contains the opening and closing statements of Frank T. Walsh on behalf of the Stock Yard Labor Council.

44. Judge Samuel Alschuler, "In the Matter of the Arbitration of Six Questions Concerning Wages, Hours, and Conditions of Labor in Certain

Packing House Industries, by Agreement Submitted for Decision to a United States Administrator," copy at Chicago Historical Society.

45. Mary E. McDowell, "Easter Day After the Decision," *Survey* 40 (April 13, 1918); 38.

46. Joe Manley to John Fitzpatrick, March 14, 1918, Fitzpatrick Papers, box 6, folder 46.

47. Jack M. Stein, "A History of Unionization in the Steel Industry in the Chicago Area" (M.A. thesis, University of Chicago, 1948), pp. 1–2.

48. David Brody, *Steelworkers in America: The Nonunion Era* (New York: Harper Torchbooks, 1969), pp. 50–57, 67–70; Stein, "History of Unionization," pp. 3–5.

49. Phyllis Bate, "The Development of the Iron and Steel Industry of the Chicago Area, 1900–1920" (Ph.D. diss., University of Chicago, 1948), pp. 175–77; Brody, *Steelworkers*, pp. 140–41, 145–46; Stein, "History of Unionization," p. 10.

50. William Z. Foster, *The Great Steel Strike and its Lessons* (New York: B. W. Huebsch, 1920), pp. 18–19; telegram, William Z. Foster to John Fitzpatrick, June 13, 1918, Fitzpatrick Papers, box 7, folder 49.

51. David J. Saposs, "How the Steel Strike Was Organized," *Survey* 41 (November 8, 1919):68–69; Foster, *Steel Strike*, pp. 21–22; Brody, *Steelworkers*, p. 217.

52. David Brody, *Labor in Crisis: The Steel Strike of 1919* (New York: Lippincott, 1965), pp. 54, 66–76; Foster, *Steel Strike*, p. 29.

53. The classic study of Polish politics in Chicago is Kantowicz, *Polish-American Politics in Chicago, 1888–1940.*

54. *Chicago Society News* (CFLPS), September 1923.

55. *Dziennik Zjednoczenia* (CFLPS), November 23, 1922; April 4, 1922; March 17, 1922.

56. *Dziennik Związkowy* (CFLPS) October 11, 1916; November 2, 1914.

57. *Dziennik Chicagoski* (CFLPS) March 31, 1891; February 4, 1922.

58. *Zgoda* (CFLPS) April 15, 1897.

59. *Dziennik Chicagoski* (CFLPS) October 19, 1894. For Kowalski's background see Kantowicz, *Polish-American Politics*, pp. 45–48, 62.

60. *Dziennik Chicagoski* (CFLPS) March 9, February 12, 1894.

61. Ibid., March 26, 1895.

62. *Polonia* (CFLPS), November 2, 1916.

63. *Dziennik Chicagoski* (CFLPS) November 14, 1892; March 18, 1895.

64. Ibid., March 28, 24, 1896.

65. Ibid., September 16, 1905.

66. Kantowicz, *Polish-American Politics*, pp. 84, 181.

67. *Dziennik Związkowy* (CFLPS) September 8, 1914; *Dziennik Chicagoski* (CFLPS) March 2, 1908.

68. *Dziennik Chicagoski* (CFLPS) March 25, 1896; December 18, 1893.

69. Ibid., January 24, March 15, 1894.

70. Ibid., August 7, 1894.

71. Ibid., March 20, 1897.

72. *Dziennik Związkowy* (CFLPS) April 20, 1912.

73. Ibid., September 12, 1912.

74. Kantowicz, *Polish-American Politics*, p. 178.

75. *Dziennik Związkowy* (CFLPS) August 23, June 25, 1918.

Chapter 6

1. Alfred W. Crosby, *Epidemic and Peace, 1918* (Westport, Conn.: Greenwood Press, 1976), pp. 18–21, 30–31, 37–39.

2. Department of Health of the City of Chicago, "Report on an Epidemic of Influenza in Chicago Occurring During the Fall of 1918," in *Report and Handbook of the Department of Health of the City of Chicago for the Years 1911 to 1918, Exclusive* (Chicago: House of Severinghous, 1919), p. 40; Crosby, *Epidemic and Peace*, p. 57.

3. Department of Health of the City of Chicago, *Report and Handbook, 1911–1918*, pp. 62, 80–82.

4. Quoted in A. A. Hoehling, *The Great Epidemic* (Boston: Little, Brown, 1961), p. 62.

5. Department of Health of the City of Chicago, *Report and Handbook, 1911–1918*, pp. 40, 53, 59–61, 70–72, 82–85, 91–92, 106–15.

6. *Report of the University of Chicago Settlement House, July 1, 1918, to July 1, 1919* (Chicago, 1919), p. 2, in McDowell Papers, box 2, folder 12.

7. Department of Health of the City of Chicago, *Report and Handbook, 1911–1918*, p. 136.

8. Allan H. Spear, *Black Chicago: The Making of a Negro Ghetto, 1890–1920* (Chicago: University of Chicago Press, 1967), pp. 11, 14–20, 130; St. Clair Drayton and Dorace C. Clayton, *Black Metropolis*, 2 vols. (New York: Harcourt, Brace, and World, 1970), 1:61–62.

9. Alzada P. Comstock, "Chicago Housing Conditions, VI: The Problem of the Negro," *American Journal of Sociology* 28 (September 1912): 253–54.

10. Drayton and Clayton, *Black Metropolis*, p. 62; James T. Farrell, *Studs Lonigan* (New York: Avon, 1977).

11. William M. Tuttle, Jr., *Race Riot: Chicago in the Red Summer of 1919* (New York: Atheneum, 1970), pp. 5–7.

12. Chicago Commission on Race Relations, *The Negro in Chicago: A Study of Relations and a Race Riot* (Chicago: University of Chicago Press, 1922), pp. 2–3, 124; Tuttle, *Race Riot*, pp. 7–8, 159.

13. Tuttle, *Race Riot*, pp. 7–8, 55–60; Chicago Commission on Race Relations, *Negro in Chicago*, pp. 5–9, 656–67.

14. *New Majority*, August 9, 1919.

15. *Dziennik Chicagoski*, August 2, 4, 1919.

16. Joseph Parot, "Ethnic versus Black Metropolis: The Origin of Polish-Black Housing Tensions in Chicago," *Polish American Studies* 29 (Spring–Autumn 1972):28.

17. Illinois Regular Militia, field orders 8-2-1919, 5:30 P.M., no. 4, in Chicago Commission on Race Relations Papers at Illinois State Archives, folder 2 (henceforth referred to as Chicago Commission Papers); Tuttle, *Race Riot*, p. 61.

18. *Dziennik Chicagoski*, August 2, 4, 1919.

19. *Dziennik Związkowy*, August 2, 5, 1919; *Dziennik Chicagoski*, August 5, 1919.

20. *Dziennik Związkowy*, August 5, 1919.

21. Joseph T. Hapak, "Recruiting a Polish Army in the United States, 1917–1919" (Ph.D. diss., University of Kansas, 1985), p. 137. This study is the best account of the Polish army and the methods used to raise it in

America.

22. *Dziennik Związkowy*, August 5, 1919.

23. *Dziennik Związkowy*, July 29, 1919.

24. Ibid., July 28, 29, 1919.

25. Ibid., July 30, 1919.

26. Ibid., August 2, 1919.

27. Ibid., August 4, 1919.

28. Ibid., August 2, 8, 1919.

29. Ibid., August 5, 1919.

30. *Dziennik Chicagoski*, August 1, 1919.

31. Ibid., July 30, August 2, 1919.

32. Quoted in Parot, "Ethnic versus Black Metropolis," pp. 28–29.

33. Mary E. McDowell, "Prejudice," in Caroline M. Hill, ed., *Mary McDowell and Municipal Housekeeping: A Symposium* (Chicago: Millar, n.d.), pp. 27–32; Ernest W. Burgess and Charles Newcomb, *Census Data of the City of Chicago, 1920* (Chicago: University of Chicago Press, 1931), census tract 354.

34. Chicago Commission on Race Relations, *Negro in Chicago*, pp. 658, 664–65, 667.

35. David Dolnick, "The Role of Labor in Chicago Politics Since 1919" (M.A. thesis, University of Chicago, 1939), p. 4; broadside in Fitzpatrick Papers, box 8, folder 57.

36. David Brody, *Labor in Crisis: The Steel Strike of 1919* (New York: Lippincott, 1965), pp. 50–53; William Z. Foster, *The Great Steel Strike and Its Lessons* (New York: B. W. Huebsch, 1920), p. 29.

37. Brody, *Labor in Crisis*, pp. 76–78; Gary quoted on p. 79.

38. Ibid., pp. 82–83, 89–95.

39. Mrs. M. A. Gadsby, "The Steel Strike," *Monthly Labor Review* 9 (December 1919):79.

40. William Hannon, "Steel—Bulwark of Anti-Unionism," *Labor Age* 12 (January 1923):1; Samuel Alschuler to John Fitzpatrick, March 28, 1919, Fitzpatrick Papers, box 8, folder 58; J. W. Johnstone to William Z. Foster, March 29, 1919, in ibid.

41. Commission of Inquiry, Interchurch World Movement, *Report on the Steel Strike of 1919* (New York: Harcourt, Brace and Rowe, 1920; reprint ed., New York: Da Capo Press, 1971), pp. 34–37; Brody, *Labor in Crisis*, pp. 95–100.

42. William Z. Foster to John Fitzpatrick, July 28, 1919, Fitzpatrick Papers, box 8, folder 61.

43. Brody, *Labor in Crisis*, p. 100; Jack M. Stein, "A History of Unionization in the Steel Industry in the Chicago Area" (M.A. thesis, University of Chicago, 1948), p. 14.

44. *Iron and Steel Workers Bulletin*, No. 2, Fitzpatrick Papers, broadside collection.

45. David J. Saposs, "How the Steel Strike Was Organized," *Survey* 41 (November 8, 1919):69; idem, "Interview with Edward J. Evans," December 27, 1918, in David J. Saposs Papers at the State Historical Society of Wisconsin, box 26, folder 6. Henceforth referred to as Saposs Papers.

46. Gadsby, "Steel Strike," p. 84; Phyllis Bate, "The Development of the Iron and Steel Industry of the Chicago Area, 1900–1920" (Ph.D. diss., University of Chicago, 1948), p. 185; see n. 5.

47. *Polonia* (South Chicago), September 18, 1919.

48. Ibid., September 25, 1919.

49. *Dziennik Chicagoski*, September 24, 25, 1919.

50. *Polonia* (South Chicago), September 25, 1919.

51. "South Works Personnel Activities Record, 1917–1920," Southeast Chicago Historical Project Archives, Columbia College, Chicago.

52. D. J. Saposs, "Interview with George W. Sterling," August 20, 1920, in Saposs Papers, box 26, folder 10; idem, "Steel Strike Interviews of Workers, 1920," p. 28, in ibid., folder 7; idem, "Chat on the Street with Polish Worker, South Chicago," in ibid., folder 9.

53. D. J. Saposs, "Interview with Kowalski," n.d., in Saposs Papers, box 26, folder 10; idem, "Interview with a German Worker," August 19, 1920, in ibid.; idem, "Interview with Victor L. Roberts," August 20, 1920, in ibid.

54. *Polonia* (South Chicago), October 2, 1919.

55. Ibid., October 9, 1919; interview with Rt. Rev. Msgr. Edward Plewinski, June 16, 1973; *New Majority*, October 4, 1919.

56. *Polonia* (South Chicago), October 9, 1919; *New Majority*, October 11, 25, 1919.

57. Stein, "A History of Unionization," pp. 19–20, 29–31; Raymond A. Mohl and Neil Betten, *Steel City: Gary, Indiana, 1906–1950* (New York and London: Holmes & Meier, 1986), pp. 26–47.

58. Neil Betten, "Polish American Steelworkers: Americanization Through Industry and Labor," *Polish American Studies* 33 (Autumn 1976): 41.

59. William Z. Foster, *American Trade Unionism* (New York: International Publishers, 1947), p. 30; J. W. Johnstone to John Fitzpatrick, March 28, 1919, in Fitzpatrick Papers, box 8, folder 58; Frank Morrison to John Fitzpatrick, September 20, 1919, in ibid., folder 62.

60. *Butcher Workman*, November 1919.

61. Foster, *Unionism*, p. 30.

62. James R. Barrett, *Work and Community in the Jungle: Chicago's Packinghouse Workers, 1894–1922* (Urbana and Chicago: University of Illinois Press, 1987), p. 227.

63. *Dziennik Chicagoski*, August 8, 9, 13, 1919.

64. *Butcher Workman*, June 1919.

65. Ibid., July 1919; minutes of the Chicago Federation of Labor Meeting of January 18, 1920, in *New Majority*, January 24, 1920.

66. *Butcher Workman*, October 1919.

67. Ibid., November 1919.

68. Hapak, "Polish Army," p. 16; *Butcher Workman*, May 1920.

69. *New Majority*, January 18, 4, 1920.

70. Minutes of the Chicago Federation of Labor Meeting of October 19, 1919, in *New Majority*, October 25, 1919.

71. Minutes of the Chicago Federation of Labor Meeting of January 18, 1920, in *New Majority*, January 24, 1920; minutes of the Chicago Federation of Labor Meeting of February 1, 1920, in *New Majority*, February 7, 1920.

72. Minutes of the Chicago Federation of Labor Meeting of February 15, 1920, in *New Majority*, February 21, 1920; *New Majority*, February 28, 1920; Barrett, *Chicago's Packinghouse Workers*, p. 228.

73. Minutes of the Chicago Federation of Labor Meeting of May 2, 1920, in *New Majority*, May 8, 1920; minutes of the Chicago Federation of Labor Meeting of May 16, 1920, in *New Majority*, May 22, 1920.

74. *Butcher Workman*, June 1920; *Dziennik Chicagoski*, May 18, 22, 1920.
75. *Dziennik Chicagoski*, May 26, 1920; *Butcher Workman*, June 1920.
76. *Butcher Workman*, May 1921.
77. Barrett, *Chicago's Packinghouse Workers*, p. 229.
78. *New Majority*, August 21, 1920; *Naród Polski*, September 1, 1920.
79. *New Majority*, March 12, 1921.
80. Alma Herbst, "The Negro in the Slaughtering and Meat Packing Industry in Chicago" (Ph.D. diss., University of Chicago, 1930), pp. 86–87, 94–101, 192.
81. *Armour and Company Annual Report, 1920*, p. 4; *Armour and Company Annual Report, 1921*, p. 4; *Armour and Company Annual Report, 1922*, p. 5.
82. *New Majority*, March 19, 26, May 7, 1921; *New York Times*, June 18, 1921.
83. *New York Times*, November 2, 10, 1921; *National Provisioner* 65 (November 12, 1921):22.
84. *New York Times*, November 10, 1921.
85. Ibid., November 19, 1921.
86. *Dziennik Związkowy*, December 6, 1921.
87. Ibid., December 7, 1921.
88. Ibid., December 8, 1921; *Dziennik Ludowy*, December 8, 1921; *Chicago Daily Tribune*, December 8, 1921.
89. *Dziennik Związkowy*, December 8, 1921; interview with Stanley Novak, 1985.
90. *Chicago Daily Tribune*, December 9, 1921.
91. *New York Times*, December 10, 1921.
92. *Dziennik Związkowy*, December 9, 1921; quotation in Howard Baron Meyers, "The Policing of Labor Disputes in Chicago: A Case Study" (Ph.D. diss., University of Chicago, 1929), p. 888; Barrett, *Chicago's Packinghouse Workers*, p. 261.
93. *Dziennik Chicagoski* (CFLPS), December 9, 1921. I used the Chicago Foreign Language Press Survey to look at several of the Polish newspapers of this period. These notes will be marked by CFLPS.
94. *Dziennik Ludowy*, December 9, 1921.
95. *Dziennik Zjednoczenia* (CFLPS), December 9, 1921.
96. *Chicago Daily Tribune*, December 9, 1921.
97. Ibid., December 10, 1921; Herbst, "Negro in Meat Packing," pp. 31, 112–16.
98. *Dziennik Chicagoski* (CFLPS), December 31, 1921; *Dziennik Związkowy*, December 31, 1921; *New Majority*, December 17, 1921; *Butcher Workman*, December 1921.
99. *Dziennik Chicagoski* (CFLPS), January 18, 1922.
100. Ibid., January 9, 30, 1922.
101. *Dziennik Związkowy*, December 31, 1921; *New York Times*, December 10, 1921.
102. Minutes of the Chicago Federation of Labor Meeting of December 18, 1921, in *New Majority*, December 24, 1921; Barrett, *Chicago's Packinghouse Workers*, p. 262.
103. John J. Bukowczyk, "The Transformation of Working-Class Ethnicity: Corporate Control, Americanization, and the Polish Immigrant Middle Class in Bayonne, New Jersey, 1915–1925," *Labor History* 25 (Winter 1984):54.

104. Victor R. Greene, *American Immigrant Leaders, 1800–1910: Marginality and Identity* (Baltimore: Johns Hopkins University Press, 1987), pp. 105–21.

105. *Dziennik Zjednoczenia* (CFLPS), February 3, July 24, 1922.

106. *Dziennik Chicagoski* (CFLPS), December 21, 1921, January 3, 7, 9, 11, 19, 1922; *Dziennik Zjednoczenia* (CFLPS), February 15, 1922.

107. *New World* (Chicago), December 2, 16, 1921, January 13, 1922.

108. Bukowczyk, "Transformation of Working-Class Ethnicity," p. 70. See also John Bukowczyk, *And My Children Did Not Know Me: A History of the Polish Americans* (Bloomington: Indiana University Press, 1987), pp. 36–37.

109. *New York Times*, January 19, 1922.

110. *Dziennik Chicagoski* (CFLPS) February 15, 1922.

Conclusion

1. The CIO proved successful in organizing both the steel and meatpacking industries in the late 1930s. Residents in both the Back of the Yards and South Chicago organized themselves into powerful local action groups during the same decade. The Back of the Yards Council and the Russell Square Community Committee proved to be effective neighborhood organizations. See Robert Slayton, *Back of the Yards: The Making of a Local Democracy* (Chicago: University of Chicago Press, 1986), and Dominic A. Pacyga, "The Russell Square Community Committee: An Ethnic Response to Urban Problems," *Journal of Urban History* 15 (November 1988), pp. 159–84.

2. Caroline Golab, *Immigrant Destinations* (Philadelphia: Temple University Press, 1977), p. 112.

3. Louis Wirth, *The Ghetto* (Chicago: University of Chicago Press, 1928), pp. 282–83.

4. Gerald Suttles, *The Social Order of the Slum* (Chicago: University of Chicago Press, 1968).

Index